The Early Medieval Settlement Remains from Flixborough, Lincolnshire: the Occupation Sequence, *c.* AD 600–1000

EXCAVATIONS AT FLIXBOROUGH

The Early Medieval Settlement Remains from
Flixborough, Lincolnshire:
The Occupation Sequence, *c.* AD 600–1000

by
Christopher Loveluck and David Atkinson

with contributions by
Matthew G. Canti, Peter Didsbury, Geoff Gaunt,
Helen Geake, Simon Mays, Andrew Payne and Jane Young

OXBOW BOOKS

Published by
Oxbow Books, Oxford, UK

ISBN 978-1-84217-255-1

A CIP record for this book is available from the British Library

This book is available direct from

Oxbow Books, Oxford, UK
(Phone: 01865-241249; Fax: 01865-794449)

and

The David Brown Book Company
PO Box 511, Oakville, CT 06779, USA
(Phone: 860-945-9329; Fax: 860-945-9468)

or from our website

www.oxbowbooks.com

This book is published with the aid of a grant from English Heritage.

Front cover: Excavating one of the skeletons.
Back cover: General view of the excavations in progress,
with the Trent valley in the background.

Printed in Great Britain by
Short Run Press Ltd, Exeter

Contents

List of Figures

Figures marked with an asterisk (*) are colour plates and can be found in a separate section at the back of the volume.

List of Contributors to the Flixborough Volumes

ARCHIBALD, MARION, Formerly Dept. of Coins and Medals, British Museum.

ATKINSON, DAVID, Senior Project Officer, Humber Field Archaeology.

BARRETT, JAMES, Dept. of Archaeology, University of York.

BLINKHORN, PAUL, Northamptonshire Archaeology Unit.

BRETMAN, AMANDA, University of Leeds (biological work on geese bones).

BROOKS, MARGARET, English Heritage project conservator, Wiltshire Conservation Centre.

BROWN, MICHELLE P., Dept. of Manuscripts, British Library.

†CAMERON, KENNETH, Formerly Professor Emeritus, School of English, University of Nottingham.

CANTI, MATTHEW, English Heritage Archaeological Science.

CARROTT, JOHN, Palaeocology Research Services and Dept. of Archaeology, University of Durham.

COPELAND, PENELOPE, Illustrator for much of Vol. 4.

COWGILL, JANE, Private consultant.

CRAMP, ROSEMARY, Professor Emeritus, Dept. of Archaeology, University of Durham.

DARRAH, RICHARD, Freelance consultant on historical uses of wood in buildings.

DIDSBURY, PETER, Freelance pottery consultant.

DOBNEY, KEITH, Dept. of Archaeology, University of Durham.

†EDWARDS, GLYNIS, English Heritage Archaeological Science.

EVANS, D. H., Archaeology Manager, Humber Archaeology Partnership. Joint editor of Vol. 2, and assistant editor for Vol. 1; project manager 2000–2007.

EVERSHED, RICHARD, Dept. of Biochemistry, University of Bristol; organic residue analysis.

EVISON, VERA L., Professor Emeritus, Institute of Archaeology, UCL, London.

FOOT, SARAH, Dept. of History, University of Sheffield.

FOREMAN, MARTIN, Assistant Keeper of Archaeology, Hull Museums and Galleries.

FRANKLAND, MICHAEL, Humber Field Archaeology; principal illustrator for these volumes.

GAUNT, GEOFF, Dept. of Archaeological Sciences, University of Bradford; formerly British Geological Survey.

GEAKE, HELEN, Dept. of Archaeology, University of Cambridge.

HALL, ALLAN, Dept. of Archaeology, University of York.

HAYNES, SUSAN, UMIST (DNA research on geese bones).

HERMAN, JERRY, National Museum of Scotland, Edinburgh (cetacean remains).

HINES, JOHN, Professor, School of History and Archaeology, Cardiff University.

HUGHES, MICHAEL, Freelance specialist on ICPS analysis of pottery.

JAQUES, DEBORAH, Palaeoecology Research Services and Dept. of Archaeology, University of Durham.

JOHNSTONE, CLUNY, Dept. of Archaeology, University of York.

JONES, JENNIFER, English Heritage conservator, Dept. of Archaeology, University of Durham.

KENWARD, HARRY, Dept. of Archaeology, University of York.

LA FERLA, BEVERLEY, Dept. of Biology, University of York (linear enamel hypoplasia in pigs).

LOVELUCK, CHRISTOPHER, Dept. of Archaeology, University of Nottingham. Principal author and series editor; project manager 1996–2000.

MAKEY, PETER, Freelance lithics specialist.

MARSDEN, BILL, BM Photographic Services, Hull (detailed finds photographs).

MARSHALL, JOHN, Formerly Senior Illustrator with the Humber Archaeology Partnership.

MAYS, SIMON, English Heritage Archaeological Science.

MORTIMER, CATHERINE, Freelance archaeo-materials analyst.

MULDNER, GUNDULA, Dept. of Archaeological Sciences, University of Bradford (stable isotope analysis of dolphins).

NICHOLS, COURTNEY, Dept. of Biological Sciences, University of Durham (DNA analysis on the dolphins).

O'CONNOR, SONIA, Conservation Laboratory, Dept. of Archaeological Sciences, University of Bradford.

O'CONNOR, T. P., Professor, Dept. of Archaeology, University of York.

OKASHA, ELISABETH, Dept. of English, University College, Cork.

OTTAWAY, PATRICK, Freelance specialist, formerly York Archaeological Trust.

PANTER, IAN, Head of Conservation, York Archaeological Trust.

PARKHOUSE, JONATHAN, Warwickshire Museum Field Services (Archaeology).

PATTERSON, ZOE, Freelance illustrator (Anglo-Saxon pottery).

PAYNE, ANDREW, English Heritage Archaeological Science.

PESTELL, TIM, Curator of Archaeology, Norwich Castle Museum & Art Gallery.

†PIRIE, ELIZABETH, Numismatic specialist.

ROFFE, DAVID, Independent scholar.

ROGERS, N. H., York Archaeological Trust.

ROGERS, PENELOPE WALTON, The Anglo-Saxon Laboratory.

SITCH, BRYAN, Head of Humanities, The Manchester Museum.

SLATER, DAVID, Dept. Biology, University of York.

SMITH, LINDA, Formerly Illustrator with the Humberside Archaeology Unit.

SMITH, REBECCA, Former Contract Illustrator, Humber Field Archaeology.

STARLEY, DAVID, Royal Armouries, Leeds (formerly Ancient Monuments Laboratory, English Heritage).

THOMAS, GABOR, Dept. of Archaeology, University of Kent (Canterbury).

TURNER, LESLIE, Former Contract Illustrator, Humber Field Archaeology.

VINCE, ALAN, Freelance ceramic consultant.

WASTLING, LISA M., Senior Finds Officer, Humber Field Archaeology.

WATSON, JACQUI, English Heritage Archaeological Science.

YOUNG, JANE, Lindsey Archaeological Services.

YOUNGS, SUSAN M., formerly Dept. of Prehistory & Europe, British Museum.

Abstract

Between 1989 and 1991, excavations adjacent to the former settlement of North Conesby, in the parish of Flixborough, North Lincolnshire, unearthed remains of an Anglo-Saxon settlement associated with one of the largest collections of artefacts and animal bones yet found on such a site. Analysis has demonstrated that the excavated part of the settlement was occupied, or used for settlement-related activity, throughout what have been termed the 'Mid' and 'Late' Anglo-Saxon periods. In an unprecedented occupation sequence from an Anglo-Saxon rural settlement, six main periods of occupation have been identified, with additional sub-phases, dating from the seventh to the early eleventh centuries; with a further period of activity, between the twelfth and fifteenth centuries AD.

The seventh- to early eleventh-century settlement remains were situated on a belt of windblown sand, overlooking the floodplain of the River Trent, eight kilometres south of the Humber estuary. The windblown sand had built up against the Liassic escarpment, to the east of the excavated area. The remains of approximately forty buildings and other structures were uncovered; and due to the survival of large refuse deposits, huge quantities of artefacts and faunal remains were encountered compared with most other rural settlements of the period. Together, the different forms of evidence and their depositional circumstances provide an unprecedented picture of nearly all aspects of daily life on a settlement which probably housed elements of the contemporary social elite amongst its inhabitants, between the seventh and eleventh centuries. Furthermore, and perhaps even more importantly, the detailed analysis of the remains also provides indications of how the character of occupation changed radically during the later first millennium AD, when the area of what is now North Lincolnshire was incorporated, in chronological succession, within the Kingdom of Mercia, the Danelaw, and finally, the West Saxon and then Anglo-Danish Kingdom of England.

The publication of the remains of the Anglo-Saxon settlement is achieved in four volumes, and will be supported by an extensive archive on the Archaeological Data Service (ADS) for the United Kingdom. The excavation, post-excavation analysis and publication phases of the project have been funded principally by English Heritage, and the project has been run through the Humberside Archaeology Unit – now the Humber Archaeology Partnership. The different volumes within the series of publications serve slightly different purposes. This volume presents an integrated analysis of the stratigraphic and chronological sequence of activity, with analysis of the contents of the archaeological deposits in preparation for wider interpretation. The reasoning is also presented for judging whether the remains are representative of the excavated area alone, or a wider settlement area. Thus, this volume provides the analytical narrative of the nature of occupation and the use of space through time, integrating the results from all the forms of data. It constitutes the primary level in the post-excavation analysis and interpretation of the evidence, to which all the other publications refer for their archaeological and chronological context.

Between 1991 and 1995, further geophysical, magnetic susceptibility and surface collection surveys were undertaken, and additional evaluation trenches were excavated. They demonstrated that Mid- and Late-Saxon archaeological evidence, as well as scatters of Romano-British and later medieval artefacts, extended to the north and south of the excavated site. Remains also continued to the east towards the escarpment and the church of All Saints', variously referred to in the past as North Conesby church or Flixborough *Old church*. Iron slag heaps, to the east of the church, are also known to have covered a moated enclosure between 1922 and 1924. They subsequently covered the intervening area between the moated site and All Saints' church, between the 1940s and 1970s. A map of Flixborough parish produced by Snape in 1778 and the Ordnance Survey map of 1907 both show the moated enclosure, which was the site of the medieval manor house of North Conesby, in relation to the church. Their positions are likely to reflect the two extremities of the medieval settlement of North Conesby. Medieval tenements may have been situated between the religious and secular foci of the settlement.

At present, archaeological evaluation immediately to the east of All Saints' church has been too limited to confirm this hypothesis, but recent trial excavation of the moated site and its environs has confirmed medieval and post-medieval settlement activity, between 300 and 400m to the east of the 1989-91 excavations. Furthermore, additional chance discoveries while quarrying have also uncovered Mid- to Late- Saxon finds and Iron Age settlement remains to the north-west of the excavations, again located beneath blown sand. These comprised a hoard of wood-working tools housed inside two lead tanks, probably dating from between the eighth and eleventh centuries AD; and the Iron Age settlement deposits were found approximately 300 metres to the north-west. In reality, therefore, the remains from the 1989–91 excavations labelled with reference to Flixborough probably represent only a sample of the surface area of multi-period settlement activity in the vicinity. The nature of the archaeological deposits uncovered between 1989 and 1991, and the vertical stratigraphic sequence identified, provide an exceptional 'window' on the complexity and dynamism of life within this larger zone of settlement activity, for the period between the seventh and early eleventh centuries AD.

The excavated settlement remains were both located upon, and sealed by blown sand; and the sealing deposits were up to two metres deep in places. Below this sand inundation, post-excavation analysis has identified evidence of six broad periods of settlement activity, with definable phases within them, dating from at least the early seventh century AD until the mid fourteenth/early fifteenth century. The overall stratigraphic sequence can be summarised as a series of phases of buildings and other structures, associated at different periods with refuse dumped around them in middens and yards, or with a central refuse zone in the shallow valley that ran up into the centre of the excavated area. Several of the main structural phases were also separated by demolition and levelling dumps and it is this superimposition that has resulted in the exceptional occupation sequence. The majority of the recovered finds, approximately 15,000 artefacts and hundreds of thousands of animal bone fragments, were found within these refuse, levelling and other occupation deposits. The high wood-ash content of a significant number of the dumps, their rapid build up, and the constant accretion of sand within them, formed a soil micro-environment which was chemically inert - the alkalinity of the wood-ash and sand accretion preventing acid leaching. It was this fortuitous burial environment that ensured the excellent preservation conditions for the artefact and vertebrate skeletal assemblages.

In order to establish the character of lifestyles, and to enable comparative analysis and interpretation of wider research themes, two tasks had to be completed. First, a site-wide chronology had to be established; and secondly, study of discard patterns of artefacts and bones, and their condition, needed to be achieved to arrive at an under-standing of site formation processes, and hence come to a conclusion on the representativity of data for inter-pretation. Without such critical analyses of the deposits and their contents, it would not have been possible to arrive at an interpretation of whether the remains were representative of the settlement as a whole or only part of it, at different periods in the occupation sequence. These tasks constituted the primary level of interpretation of the Flixborough settlement evidence, and due to the scale of the task - integrating the evidence from thousands of stratigraphic units/contexts, thousands of artefacts, and hundreds of thousands of animal bones – its realisation is the subject of the entire first volume of the publication series.

The chronology of the Flixborough settlement sequence was established by integrated analysis of the vertical and horizontal stratigraphic relationships of structural evidence and refuse deposits, in conjunction with analysis of datable chronological indicators found within them. The evidence for attributing calendar-based date ranges to the relative chronology of the stratigraphic sequence was provided mainly by pottery, coinage, dress accessories with diagnostic stylistic decoration, certain glass vessels, and to a lesser extent by archaeomagnetic dates from fired-clay oven and hearth bases. Some assessment and estimation was also made concerning the longevity of structures built on the site, on the basis of their architectural features, limited charred timber remains, and an awareness of the hostile nature of the calcareous windblown sand, which was subject to acid leaching in the absence of deposits ameliorating its effects.

An exceptional feature of the Flixborough remains is the relative abundance of datable material amongst the artefact assemblages. Certain periods in the occupation sequence, however, provided far more datable material than others. For example, artefacts dated to the eighth and ninth centuries are very numerous; and due to their abundance and the extent of refuse re-organisation in most periods, they are often the most numerous artefacts in later phases too. Consequently, great care had to be taken in attributing smaller quantities of datable artefacts from other periods their appropriate significance. This is particularly true for the structural and depositional remains from Period 6, which contained small quantities of material datable to the tenth century, alongside the largest buildings and some of the largest animal bone deposits from the settlement's history. A uniform expectation of equivalent quantities of datable material in different periods might have led to the assumption that there was a diminution of settlement activity on the basis of datable artefacts. Yet, the structural, depositional and vertical stratigraphic data demonstrated that such an assumption would be false. Consequently, the account and interpretation of the history of occupation within the settlement area relies on the integrated analysis of all the different forms of evidence, and is not disproportionately led by archaeological visibility factors relating to certain types of artefact, such as coinage and dress accessories.

Interpretation of the settlement remains relating to themes such as the agricultural economy, craft-working, exchange, and problems of defining settlement character is of necessity viewed through the filter of site taphonomy and discernible patterns in the discard of artefacts and faunal remains. The undertaking of the thematic social analysis presented in Volume 4 depended on the extent to which deposits and their contents could be shown to be representative of the settlement as a whole, or the excavated area alone. Furthermore, analysis of changing trends through time could be achieved only through establishment of the existence of like deposits in different periods of the occupation sequence. Assessment of the parameters of interpretation possible in different periods of occupation rested on a range of factors. These comprised the refuse disposal strategies used; the extent of artefact residuality and re-deposition; survival factors relating to particular types of evidence: for example, artefact fragmentation and animal bone taphonomy; and the presence of intact occupation surfaces, within or in association with structures, e.g. floors within buildings.

Varied organisation of refuse disposal in different periods of occupation had a great impact on ability to associate specific activities with particular parts of the excavated area. The re-working of earlier refuse material as disposal strategies changed also resulted in a high degree of residuality of eighth- and ninth-century artefacts throughout the settlement's occupational history. In most cases, the identification of any patterning in the finds profiles related to the association of large refuse dump deposits with neighbouring buildings. It is the analysis of what Michael Schiffer has called *waste streams*, associated with different refuse discard strategies, that has provided the key to understanding the human agency associated with rubbish accumulation at Flixborough. This, in turn, has enabled the interpretation of the range of actions that made up the lifestyles of the inhabitants through time.

A contrast exists in our ability to draw conclusions relating to social practices in different periods due to changes in *waste streams*, i.e. demonstrable changes in the origins of components of the refuse. For example, floor deposits and external yard deposits were found in association with buildings in Periods 1 and 2, dated to between the mid to late seventh century and early eighth century, but the floors were kept relatively clean and very few finds were recovered from the yards. As a result, the majority of the finds from the seventh-century phases were found in the fills of post-holes, and in comparison with other periods of occupation the numbers of finds are small (although large in comparison with most other Anglo-Saxon rural settlements of the same date).

Whereas, for much of the eighth, ninth and tenth centuries, refuse was collected and dumped in the central part of the site. Artefact residuality and fragmentation studies suggest that during these three latter centuries both heavily reworked and 'pristine', undisturbed refuse deposits were dumped in this central area. Presence of debris from activities for which there was no trace in the excavated area also showed importation of material from other parts of the settlement. The pristine and fragmented artefacts, and the identifiable components of eighth- to late tenth-century refuse imported from outside the excavated area, suggest focused use of a designated refuse zone for the settlement. Therefore, the extent to which trends from the seventh century can be compared to those from the eighth, ninth and tenth centuries demanded critical consideration of the different depositional circumstances.

Chapters 3 to 7 present an interpretation of occupational history for the period between the mid to late seventh century and the late fourteenth/early fifteenth century. The defined periods of settlement activity are differentiated on the basis of similar use of space within the excavated area, and by the various indicators of the chronology of that particular use of space. Within the narratives, stratigraphic and structural evidence is presented for each period, combined with an integrated analysis of the evidence provided by artefacts, industrial residues and biological remains. The character and condition of key artefacts, industrial residues and biological remains are also discussed in relation to their varied depositional circumstances, in order to enable an assessment of the representativity of the recovered finds assemblages for interpretation. Due to the huge quantity of finds, it has not been possible to present and discuss every individual artefact, animal bone and industrial residue encountered, in these chapters. The narratives present the most important, and a very significant proportion of all the finds, integrated within the stratigraphic and structural sequence of activity for each period. Nevertheless, the presented and interpreted evidence reflects analysis of all the different sets of data, even though not all are presented in Volume 1 (see the ADS archive for a total, phased presentation of the finds assemblages, and Volume 2 for all individual material and artefact-specific reports). The overall result of this integrated analysis is an interpretation of the occupation sequence at Flixborough, on which all the thematic discussions, presented in Volumes 3 and 4, are based. The volume concludes with consideration of the burial practices and associations created by the inhabitants and their wider parallels; followed by discussion of the osteological remains themselves, giving hints of the demographic spectrum of the inhabitants, their lifestyles and ailments.

Zusammenfassung

Von 1989 bis 1991 fanden in der Nähe des aufgegebenen mittelalterlichen Dorfes North Conesby in der Gemeinde Flixborough, North Lincolnshire, Ausgrabungen statt, die eine angelsächsische Siedlung mit einem für derartige Fundplätze außergewöhnlich umfangreichen Kleinfund- und Tierknochenspektrum aufdeckten. Die Auswertung des Fundmaterials zeigte, dass der ergrabene Teil der Siedlung während der „mittleren" und „späten" angelsächsischen Zeit durchgehend bewohnt oder für siedlungsähnliche Tätigkeiten verwendet wurde. Anhand einer für eine ländliche angelsächsische Siedlung bisher einmaligen Nutzungsabfolge konnten sechs Haupt-perioden mit mehreren Phasen identifiziert werden, die schwerpunktmäßig vom 7. bis zum 11. Jahrhundert, mit einer jüngsten Nutzung vom 12. bis in das 15. Jahrhundert, reichen.

Die Ansiedlung des 7. - 11. Jahrhunderts befand sich ca. acht Kilometer südlich des Humber-Mündungsgebiets in der Flussebene des Trent auf einer Erhebung aus Flugsand. Dieser hatte sich vor einem östlich der ergrabenen Fläche gelegenen liassischen Geländeabbruch angesammelt. Während der Ausgrabungen konnten die Reste von ca. 40 Gebäuden und anderen Strukturen, sowie Überreste von Abfallgruben, die im Vergleich mit ähnlichen Siedlungen erstaunlich große Mengen an Kleinfundmaterial und Tierknochen enthielten, identifiziert werden. Insbesondere wegen ihres guten Erhaltungszustands bieten die verschiedenen Gattungen von Fundmaterial einen einmaligen Einblick in fast alle Aspekte des täglichen Lebens einer Siedlung des 7. bis 11. Jahrhunderts, in der unter anderem Angehörige der damaligen sozialen Elite wohnten. Von größerer Relevanz ist jedoch, dass die detaillierte Analyse des Fundmaterials deutlich macht, wie drastisch sich die Nutzungscharakteristika der Siedlung im Laufe des ersten Jahrtausends nach Christus veränderten. Während dieser Zeit gehörte das heutige nördliche Lincolnshire nacheinander zum Königreich Mercia, dem Danelag und dem westsächsischen, später anglo-dänischen, König-reich England.

Die Publikation der Ausgrabungen der angel-sächsischen Siedlung umfasst vier Bände und wird durch ein umfangreiches Archiv im digitalen *Archaeological Data Service* (ADS) Großbritanniens ergänzt. Ausgrabungen, Auswertung und Publikation des Projekts wurden finanziell hauptsächlich von *English Heritage* getragen und von der *Humberside Archaeological Unit*, jetzt *The Humber Archaeology Partnership*, durchgeführt. Die verschiedenen Bände der Publikation erfüllen je unterschiedliche Rollen: Der vorliegende Band enthält eine durchgängige Analyse der stratigraphischen und chronologischen Abfolge des Fundplatzes sowie Befund- und Fundbesprechungen als Grundlage für weiterreichende Interpretationen. Die gesamte Argumentationskette ist bewusst komplett dargestellt, um eine Beurteilung, inwiefern die Funde und Befunde nur für die ergrabene Fläche, oder aber eine größere Siedlungsfläche, repräsentativ sind, zu ermöglichen. Dieser Band stellt somit die Diskussion der Siedlungsgeschichte und der chronologischen Entwicklung der räumlichen Nutzung im Rahmen sämtlicher archäologischer Funde und Befunde dar. Folglich ist Band 1 die archäologische und chronologische Grundlage sämtlicher Auswertungen und Interpretationen des Fundmaterials, auf die sich alle anderen Bände der Publikation beziehen.

Zwischen 1991 und 1995 wurden am Fundplatz einige weitere Suchschnitte geöffnet und Oberflächensurveys, sowie geophysische und geomagnetische Untersuchungen durchgeführt. Diese Untersuchungen zeigten, dass Funde aus der mittleren bis späten angelsächsischen Zeit, sowie romano-keltisches und spätmittelalterliches Fund-material, weit nördlich und südlich des ergrabenen Bereichs streuen. Archäologische Befunde konnten nach Osten in Richtung des Geländeabbruches und der *All Saints'* Kirche, die sowohl als *North Conesby church* als auch als *Old Church* angesprochen wird, verfolgt werden. Zwischen 1922 und 1924 wurden östlich der Kirche Eisenschlackeschüttungen über einem Bereich, der mit einem Graben umwehrt war, angehäuft. Diese wurden von den 1940er bis in die 1970er Jahre ausgedehnt, bis sie auch das Areal zwischen der Kirche und selbigem Bereich bedeckten. Ein Plan von Flixborough, der 1778 von Snape erstellt wurde, sowie eine *Ordnance Survey*

Karte von 1907, zeigen beide diesen mit einem Graben umwehrten Bereich, der als mittelalterliches Herrenhaus von North Conesby angesprochen wird, und seine relative Position zur Kirche. Diese beiden Gebäude scheinen das Ausmaß der mittelalterlichen Siedlung von North Conesby anzudeuten, da mittelalterliche Wohngebäude wahrscheinlich zwischen dem religiösen und dem weltlichen Zentrum des Ortes angesiedelt waren.

Die bisher östlich der Kirche ausgeführten archäologischen Untersuchungen reichen nicht aus, um diese Hypothese zu bestätigen. Probegrabungen in dem umwehrten Bereich und seiner Umgebung, die vor kurzem durchgeführt wurden, erbrachten jedoch klare Nachweise für mittelalterliche und jüngere („post-medieval") Siedlungstätigkeit ungefähr 300-400m östlich der Grabungen von 1989-91. Bei Sandabbauarbeiten in der Nähe der Grabungen kamen nicht nur Funde der mittleren bis späten angelsächsischen Zeit zu Tage, sondern, ca. 300m nord-westlich der Grabungsfläche selbst, auch Reste einer eisenzeitlichen Siedlung, die unter dem verwehten Sand erhalten geblieben waren. Zu den angelsächsischen Funden zählt ein Werkzeughort, der hauptsächlich aus Stücken zur Holzbearbeitung besteht und in zwei Bleitanks deponiert worden war. Die Werkzeuge sind vom 8. bis in das 11. Jahrhundert zu datieren. Es scheint also, dass die 1989-91 für Flixborough aufgenommenen Befunde nur einen Teil einer komplizierten und mehrphasigen Siedlungsabfolge in der gesamten Gegend darstellen. Sowohl die von 1989-91 entdeckten Schichten selbst, als auch ihre stratigraphische Abfolge, ermöglichen somit einen außergewöhnlichen Einblick in die Komplexität und Dynamik des täglichen Lebens dieses ausgedehnten Siedlungsgebiets des 7. bis frühen 11. Jahrhunderts.

Die ergrabenen Siedlungsreste waren auf eine Schicht aus Flugsand gesetzt. Eine ähnliche Wehschicht, teils bis zu 2m tief, bedeckte sämtliche Funde. Unter dieser Sandmenge konnten 6 Hauptperioden der Ansiedlung mit zugehörigen, gut definierbaren Unterphasen identifiziert werden. Insgesamt datieren diese vom frühen 7. bis zur Mitte des 14. Jahrhunderts bzw. in das frühe 15. Jahrhundert. Die gesamte Schichtenabfolge kann als eine Reihe verschiedener Gebäude und anderer Strukturen mit zugehörigen Höfen und Abfallhäufen bzw. -gruben sowie einer zeitweise genutzten zentralen Abfallgrube im Bereich des flachen Tals im Zentrum der Grabungen zusammengefasst werden. Mehrere der Hauptbesiedlungsperioden sind durch Zerstörungsschichten und deren Einebnungen klar trennbar, wodurch sich eine außergewöhnlich klare Nutzungssequenz ergibt. Der größte Teil der ungefähr 15.000 Kleinfunde und unzähligen (100.000+) Tierknochenfragmente stammt aus diesen Abfall-, Aufschüttungs- und anderen Nutzungsschichten. Eine bemerkenswerte Anzahl der Abfallgruben enthielt große Mengen von Holzasche. Dieser Faktor, sowie der schnelle Aufbau der Schichten und die konstante Ablagerung von Sand erzeugten ein

konservierungstechnisches Mikroklima mit chemisch inaktivem Boden – die alkalische Holzasche verhinderte ein Zersetzen durch Säuren, die durch die Sandschicht drangen und deren Alkalinität aufhoben. Aufgrund dieses glücklichen Umstands waren sowohl Klein- als auch Knochenfunde außerordentlich gut erhalten.

Für eine Rekonstruktion des täglichen Lebens und vergleichende Analysen und Interpretationen im Rahmen weiterreichender Forschungsthemen, waren zwei weitere Schritte notwendig: Für den gesamten Fundplatz mussten eine Gesamtchronologie erarbeitet und „Entsorgungsparameter" für Kleinfunde und Knochen, die den Erhaltungszustand berücksichtigen, festgelegt werden. Die „Entsorgungsparameter" sind Grundlage für ein Verständnis der Umstände, die zur Entwicklung des Platzes geführt haben und als solche zentral für jede Bewertung der Aussagekraft des Fundmaterials in weiterreichenden Auswertungen. Ohne diese wichtige Auswertung der Schichten und ihrer Inhalte wäre es unmöglich gewesen festzustellen, ob die Funde und Befunde zu verschiedenen Zeitpunkten für die gesamte Ansiedlung oder nur für einen Teil davon maßgeblich waren. Diese Untersuchungen stellen die Grundlage für das Projekt Flixborough dar und bilden aufgrund ihres Umfangs – es mussten über tausend Kontexte, tausende Kleinfunde und mehrere hunderttausend Tierknochen integriert werden – den gesamten ersten Band dieser Publikationsserie.

Die zeitliche Abfolge der Okkupation von Flixborough wurde durch eine durchgehende Analyse der vertikalen und horizontalen stratigraphischen Verhältnisse von Befunden und Abfallhäufen bzw. -gruben, die mit datierbarem Fundmaterial korreliert wurden, erstellt. Grundlage für eine klare, kalender-basierte Datierung der stratigraphischen Verhältnisse waren gut datierbare Kleinfunde wie Keramik, Münzfunde, Trachtbestandteile mit diagnostischen Dekorationsstilen und spezielle Glasfunde. Diese wurden, in geringerem Maße, durch archäometrische Daten aus Öfen aus gebranntem Lehm und Feuerstellen ergänzt. Weiterhin wurde anhand von Architekturmerkmalen und verbrannten Holzresten, unter Rücksichtnahme der destruktiven Kraft des kalkhaltigen Flugsandes, der ohne die Dämmwirkung anderer Ablagerungen wie Asche (s.o.) zu einem Aufbau an Regensäuren führte, geschätzt, wie lange Strukturen am Fundplatz in Benutzung gewesen sein könnten.

Die reine Menge an datierbarem Fundmaterial aus Flixborough an sich ist bemerkenswert. Manche Schichten enthielten jedoch wesentlich mehr datierbare Funde als andere. So kommen Funde des 8. und 9. Jahrhunderts sehr häufig vor und sind oft, aufgrund ihrer Menge und der häufigen Umschichtung der Abfallhäufen und -gruben, auch in späteren Phasen die am häufigsten angetroffenen Fundgruppen. Daher musste mit großer Vorsicht versucht werden, kleineren Mengen von Funden aus anderen Perioden eine gerechtfertigte Rolle einzuräumen. Dies war im Rahmen der Auswertung der

Funde und Befunde der Periode 6 besonders wichtig, da diese kleine Fundmengen enthielt, die in das 10. Jahrhundert datieren. Gleichzeitig finden sich in dieser Periode jedoch die größten Gebäudestrukturen und die mitunter größten Knochenansammlungen in der gesamten Geschichte des Fundplatzes. Eine einheitliche Einstufung gleichartiger Fundmengen in unterschiedlichen Perioden würde anhand der geringeren Menge datierbarer Kleinfunde reduzierte Siedlungsaktivität andeuten. Sowohl die Befunde als auch die Aufarbeitung der Stratigraphie zeigen jedoch, dass eine solche Annahme falsch wäre. Die hier präsentierten Interpretationen und Rekonstruktionen der Geschichte Flixboroughs basieren daher auf einer integrierten Analyse aller verfügbaren Daten, und sind nicht durch eine Überbewertung gewisser archäologisch leicht verständlicher Fundgattungen wie Münzfunde oder Trachtbestandteile verzerrt.

Aussagen zur landwirtschaftlichen Nutzung Flixboroughs, dem Handwerk vor Ort und Siedlungscharakteristika konnten nur mit Rücksichtnahme auf erarbeitete „Entsorgungs-parameter" von Kleinfunden und Knochenresten in Abfallhäufen und Gruben, sowie taphonomischen Studien, gemacht werden. Für den Versuch einer soziologischen Studie wie in Band 4 war es daher notwendig festzustellen, in welchem Maße einzelne Schichten oder deren Fundmaterial repräsentativ für die gesamte Ansiedlung, oder aber nur die ergrabene Fläche, sind. Graduelle Veränderungen in der Nutzung des Fundplatzes konnten nur anhand ähnlicher Befunde in unterschiedlichen Siedlungsperioden erarbeitet werden. Mehrere Faktoren bestimmten dabei, zu welchem Grad Aussagen für einzelne Perioden gemacht werden konnten: Parameter nach denen Abfall zu verschiedenen Zeitpunkten deponiert wurde, Verfälschung des Fundbilds durch Altfunde und Umlagerung, spezielle Erhaltungsfaktoren für bestimmte Fundgattungen wie Kleinfundzerfall oder Tierknochen taphonomie und die Existenz von intakten Siedlungsschichten wie existierenden Laufniveaus, die innerhalb von Strukturen gefunden wurden oder mit diesen assoziiert waren.

Die Abfallentsorgung wurde in unterschiedlichen Nutzungsperioden nach verschiedenen Parametern organisiert. Dies hat einen direkten Einfluss auf die Interpretationsmöglichkeiten verschiedener Sektoren der Ausgrabungen und bestimmter Nutzungsformen. So wurden zum Beispiel aufgrund von Veränderungen in der Organisation der Abfallentsorgung frühere Abfälle wieder verwendet bzw. verändert genutzt, was ein hohes Aufkommen von Funden aus dem 8. und 9. Jahrhundert in allen Nutzungsschichten der Siedlung zur Folge hatte. Meistens war es möglich, derartige Verzerrungen der Fundprofile direkt mit Strukturen, die mit benachbarten Abfallhäufen, bzw. -gruben assoziiert waren, in Verbindung zu bringen. Michael Schiffer nannte das Resultat solcher verschiedener Entsorgungsstrategien „waste streams". Die Analyse solcher „waste streams"

war die einzige Möglichkeit, die menschlichen Faktoren hinter den Abfallablagerungen Flixboroughs zu rekonstruieren. Dies wiederum ermöglichte Aussagen zu den verschiedenen Siedlungsaktivitäten, die das tägliche Leben der Bewohner während den verschiedenen Perioden ausmachten.

Was die Möglichkeit soziologischer Schlüsse angeht, verursachen Veränderungen in den „waste streams" in Form merklicher Herkunftsunterschiede von Abfallkomponenten einen deutlichen Kontrast zwischen verschiedenen Perioden. So konnten zum Beispiel für Perioden 1 und 2 klar mit Gebäuden assoziierte interne Fußbodenniveaus und externe Laufniveaus, die zwischen der Mitte des 7. Jahrhunderts und dem frühen 8. Jahrhundert datieren, identifiziert werden. Diese Böden schienen jedoch relativ sauber gehalten worden zu sein und enthielten vergleichsweise wenig Fundmaterial. Ein Großteil des Fundmaterials des 7. Jahrhunderts stammt daher aus Verfüllungen von Pfostenlöchern, was die Fundmenge für diese Zeit im Vergleich zu anderen Perioden relativ klein erscheinen lässt (wobei die Fundmenge im Vergleich zu anderen ländlichen angelsächsischen Siedlungen immer noch groß ist). Vom 8. bis 10. Jahrhundert wurde Abfall dagegen gesammelt und in einem zentral gelegenen Bereich deponiert. Die Funde aus dieser „Deponie" und ihr Erhaltungszustand weisen darauf hin, dass während diesen 3 Jahrhunderten sowohl neue, „ungestörte" Anschüttungen, als auch ältere, umgelagerte Abfälle hier deponiert wurden. Materialreste aus Prozessen, die im ergrabenen Bereich nicht nachweisbar waren, weisen ferner darauf hin, dass Abfälle auch aus anderen Teilen der Ansiedlung bewusst zu dieser „Deponie" transportiert wurden. Da dieses Areal sowohl intaktes als auch fragmentiertes Fundmaterial sowie Abfallkomponenten des 8. – 10. Jahrhunderts von Außerhalb des ergrabenen Bereichs erbrachte, kann man annehmen, dass es während dieser Zeit als zentrale Abfalldeponie für den gesamten Siedlungsbereich genutzt wurde. Um die Vorgänge des 7. Jahrhunderts mit denen des 8., 9. und 10. Jahrhunderts zu vergleichen, bedurfte es daher eines kritischen und differenzierten Ansatzes, der diese unterschiedlichen Umstände in Betracht zog.

Kapitel 3 bis 7 fassen die Siedlungsgeschichte Flixboroughs vom späten 7. bis ins späte 14./ frühe 15. Jahrhundert zusammen. Die einzelnen Siedlungsperioden wurden anhand von ähnlicher Raumnutzung innerhalb des ergrabenen Bereichs und verschiedenen chronologischen Hinweisen auf diese Arten von räumlicher Nutzung unterschieden. Für jede Periode sind stratigraphisches und strukturelles Beweismaterial, sowie übergreifende Diskussionen des Fundmaterials, biologischer Überreste und etwaiger Spuren industrieller Tätigkeiten, im Text integriert. Herausragende Funde samt ihres Zustands, sowie Spuren industrieller Tätigkeit und biologische Überreste werden dazu im Rahmen ihrer jeweiligen Fundumstände besprochen, um festzulegen, inwiefern die vorliegenden Fundkomplexe repräsentativ für weitere Interpretationen sind. Angesichts der großen Fundmenge war es leider nicht möglich, in diesen Kapiteln alle Fundstücke, Tierknochen und Werkstattabfälle einzeln vorzulegen und zu besprechen. Der Text enthält einen Großteil des gesamten Fundmaterials, vor allem die wichtigsten Bestandteile, die in die stratigraphische und strukturelle Rekonstruktion der Siedlungsaktivität für jede Periode integriert wurden. Obwohl in Band 1 nicht alle Datensets enthalten sind, reflektiert das hier dargelegte und diskutierte Material die komplette Analyse aller Daten aus Flixborough (eine komplette, periodisierte Vorlage aller Fundkomplexe ist im ADS eingehängt, während Band 2 sämtliche einzelnen material- und klein-

fundspezifischen Fundberichte enthält). Das Gesamtergebnis dieser umfassenden Diskussion ist eine Interpretation der kompletten Siedlungsgeschichte Flixboroughs, auf der sämtliche thematischen Analysen, die in den Bänden 3 und 4 enthalten sind, basieren. Der Band schließt mit einer Besprechung der Begräbnisrituale der Bewohner und entsprechender weitläufigerer Parallelen. Dieser folgt die Erörterung der osteologischen Überreste selbst, die demographische Schlüsse auf die Bewohner der Siedlung, sowie Aussagen zu deren Lebensstil und Gesundheitszustand, zulässt.

Translation by Christoph Rummel

Résumé

Entre 1989 et 1991, des fouilles adjacentes à l'ancien établissement de North Conesby, dans la paroisse de Flixborough, Lincolnshire Nord, mirent à jour les vestiges d'un établissement Anglo-saxon associés à l'une des plus larges collections d'artefacts et d'ossements animaux jamais trouvée sur un tel site. Les analyses ont montré que la partie fouillée de l'établissement était occupée, ou utilisée pour des activités liées à l'établissement, pendant ce qu'on a appelé le « Milieu » et la « Fin » de l'époque Anglo-saxonne. Grâce à cet exemple sans précédent de séquence d'occupation d'un établissement Anglo-saxon rural, on a identifié six périodes d'occupation principales, avec des sous phases supplémentaires, qui vont du septième au début du onzième siècle ; avec une autre période d'activité située entre le douzième et le quinzième siècle après JC.

Les vestiges de l'établissement datant du septième au début du onzième siècle se trouvaient sur une région de sablon, qui dominait la plaine inondable de la rivière Trent, située à huit kilomètres au sud de l'estuaire de la rivière Humber. Le sablon s'était accumulé le long de l'escarpement liasique, à l'est de la zone fouillée. On mit à jour les restes d'environ quarante bâtiments et autres structures ; et, grâce à la présence d'importants dépôts de détritus, on a découvert de grandes quantités d'artefacts et de restes animaux, contrairement à la plupart des autres établissements ruraux de la période. Les différentes formes de preuves, ainsi que les circonstances de leur déposition, fournissent une image sans précédent de presque tous les aspects de la vie quotidienne dans un établissement qui comptait certainement, entre le septième et le onzième siècle, des membres de l'élite sociale de l'époque parmi ses habitants. De plus, et peut-être surtout, les analyses détaillées des vestiges fournissent aussi des indications quant au changement radical du caractère de l'occupation pendant la fin du premier millénaire après JC, quand la région de l'actuel North Lincolnshire fut incorporée, chronologiquement, au Royaume de Mercie, au Daneslaw, et enfin au Royaume d'Angleterre Saxon de l'Ouest, puis Anglo-Danois.

La publication des vestiges de l'établissement Anglo-saxon se compose de quatre volumes, et s'appuiera sur les nombreuses archives du Service de Données Archéologiques (*Archaeological Data Service,* ou *ADS*) du Royaume-Uni. Les fouilles, analyses post-fouilles, et les phases de publication du projet ont été financées principalement par English Heritage (organisme Britannique de protection du patrimoine historique), et le projet fut mené à bien par l'Unité Archéologique du Humberside (Humberside Archaeology Unit), désormais connue sous le nom de Humberside Archaeology Partnership. Les différents volumes qui composent la série de publication ont des objectifs qui diffèrent quelque peu. Ce volume-ci présente une analyse combinée des séquences d'activités stratigraphiques et chronologiques, avec des analyses du contenu des dépôts archéologiques en vue d'une interprétation plus générale. Le raisonnement est également présenté pour permettre de juger si les restes sont représentatifs de la zone fouillée seule, ou d'une zone d'établissement plus large. Ainsi, ce volume fournit une analyse de la nature de l'occupation et de l'utilisation de l'espace à travers les époques, en prenant compte des résultats de toutes les différentes formes de données. Il constitue la première étape de l'analyse post-fouille et de l'interprétation des preuves, auxquelles toutes les autres publications se réfèrent pour leurs contextes archéologiques et chronologiques.

Entre 1991 et 1995, de nouvelles prospections géophysiques et magnétiques, et des ramassages de surface furent entrepris, et des tranchées de sondage supplémentaires furent fouillées. Ceci permit de mettre en évidence que les preuves archéologiques du milieu et de la fin de l'époque Saxonne, ainsi que les dispersions d'objets Britanico-Romains et ensuite médiévaux, s'étendaient au nord et au sud du site fouillé. Les restes se retrouvaient également à l'est, vers l'escarpement et l'église des All Saints, aussi appelée église de North Conesby ou *Old Church* de Flixborough par le passé. On sait aussi que des crassiers de fer ont recouvert un système de fossés à l'est de l'église entre 1922 et 1924. Par la suite, ils couvrirent la zone située entre le site de fossés et l'église des All Saints, entre les années 1940 et 1970. Une carte de la paroisse de Flixborough produite par

Snape en 1778, et la carte d'état major de 1907 montrent toutes les deux le système de fossés, qui se trouvait sur le site du domaine seigneurial médiéval de North Conesby, lié à l'église. Leur situation représente vraisemblablement les deux extrémités de l'établissement médiéval de North Conesby. Les logements médiévaux se situaient probablement entre les sièges religieux et non-religieux de l'établissement.

Jusqu'à maintenant, l'évaluation archéologique directement à l'est de l'église des All Saints a été trop limitée pour confirmer cette hypothèse, mais des tranchées de sondage récentes du système de fossés et de ses alentours ont confirmé des activités liées à l'établissement médiéval et postmédiéval, entre 300 et 400m à l'est des fouilles de 1989-91. De plus, des découvertes occasionnelles lors d'extraction de carrière ont également mis à jour des découvertes du milieu et de la fin de la période Saxonne, ainsi que des vestiges de village de l'Age du Fer au nord-ouest des fouilles, pareillement situé sous du sablon. Ces découvertes comportaient une cache d'outils à bois dissimulés à l'intérieur de deux réservoirs en plomb, datant probablement d'entre le huitième et onzième siècle après JC. Les dépôts du village de l'Age du Fer se situaient à environ 300 mètres au nord-ouest. En réalité, les vestiges provenant des fouilles de 1989–91 connus sous le nom de Flixborough ne représentent probablement qu'un échantillon de la zone d'activité d'établissements à multiple périodes, situés dans le voisinage. La nature du dépôt archéologique mis à jour entre 1989 et 1991, et la séquence stratigraphique verticale identifiée, fournissent une "fenêtre" exceptionnelle sur la complexité et le dynamisme de la vie au sein de cette zone élargie d'activité d'établissement, du septième au début du onzième siècle après JC.

Les vestiges de l'établissement qui ont été fouillés se situaient sur le sablon, et ils en étaient également recouverts. Ce dépôt de couverture mesurait jusqu'à 2 mètres de profondeur par endroit. Sous cette épaisseur de sable, les analyses post-fouilles ont pu identifier 6 périodes d'activités de l'établissement, qui comprennent leurs propres sous-phases, et qui dataient au moins du début du Septième siècle et allaient jusqu' au milieu du quatorzième/début du quinzième siècle après JC. La séquence stratigraphique générale peut se résumer à une série de phases de construction de bâtisses et autres structures, associée au cours de différentes périodes à des détritus répandus ou amassés autours des structures, ou encore à une zone centrale d'amoncellement de détritus dans la petite vallée qui s'étendait jusqu'au centre de la zone de fouilles. Plusieurs de ces phases structurelles principales étaient aussi séparées par des couches de gravats provenant de démolition et de nivellement, et c'est cette superposition qui rend la séquence d'occupation exceptionnelle. La plupart des découvertes (environ 15000 artefacts et des centaines de milliers de fragments d'os animaux) provenaient de ces amas de détritus, couches de déblaiement, et autres dépôts liés à l'occupation. Un nombre significatif de ces amas se distinguent par une forte proportion de cendre de bois, leur formation rapide, et l'apport constant de sablon, ce qui a provoqué la formation d'un microenvironnement du sol qui était chimiquement inerte: Les cendres de bois alcalines et l'apport de sablon ont empêché le lessivage acide. Cet ensevelissement fortuit a permis d'excellentes conditions de conservation des artefacts et d'ensembles d'ossements articulés.

Deux tâches ont dû être effectuées afin de déterminer le caractère des styles de vie, et pour permettre l'analyse comparative et l'interprétation de thèmes de recherche plus étendus. Tout d'abord, il fallait établir une chronologie pour le site entier; ensuite, il fallait étudier la manière dont les artefacts et ossements étaient déposés, ainsi que leur état, afin de pouvoir comprendre les processus de formation du site, et ainsi parvenir à une conclusion pour déterminer si les données interprétées étaient représentatives du site. Sans de telles analyses critiques des dépôts et de leurs contenus, il n'aurait pas été possible de déterminer si les restes étaient représentatifs de l'établissement dans son ensemble ou en partie, aux différentes périodes de la séquence d'occupation. Ces tâches constituent le niveau premier d'interprétation des preuves de l'établissement de Flixborough, et la réalisation de cette étude, à cause son ampleur (intégrer les preuves de milliers de contextes stratigraphiques, de milliers d'objets, et de centaines de milliers d'ossement animaux), est le sujet de l'intégralité du premier volume de cette série de publication.

Les analyses intégrées des relations stratigraphiques verticales et horizontales des restes de structures et de dépôts de détritus, en conjonction avec les analyses d'indicateurs chronologiques datables qu'ils contenaient, ont permis d'établir la chronologie de la séquence d'établissement de Flixborough. La poterie, le système monétaire, les accessoires vestimentaires avec des décorations de styles caractéristiques, certains vases de verre, et dans une moindre mesure la datation par l'archéomagnétisme de fours de terre cuite et de foyers ont fournis des preuves datables dans la chronologie relative de la séquence stratigraphique. On a aussi eu recours à l'évaluation et l'estimation de la longévité des structures construites sur le site, en prenant en compte leurs caractéristiques architecturales, de la quantité restreinte des restes de bois de construction carbonisées, et en ayant conscience de la nature hostile du sablon calcaire, sujet au lessivage acide en l'absence d'autres dépôts qui auraient amélioré ses effets.

L'abondance relative de matériaux datables parmi les ensembles d'artefacts est une caractéristique exceptionnelle des restes de Flixborough. Toutefois, certaines périodes de la séquence d'occupation ont fourni bien plus de matériaux datables que d'autres. Par exemple, les objets datant du huitième et neuvième siècle sont très nombreux; et, à cause de leur abondance et de l'étendue de la réorganisation des déchets à la plupart des époques, ils sont souvent les plus nombreux aux phases suivantes également. Par conséquent, il a fallu prendre beaucoup de précautions pour attribuer l'importance qu'il leur revenait aux plus petites quantités d'artefacts datables des autres périodes. Ceci est particulièrement vrai pour les restes structurels et déposés de la Période 6, qui contenaient de petites quantités de matériaux datés du dixième siècle, avec en même temps les plus grands bâtiments et certains des plus grands dépôts d'ossements animaux de l'histoire de l'établissement. Si l'on s'était attendu à trouver des quantités similaires de matériaux datables à toutes les périodes, la réduction du nombre d'objets datables aurait pu nous faire supposer que l'activité de l'établissement était également diminuée. Pourtant, les données stratigraphiques structurelles, verticales, et de déposition montrent qu'une telle supposition serait fausse. Par conséquent, le compte rendu et l'interprétation de l'histoire de l'occupation au sein de la zone d'établissement reposent sur l'analyse intégrée de toutes les différentes formes de preuves, et ne sont pas influencés de manière disproportionnée par des facteurs archéologiques visibles se rapportant à certains types d'artefacts, tels que la monnaie ou les accessoires vestimentaires.

L'interprétation des restes de l'établissement par rapport à des thèmes tels que l'économie agricole, l'artisanat, l'échange, et par rapport aux problèmes quant à la définition du caractère de l'établissement, est nécessairement vue à travers le filtre de la taphonomie du site et des schémas discernables de déposition d'objets et restes animaux. Le déroulement de l'analyse sociale thématique présentée dans le Volume 4 dépendait de la possibilité de montrer à quel point les dépôts et leurs contenus étaient représentatifs de l'établissement entier, ou de la zone fouillée seule. De plus, les analyses de l'évolution des tendances à travers le temps n'ont été possibles qu'après avoir déterminé l'existence de dépôts similaires à différentes périodes de la séquence d'occupation. L'évaluation des paramètres d'interprétations possibles à différentes périodes d'occupation reposait sur plusieurs facteurs. Ceux-ci comprenaient les stratégies d'élimination des détritus utilisées; la quantité d'artefacts résiduels et redéposés; les facteurs de survie de certains types de preuves: par exemple, la fragmentation des artefacts, et la taphonomie des ossements animaux; ainsi que la présence de surfaces d'occupation intactes, à l'intérieur ou associées à des structures, comme par exemple les sols à l'intérieur de bâtiments.

Les différentes méthodes d'élimination des déchets aux diverses périodes d'occupation ont eu un fort impact sur la possibilité d'associer des activités particulières à des parties spécifiques de la zone fouillée. Le remaniement de déchets antérieurs avec l'évolution des stratégies de traitement des détritus a aussi provoqué une

hausse résiduelle des artefacts du huitième et neuvième siècle pendant toute la durée de l'occupation de l'établissement. Dans la plupart des cas, l'identification de schémas dans les profils de découvertes était en rapport avec l'association d'importants amoncellements de détritus avec les bâtiments environnant. C'est l'analyse de ce que Michael Schiffer appelle les *flux de déchets* (*waste streams*), associés à différentes méthodes d'élimination des détritus qui a fourni la clé pour comprendre l'action humaine en relation avec l'accumulation de détritus à Flixborough. Ceci, à son tour, a permis l'interprétation de l'éventail des actions qui constituaient les styles de vie des habitants à travers le temps.

Il existe un contraste dans notre capacité à tirer des conclusions sur les pratiques sociales de différentes périodes dû aux changements dans les *flux de déchets*, c'est-à-dire des changements manifestes de l'origine des éléments qui composaient les déchets. Par exemple, les dépôts de revêtements des sols et des dépôts des cours extérieures ont été découverts, associés à des bâtiments de la Période 1 et 2, datant d'entre le milieu et la fin du septième siècle et le début du huitième siècle, mais les sols étaient relativement bien nettoyés, et très peu de découvertes furent mises à jour dans les cours. Par conséquent, la plupart des découvertes des phases du septième siècle furent trouvées dans le remplissage des trous de poteaux, et la quantité de découvertes est moins importante que celle des autres périodes (mais néanmoins importante comparée aux autres établissements Anglo-saxons ruraux de la même date). Alors que pour la majeure partie des huitième, neuvième et dixième siècles, les détritus étaient collectés et amassés dans la zone centrale du site. Les restes d'artefacts et les études de fragmentation suggèrent que pendant ces trois derniers siècles, aussi bien les dépôts de détritus fortement remaniés que les "intacts" et non perturbés étaient amassés dans cette zone centrale. La présence de débris provenant d'activités n'ayant laissé aucune trace dans la zone fouillée suggérait également l'importation de matériaux d'autres parties de l'établissement. Les artefacts intacts et ceux fragmentés, ainsi que les composants des détritus importés de l'extérieur de la zone fouillée et identifiables du huitième à la fin du dixième siècle, laissent à penser qu'une zone de détritus déterminée pour l'établissement avait une utilisation ciblée. Donc, on a dû considérer de façon critique les différentes circonstances de déposition pour évaluer jusqu'à quel point les tendances du septième siècle pouvaient être comparées à celles des huitième, neuvième et dixième siècles.

Les chapitres 3 à 7 présentent une interprétation de l'histoire de l'occupation pour la période allant du milieu à la fin du septième siècle jusqu'à la fin du quatorzième/ début du quinzième siècle. Les périodes définies de l'activité de l'établissement sont différenciées par rapport à l'utilisation de l'espace similaire au sein de la zone fouillée, et par divers indicateurs de la chronologie de cette utilisation spécifique de l'espace. Au cœur des explications, les preuves stratigraphiques et structurelles sont présentées pour chaque période, avec une analyse intégrée des preuves fournies par les artefacts, résidus industriels, et restes biologiques. Le caractère et la condition des artefacts clés, des résidus industriels et des restes biologiques sont également exposés en relation avec les diverses circonstances de leur déposition, afin de permettre d'évaluer la représentativité des ensembles de découvertes mises à jour afin de les interpréter. A cause de l'énorme quantité de découvertes, il n'a pas été possible de présenter et détailler chaque artefact, os animal, ou résidu industriel individuel dans ces chapitres. Les explications décrivent les plus importants, et une proportion très significative de toutes les découvertes, intégrées à la séquence stratigraphique et structurelle d'activité de chaque période. Néanmoins, les preuves présentées et interprétées reflètent l'analyse de tous les différents groupes de données, même s'ils ne sont pas tous présentés dans le Volume 1 (voir les archives de l'*ADS* pour une présentation totale des ensembles de découvertes avec phases correspondantes, et le Volume 2 pour tous les comptes-rendus de matériaux individuels et ceux spécifiques aux artefacts). Le résultat global de cette analyse intégrée est une interprétation de la séquence d'occupation à Flixborough, sur laquelle toutes les discussions thématiques des Volumes 3 et 4 sont basées. Le volume se termine par une réflexion sur les pratiques sépulcrales et les relations créées par les habitants et leurs semblables éloignés; suivi d'une discussion sur les restes osseux eux-mêmes, qui donnent des indications quant à la diversité démographique des habitants, leurs styles de vie et leurs maux.

Traduit par Sterenn Girard-Suard

Acknowledgements

Inevitably with any major project which has run for 16 years or more, there would be a myriad of people to credit for their help, support, and advice; as Flixborough also produced an abundance of finds and raised all sorts of tantalising research questions, the number of individuals and organisations whom we need to thank is substantial. The names of the 67 individuals who have contributed directly to the production of the final text and illustrations for these four volumes can be found in the List of Contributors, and we should like to extend our grateful thanks to each of them; however, in addition to these, many others were involved in the discovery and excavation of the site, and seeing through this project to its conclusion.

As described in Section 1.2 (below), the first indications of settlement on this site were recognised in 1933, but it was unfunded field-walking in 1988 by Irene McGrath and Phil Lings which suggested the presence of a Middle Saxon settlement; and it was the excavations conducted by Dr Kevin Leahy during that summer which were to uncover not only part of a cemetery, but also to suggest the proximity of an adjacent enclosure. Kevin was involved closely in this project for the best part of the next decade, and has done much to publicise the site; we have continued to liaise closely with him, as he will be the recipient curator of the archive. The excavations would not have been possible, without the support of the landowners, Sir Reginald Sheffield, and his tenant, Mr Peter Ogg; we are also grateful for the support of the Sheffield family during the post-excavation process, and for allowing us access to this material during the last 14 years. The main reason for excavating the site was that it was threatened with destruction by sand quarrying; Messrs G. S. and J. Jewitt Estate Development Co. helped us throughout the process, by rescheduling their extraction programme around our requirements, and offering help in kind by supplying us with earthmoving machinery and operators, whenever they were needed.

Another key person who was involved in this project from its inception was the former County Archaeologist, Dr Ben Whitwell. This was a project which was very close to Ben's heart, and he poured an enormous amount of energy into trying to raise local consciousness about the site, and to secure funding for its investigation and study; right up until his retirement in early 1995, he did much to champion the importance of this project. Thanks to his efforts, not only was substantial funding secured from English Heritage, but significant contributions were also given during the excavations of 1989 to 1991 by Humberside County Council, Scunthorpe Borough Council, British Steel, Glanford Borough Council, Clugstons, and Rugby Cement; our grateful thanks are due to all of these, and we should also like to acknowledge the support of the late Mike Symmons and the late Bob Hallas (who were respectively the County Council's Chief Property Services Officer and his deputy), who did much to raise political support for this project.

The excavations were supervised by David Tomlinson, and were undertaken by a small team consisting of the following: David Atkinson, Kath Crooks, Andrew DesForges, Gail Drinkall, Richard George, Tony German, Phil Lings, Irene McGrath, Lousie Muston, and Jon Watt. They were supplemented at various times by Ian Beck, Michael Cressey, Mike Frankland, John Tibbles, and Dawn Briggs; the volunteers included Anthony Martinson, and were assisted at various times by members of our ET scheme, Lorraine White, Simon Small, and Jim Firmage. Peter Fox, Dawn Dickinson and Mathew Sallis (of the County Surveyors team) helped to tie in the site survey grid.

Post-excavation work began in 1992, and was co-ordinated by Ben Whitwell, Gareth Watkins and David Tomlinson – with Gareth largely being responsible for finds co-ordination. Although many of the final members of the project team have been involved from those early days onwards, a number of other people kindly offered opinions on material, or took part in preliminary assessments of individual categories of finds or residues. Amongst those whom we should like to thank for their contributions are: Mrs Leslie Webster (British Museum), Dr Seamus Ross (British Academy), Dr Richard Morris, Professor Peter Sawyer, Professor Ray Page, Christine Fell, Dr Phil Dixon, Dr Simon James, Dr Helena Hamerow, Professor Martin Carver, Dr Tania Dickinson,

Dr Andrew Rogerson, Dr Dawn Hadley and Bob Carr. In addition, Dr Ailsa Mainman, Simon Trafford, Elaine Campbell, Annie Milles, Dr Alex Woolf, Professor Ian Wood, Gail Drinkall, and Jon Watt all gave valuable input. Many of the early drawings which were prepared for interim reports and enabling documents were the work of John Marshall and Linda Smith, who were the two permanent illustrators for the Humberside Archaeology Unit.

The support of key figures such as Professor Rosemary Cramp, Dr Richard Morris and Dr Geoff Wainwright was invaluable in securing English Heritage grant aid. Over the last 15 years many people in that organisation have helped to steer the project through to publication; in addition to the specialist contributors, the support of Geoff Wainwright, Tim Williams, Chris Scull and Barney Sloane has been invaluable. We should also like to thank the successive Regional Inspectors of Ancient Monuments for this area for their continued interest and support – Andrew Davison, Dr David Fraser, Jon Etté, and Keith Miller. Sarah Jennings and Sebastian Payne gave of their expertise in matters concerning, respectively, ceramics and environmental science. Throughout the last 14 years our Project Officer has been Fachtna McAvoy, who has patiently coaxed the team through its paces. The interpretation of the Flixborough remains within their wider context, involving comparative analysis with evidence from other parts of the British Isles and Continental Europe, was achieved primarily during a British Academy postdoctorial fellowship awarded to Dr Chris Loveluck, and in his academic posts at the Universitites of Southampton and Nottingham.

Special thanks are extended to Frans Verhaeghe, Dries Tys, Elisabeth Zadora-Rio, Henri Galinié, Elisabeth Lorans, Anne Nissen-Jaubert, François Gentili, Isabelle Catteddu and Alain Ferdière for discussions on published work and research in progress in France and the Low Countries, relating to early medieval rural settlement.

Many of the photographs are by Bill Marsden, who has also been responsible for producing many prints over the years for exhibitions and interim publications. Administrative support was provided successively by Zena Ahmed, Claire Hampshire and Georgina Richardson. Lastly, we should like to thank the Departments of Archaeology at Southampton and Nottingham Universities for allowing Dr Chris Loveluck to finish these reports.

1 Introduction

Christopher Loveluck and Geoff Gaunt

1.1 Background, aims and structure of the Flixborough publications

by Christopher Loveluck

1.1.1 Background and scope

Between 1989 and 1991, excavations adjacent to the former settlement of North Conesby, in the parish of Flixborough, North Lincolnshire, unearthed remains of an Anglo-Saxon settlement associated with one of the largest collections of artefacts and animal bones yet found on such a site (FIGS 1.1, 1.2*, 1.3–1.4). Analysis has demonstrated that the excavated part of the settlement was occupied, or used for settlement-related activity, throughout what have been termed the 'Mid' and 'Late' Anglo-Saxon periods. In an unprecedented occupation sequence from an Anglo-Saxon rural settlement, six main periods of occupation have been identified, with additional sub-phases, dating from the seventh to the early eleventh centuries; with a further period of activity, between the twelfth and fifteenth centuries AD.

The remains of approximately forty buildings and other structures were uncovered; and due to the survival of large refuse deposits, huge quantities of artefacts and faunal remains were encountered compared with most other rural settlements of the period. Together, the different forms of evidence and their depositional circumstances provide an unprecedented picture of nearly all aspects of daily life on a settlement which probably housed elements of the contemporary social elite amongst its inhabitants, between the seventh and eleventh centuries. Furthermore, and perhaps even more importantly, the detailed analysis of the remains also provides indications of how the character of occupation changed radically during the later first millennium AD, when the area of North Lincolnshire was incorporated, in chronological succession, within the Kingdom of Mercia, the Danelaw, and finally, the West Saxon and then Anglo-Danish Kingdom of England.

The quality of the overall archaeological data contained within the settlement sequence is particularly important for both the examination of site-specific issues, and also for the investigation of wider research themes and problems, currently facing settlement studies in England, for the period between AD 600 and 1050. For example, with regard to site-specific research, the remains provide an exceptional opportunity for examining local dynamism in settlement evolution, and for reconstructing the changing lifestyles of the inhabitants and their changing relationships with the surrounding locality, the trans-Humber region, and the wider world. At a broader level, amongst other themes, the wider comparison of the material culture traits evident at Flixborough enables a re-assessment of the problems of defining the character and social complexity of rural settlements, dating from the seventh to eleventh centuries AD.

1.1.2 Aims, structure and inter-relationship of the Flixborough publications

The publications of the Flixborough settlement remains aim to present the evidence in a way that will enable readers to understand the process of analysis and interpretation, from the micro-level of the excavated deposits themselves, to the macro-level of appreciating their importance for our knowledge of seventh- to eleventh-century England, and to a certain extent neighbouring areas of Continental Europe. The presentation, analysis and interpretation of the archaeological evidence are divided into four volumes, with the ultimate goal of a fully integrated understanding of the lifestyles of the inhabitants of the settlement. This entailed complex interweaving and interpretation of stratigraphical, structural, biological and artefact remains, within the chronological occupation sequence in the excavated area. It also required assessment of the representativity of the evidence for the scale of interpretation possible from the data.

The different volumes within the series of publications

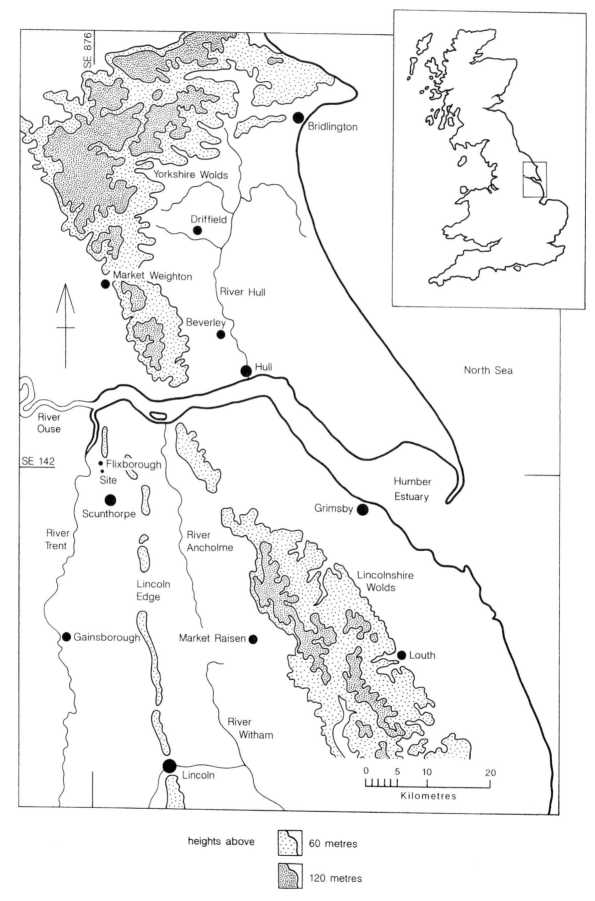

FIG. 1.1. Location Map – Flixborough within the trans-Humber region (M. Frankland).

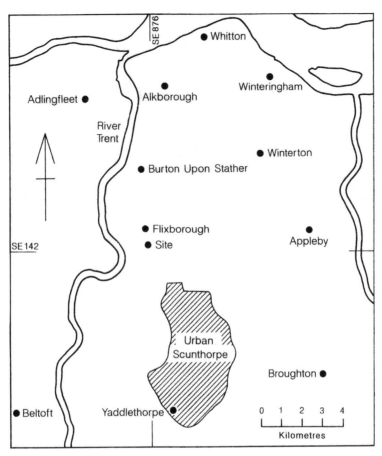

Fig. 1.3. Local settlement geography around the parish of Flixborough, North Lincolnshire (M. Frankland).

serve slightly different purposes. This volume, the first in the series, presents an integrated analysis of the stratigraphic and chronological sequence of activity on the excavated site, with analysis of the contents of the archaeological deposits in preparation for wider interpretation. The reasoning is also presented for judging whether the remains are representative of the excavated area alone, or a wider settlement area. Thus, this volume provides the analytical narrative of the nature of occupation and the use of space through time, integrating the results from all the forms of data. This narrative does not, however, discuss approaches to wider interpretation of the settlement remains from the seventh to eleventh centuries AD. These are informed by comparative analysis and assessment of different contemporary influences on interpretation of archaeological evidence and are presented in Volume 4. Hence, this first volume provides the primary level in the post-excavation analysis and interpretation of the evidence from Flixborough, to which all the other publications refer for their archaeological and chronological context.

Detailed presentation of the many thousands of artefacts recovered from the archaeological deposits, and discussion of their comparisons is presented in Volume 2 of the series. The occurrence of many of these artefacts, especially those critical for dating the occupation

sequence and interpretation of activities is contained within Volume 1, and the full catalogues are presented in Volume 2. The site chronology, the analysis of archaeological site formation processes and the representativity of the remains for interpretation were achieved by the integrated and reflexive analysis of the stratigraphical and structural data, together with the artefact and animal bone evidence. Presentation of the artefact, and also the biological remains, in separate volumes is a reflection of the scale and importance of the different types of data by themselves, and as an integrated assemblage. Both the discussion in Volumes 1 and 4 is cross-referenced to the material-specific analyses in Volumes 2 and 3.

Volume 3 presents the nature of the biological remains from the site, above all represented by animal bones. Due to the exceptional circumstances of the occupation sequence and the unprecedented size of the assemblage represented by the faunal remains, Volume 3 is designed to present the evidence both in its site-specific and wider comparative context, with integrated interpretation of the contribution of the animal bones for understanding aspects of the settlement's economy, status and character.

The final book, Volume 4, offers a series of thematic analyses, integrating all the forms of evidence to reconstruct the lifestyles of the inhabitants. These comprise settlement-specific aspects and wider themes.

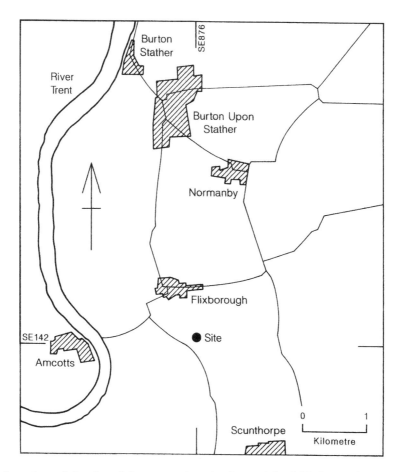

FIG. 1.4. Location of the site of the excavations in the parish of Flixborough (M. Frankland).

The former include relations with the surrounding landscape and region, trade and exchange, and specialist artisan activity. Whereas the wider themes consider approaches to the interpretation of settlement character, the social spectrum of its inhabitants, changing relationships between rural and emerging urban centres, and the importance of the excavated remains within contemporary studies of early medieval settlement and society in western Europe.

In certain instances, primarily in Volumes 1, 2 and 3, cross-referencing links to the digital archive of the research on the Flixborough remains is also presented. This digital archive is to be housed on the Archaeological Data Service (ADS) for the United Kingdom. It contains most of the principal data-bases relating to the stratigraphic data, artefacts, and environmental samples from the excavations, together with much graphical information, including certain sections and feature plans not presented in the reports, and also detailed artefact distribution plots for all the main artefact types. The latter have not been produced in the printed publications due to the sheer number of distribution plots by period and phase, and the huge quantity and density of finds by deposit, which renders printed distributions illegible except when produced at large scale. The digital archive also contains much of the data on the vertebrate remains.

The four-volume series of publications, in conjunction with the ADS digital archive, and the original excavation and post-excavation research archives will then allow ongoing re-interpretation of the early medieval settlement and its context in future years.

1.2 Topographic setting and circumstances of discovery

by Christopher Loveluck

The seventh- to early eleventh-century settlement remains were situated on a belt of windblown sand, overlooking the floodplain of the River Trent, eight kilometres south of the Humber estuary. The windblown sand had built up against the Liassic escarpment, to the east of the excavated area (FIG. 1.13; Gaunt below). Until the seventeenth and eighteenth centuries, this belt of sand was located on the interface between two environmental zones. These comprised the wetlands of the lower floodplain and estuarine areas of the River Trent, situated to the west and north; and the well-drained soils of the Lincoln Edge, on the escarpment to the east (FIG. 1.5*; Gaunt 1975, 15; Gaunt, this volume; Lillie and Parkes 1998, 51–52). Descriptive impressions of this landscape, with its marshes, sand belts of pasture and arable land,

and occasional woodland, can be gleaned to a certain extent from the Domesday survey of 1086 (Foster and Longley 1924; Darby 1987, 103–108). They can also be visualised more fully from John Leland's account of his journey of 1544, from Gainsborough through to the Isle of Axholme (Chandler 1993, 294–297).

The excavated part of the Anglo-Saxon settlement was located upon and adjacent to two spurs on the sand belt, with a shallow valley extending into the central part of the site (FIG. 1.6*). Derrick Riley first identified settlement remains in this area in 1933, following the recovery of Maxey-type pottery and loom weights. Unfortunately, this type of pottery was not identified as 'Mid' Saxon in date until Addyman's excavations at Maxey, in Northamptonshire (Addyman *et al.* 1964, 20–73). Consequently, Riley concluded that the settlement was Romano-British (Riley's unpublished notebook). Harold Dudley also referred to his recovery of Anglo-Saxon remains from nearby Conesby, although the exact geographical relationship of these finds to the excavated settlement evidence is unclear (Dudley 1931, 44).

Prior to the quarrying of sand on the site, the settlement was confirmed as dating from the Anglo-Saxon period, during an archaeological evaluation in 1988, by Dr Kevin Leahy, Principal Keeper of Archaeology and Natural History, at Scunthorpe Museum. This work had resulted from pre-development discussion between the developer – Mr Jewitt; the regional Sites and Monuments officer for Humberside, Mary Lakin; Kevin Leahy; and Ben Whitwell and David Evans of the Humberside Archaeology Unit. The 1988 evaluation uncovered the remains of eleven east-west aligned inhumation graves, without grave-goods (FIGS 1.7, 1.8 and 1.9). Some of the burials were interred in coffins or chests, with iron fittings identical to those from other Anglo-Saxon cemeteries in the surrounding region, dating from the period between the seventh and ninth centuries AD (Mortimer 1905, 254–257; Ottaway 1996, 99–100; *et al.*). The partial foundations of possible buildings were also uncovered. As a consequence, English Heritage funded the Humberside Archaeology Unit (now Humber Field Archaeology) to conduct further evaluations, which resulted in a two-year programme of excavations on the settlement, from 1989 to 1991 (FIGS 1.7 and 1.8).

Between 1991 and 1995, further geophysical, magnetic susceptibility and surface collection surveys were undertaken, and additional evaluation trenches were excavated. They demonstrated that 'Mid' and 'Late' Saxon archaeological evidence, as well as scatters of Romano-British and later medieval artefacts, extended to the north and south of the excavated site. Remains also continued to the east towards the escarpment and the church of All Saints', variously referred to in the past as North Conesby church or Flixborough *Old church* (Coppack 1986, 51). Iron slag heaps, to the east of the church, are also known to have covered a moated enclosure between 1922 and 1924. They subsequently covered the intervening area

between the moated site and All Saints' church, between the 1940s and 1970s (Foster and Longley 1924, liii; Loveluck and McKenna 1999). A map of Flixborough parish produced by Snape in 1778 and the Ordnance Survey map of 1907 both show the moated enclosure, which was the site of the medieval manor house of North Conesby, in relation to the church (FIG. 1.10). Their positions are likely to reflect the two extremities of the medieval settlement of North Conesby. Medieval tenements may have been situated between the religious and secular foci of the settlement, in an area formerly known in 1778 as 'Church Field'.

At present, archaeological evaluation immediately to the east of All Saints' church has been too limited to confirm this hypothesis, but recent trial excavation of the moated site and its environs has confirmed medieval and post-medieval settlement activity, between 300 and 400m to the east of the 1989–91 excavations (Duggan, Fraser and Steedman 2001; Bradley 2005). Furthermore, additional chance discoveries whilst quarrying have also uncovered Mid to Late Saxon finds and Iron Age settlement remains to the north-west of the excavations, again located on blown sand. These comprised a hoard of wood-working tools housed inside two lead tanks, found adjacent to the excavated site, and probably dating from between the eighth and eleventh centuries AD (FIGS 1.11* and 1.12*; see Volumes 2 and 4); and the Iron Age settlement deposits were found sealed below sand, approximately 300 metres to the north-west. In reality, therefore, the remains from the 1989–91 excavations labelled with reference to Flixborough probably represent only a sample of the surface area of multi-period settlement activity in the vicinity (Loveluck and McKenna 1999; Loveluck 2001, 81). The nature of the archaeological deposits uncovered between 1989 and 1991, and the vertical stratigraphic sequence identified, provide an exceptional 'window' on the complexity and dynamism of life within this larger zone of settlement activity, for the period between the seventh and early eleventh centuries AD.

1.3 Geological situation of the settlement and its surrounding area

by Geoff Gaunt

The site of the archaeological excavations in Flixborough parish lies close to a line, in effect coincident with the eastern edge of the Trent floodplain, which separates flat low-lying ground to the west from mainly elevated ground to the east, the latter consisting essentially of two north-to-south aligned asymmetric ridges. These topographic contrasts closely reflect the underlying geology.

Within the Flixborough area generally the solid rocks of parts of two systems, the Triassic and Jurassic, occur either at outcrop or at rockhead (i.e. directly underlying Quaternary deposits). The subdivision and distribution

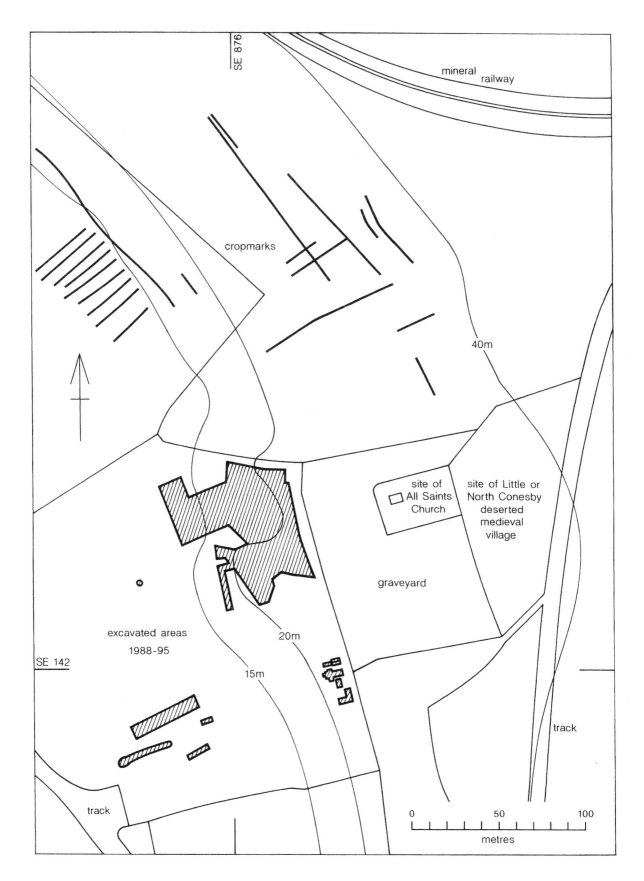

Fig. 1.7. Plan of the excavated areas and adjacent settlement features (M. Frankland).

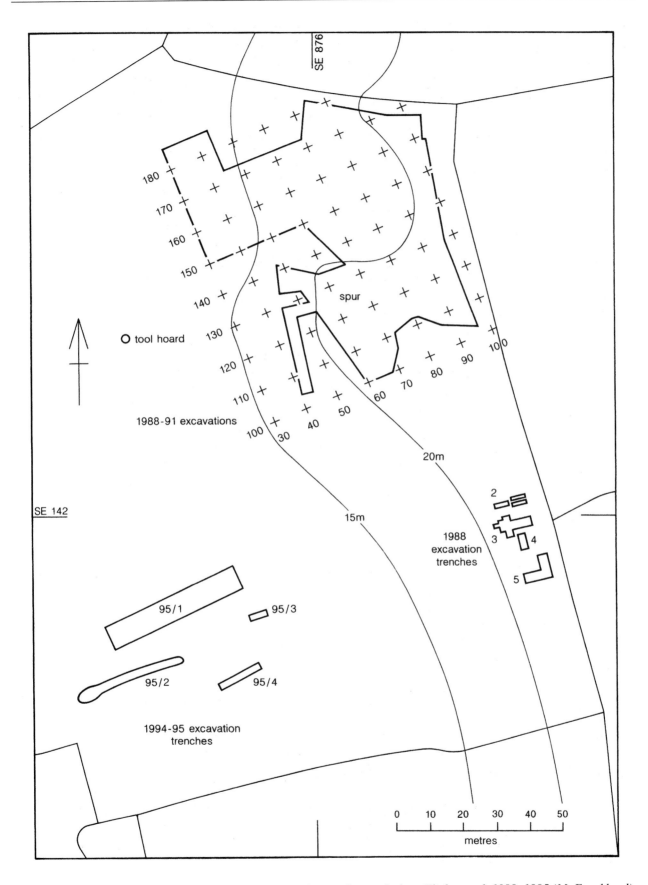

FIG. 1.8. *Location of excavations, trial excavation trenches, and stray finds at Flixborough 1988–1995 (M. Frankland).*

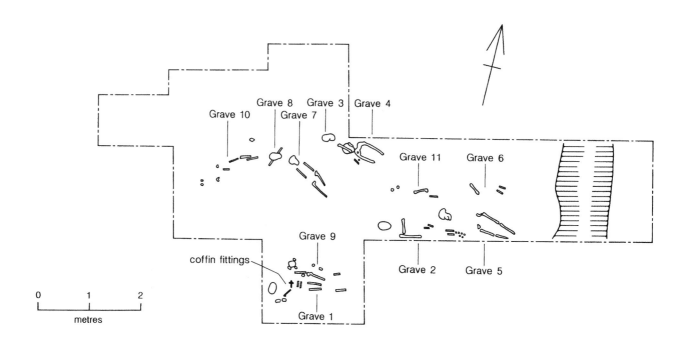

FIG. 1.9. Plan of the badly preserved inhumation graves excavated by Kevin Leahy in 1988 (courtesy of Kevin Leahy).

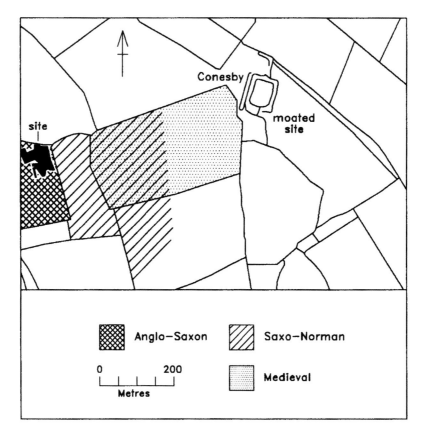

FIG. 1.10.   Schematic plan of the probable development of the settlement of North Conesby within the modern parish of Flixborough (D. Atkinson and M. Frankland).

of these rocks and deposits are shown on FIG. 1.13. All the solid rocks dip gently eastwards, so their outcrops and rockhead locations succeed each other in stratigraphically ascending order in this direction. Certain relatively hard rocks, notably limestones, form the higher parts of the two asymmetric ridges, which exhibit steep west-facing scarp slopes and long gentle eastward-declining dip slopes. The easterly offset of these two ridges and their associated outcrops to the south of a line running east-south-eastwards through Flixborough and Risby Warren is due to a zone of faulting and monoclinal folding along this line.

Summaries of the various rocks and deposits in the Flixborough area, and their relevance to the excavated settlement remains, are given below (see FIG. 1.13). More detailed information is available in two British Geological Survey Memoirs – Gaunt *et al.* (1992) for that part of the area east of the Trent, and Gaunt (1994) for that part farther west. A more generalised review of the geology of the whole of Lincolnshire and eastern Yorkshire is provided by the appropriate Regional Guide (Kent 1980).

1.3.1 Solid rocks

The solid rock geology comprises seven stratigraphical sequences.

Mercia Mudstone

The Triassic Mercia Mudstone (formerly called Keuper Marl) consists of mainly red, locally gypsiferous and generally soft mudstones and silty mudstones. The only outcrop in the Flixborough area is in the south-west around Beltoft, part of the Isle of Axholme, but Mercia Mudstone forms rockhead under virtually all the alluvium in the western half of the area.

Penarth Group

The Triassic Penarth Group (formerly called the Rhaetic) comprises a thin sequence of black, red and green, mainly soft mudstones. Exposures are generally limited to deep ditches, and the sequence is confined to a narrow (< 0.5km wide) rockhead belt under the eastern edge of the Trent alluvium and some of the adjacent landslip, head (i.e. solifluction) and blown sand deposits.

Scunthorpe Mudstones (Lias on FIG. 1.13)

The basal strata of the Scunthorpe Mudstones, *c.* 6m thick, is of Triassic age on fossil evidence, but the rest of the sequence is referable to the Lower Jurassic. As its name implies, most of the sequence consists of mudstones, which are grey to black and partly silty. A few thin limestones, mainly very fine-grained, porcellanous and concretionary but including some bioclastic layers (i.e. consisting mainly of fossils), are present in the Triassic basal strata. At present the nearest outcrops of these strata to Flixborough are near Yaddlethorpe. However, the number of fragments of limestone from the basal strata found in the archaeological excavations at Flixborough suggests that these strata were formerly exposed nearby,

either naturally or by shallow excavations through the thin head and blown sand deposits which cover them hereabouts.

Thin, hard, partly bioclastic, limestones are present also in the upper part of the Scunthorpe Mudstones (but below the Frodingham Ironstone – see below) with, in addition, a few calcareous siltstones. They occur at outcrops along the crest of the more westerly of the two asymmetric ridges, which runs from Whitton southwards, via Flixborough and Scunthorpe. The appreciable number of fragments of these limestones found from the archaeological excavations presumably came from outcrops close by to the north, where the hardness of the limestones produces narrow but prominent topographic features along the hillside.

The highest few metres of the Scunthorpe Mudstones consist of Frodingham Ironstone, which is variously fine-grained, bioclastic and oolitic (i.e. mainly comprising spherical to ovoid masses generally not more than 2mm wide and with a concentric internal structure, called ooliths). The ironstone previously formed much of the gentle easterly declining dip slope of the more westerly asymmetric ridge, but as FIG. 1.13 shows, this slope has been extensively open-cast mined. Where outcrops of long-weathered ironstone survive, their highly oxidised reddish-brown surface layer is known in the area as 'gingerbread' stone, and prior to mining as a source of iron it was used locally as a building and field-walling stone.

Coleby Mudstones (Lias on FIG. 1.13)

All the Coleby Mudstones sequence is referable to the Lower Jurassic, and most of it consists of grey to black mudstones, with thin siltstones, a few thin sandstones and two thin ironstone layers at higher stratigraphical levels. Outcrops of the Coleby Mudstones are confined to the west-facing scarp slope of the more easterly of the two asymmetric ridges, which runs southwards from Winteringham, with Winterton and Broughton on its dip slope, and which forms the northernmost part of the Lincoln Edge.

Northampton Sand and Grantham Formation

The Northampton Sand and the overlying Grantham Formation (the latter formerly called the Lower Estuarine Series) form the basal Middle Jurassic strata in the area. Both are thin, and the Northampton Sand is absent north of Winterton. Both sequences crop out close to the top of the west-facing slope of the Lincoln Edge and locally extend down the dip slope to the east.

Lincolnshire Limestone

The Middle Jurassic Lincolnshire Limestone is lithologically variable, and these variations form the basis for a four-fold subdivision, summarised here in ascending order, but not differentiated on FIG. 1.13 in the interests of simplicity. The Raventhorpe Beds consist of strongly calcareous siltstones and mudstones with only a few thin

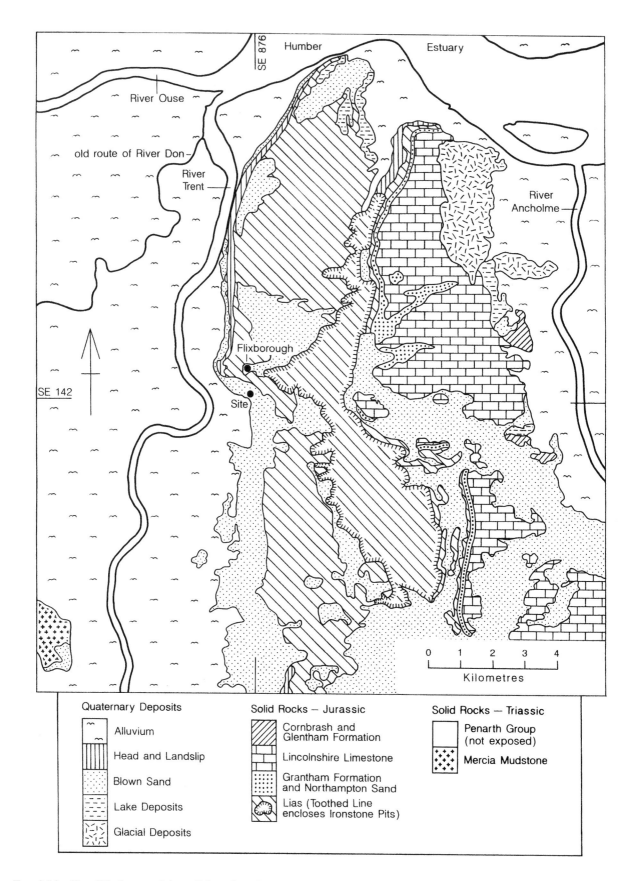

FIG. 1.13. Simplified map of the solid-rock and Quaternary geology of parts of northern Lincolnshire and the Humber estuary, after G. Gaunt (M. Frankland). [Note the basic Liassic strata are of Triassic age – see p.9, 'Scunthorpe Mudstones'.]

and locally impersistent limestones, notably the Cleatham Limestone and Ellerker Limestone. The Santon Oolite (an oolitic limestone, as its name implies) is thin, and does not extend much farther north than Winterton. The lower part of the overlying Kirton Cementstones comprises thinly interbedded fine-grained limestones and strongly calcareous mudstones, whereas the upper part is mainly calcareous mudstone with a few impersistent coral-knoll limestones. The Hibaldstow Limestones are, except for some thin fine-grained basal beds, almost entirely oolitic and mainly medium-bedded, characteristics that make this subdivision of the Lincolnshire Limestone the best building stone in Lincolnshire. The Lincolnshire Limestone as a whole forms the crest of the Lincoln Edge and extends down the easterly declining dip slope, but outcrops of the Hibaldstow Limestones are limited to discontinuous localities north of Winterton and from there south-eastwards to just beyond Appleby, with a few small outliers to the north and west of Risby Warren.

Glentham Formation and Cornbrash

The lower part of the Middle Jurassic Glentham Formation (formerly called the Upper Estuarine Series) is a friable and in places incohesive fine-grained sandstone and the upper part is mainly soft grey mudstone with some thin siltstones and fine-grained friable sandstones. The overlying Cornbrash, also referable to the Middle Jurassic, is a thin sequence of bioclastic limestones and grey calcareous sandstones. Within the Flixborough area, outcrops of both the Glentham Formation and the Cornbrash are confined to a few small locations at the foot of the Lincoln Edge dip slope, but both sequences occur at rockhead beneath the western part of the Ancholme Valley alluvium farther east.

1.3.2 Quaternary deposits

The Quaternary deposits in the area of the archaeological excavations, and in the surrounding region, have had the greatest influence on the location of the excavated settlement remains, the character of the surrounding landscape, managed or otherwise, and lifestyles reflected by the former inhabitants, from the seventh to eleventh centuries AD (Gaunt and Loveluck, Volume 4, Chapter 4; Loveluck Volume 4, Chapter 9). The existence and nature of the Quaternary deposits (especially the blown sand) have also played a critically important role in the preservation of the archaeological remains and their discovery.

Glacial Deposits

A glacial complex of clay till, sand and gravel extends north-north-eastwards from near Winterton almost to the Humber estuary, and a narrow ridge of clay till extends from Winterton eastwards more than half-way across the alluvial floodplain of the Ancholme valley, thereby forming the best natural route across the valley north of

Brigg. Most of the erratics in these deposits are of flint and (except near ground surface due to weathering) of chalk, but a few erratics consist of more far-travelled rocks. The deposits were formed approximately along the maximum south-westerly limits of ice that flowed westwards through the Humber Gap during the Devensian (i.e. last) glaciation. No distinct deposits of older glaciations are known in the Flixborough area, but scattered erratics (mainly of far-travelled rocks) resulting from older glaciations are present on solid rock outcrops in the area. Two small concentrations of these erratics are present at localities (SE 867 153; SE 870 157) near Flixborough. Old geological accounts (e.g. Ussher 1890, 134, 139) suggest that similar erratic concentrations, and possibly even distinct glacial deposits, in the area may have been removed by ironstone open-cast mining in more recent times.

Lake Deposits

A variety of deposits ranging from clay and silt to sand and gravel produce impersistent narrow terrace-like features in the area. They were formed along the margins of extra-glacial 'Lake Humber' when Devensian ice and its resulting deposits blocked drainage through the Humber Gap. The lake deposits bordering alluvium south-south-east of Whitton consist of clay and silt, but those occurring slightly higher up the slope to the west, and also those just north-west of Whitton, are of sand and gravel in which the pebbles are mainly of Liassic rocks. Two minute patches of similar sand and gravel at localities south-west of Flixborough are too small to show on Fig. 1.13. The lake deposits bordering alluvium on the western side of the Ancholme valley south-east of Winterton are mainly silty and clayey sands, locally containing pebbles of Lincolnshire Limestone.

Blown Sand

Deposits of blown sand (referred to as cover sand in some publications) are quite extensive in the Flixborough area, and vestigial dunes are present in some localities. Most of these deposits are dateable by calibrated radiocarbon and thermoluminescence age determinations to approximately between 12,500 and 11,400 calendrical years ago, in effect to little more than the last millennium of the Devensian (cold) Stage (Bateman 1998). Mesolithic and a few older artefacts have been found on and in some blown sand deposits, notably on Sheffield's Hill (NGR SE 910 158) not far from Flixborough. However, some Aeolian re-working of the original blown sand has taken place, probably starting with Bronze Age forest clearance, and Holland (1975) implies that it was still active during the Iron Age. In more recent centuries deliberate clearances to create warrens have accentuated the remobilisation process in some localities. The Anglo-Saxon settlement remains at Flixborough are located on blown sand, and both the latter and the more recently discovered Iron Age settlement evidence, to the north-west of the Anglo-Saxon site, are sealed by deposits of blown sand of varying depths (see chapter 2, this volume).

Head and landslip

Deposits of *head*, formed by solifluction down slopes, consist of clay and silt containing virtually unworn and unsorted fragments of rocks that crop out farther upslope. They are present along the steep west-facing slope between Whitton and Flixborough, along the southerly continuation of the same slope south of Yaddlethorpe, and along the steep north-facing and west-facing slope north-west and south-west of Winteringham. Most of the head deposits are thought to be of terminal Devensian age, but some downslope movement has continued into Flandrian (i.e. 'post-glacial') times. Numerous but fairly small rotational landslips are present on the steep west-facing slope between Alkborough and Flixborough, and a single landslip of this type occurs south of Yaddlethorpe. They are presumed to be mainly, and probably entirely, of Flandrian age, and some of those north of Burton-upon-Stather exhibit evidence of recent movement, almost certainly due to undercutting by the River Trent.

Alluvium

River and estuarine alluvial deposits in the Flixborough area vary from stiff, locally peaty, bluish clay to pale brown silty clay and silt. Stiff clays are most commonly found on the more low-lying, poorly drained ground at distance from the rivers and the Humber estuary, whereas the more silty deposits occur generally close to the rivers and estuary, where they formed as the elevated and normally better drained natural levées prior to construction of flood-defence embankments. Silty levées also flank the former original course of the River Don to its confluence with the River Trent north-east of Adlingfleet. In addition, much of the flood-warp (artificially induced alluvium deposited between the eighteenth and twentieth centuries to improve agricultural potential) consists of silty clay, and this extends widely along both sides of the Trent south of Flixborough.

Peat

A few small outcrops of peat are present in the Flixborough area, mainly on the western edge of the Ancholme valley floodplain, but they are insufficiently large to distinguish on Fig. 1.13.

Tufa

Lime-rich springs have deposited calcareous tufa in several localities near Flixborough, notably the 'dragon'

at Dragonby (SE 9044 1418), but these deposits also are too small to show on Fig. 1.13.

1.4 The structure of this volume
by Christopher Loveluck

The purpose of this volume is to present the primary level of post-excavation analysis and interpretation, resulting in a narrative of the chronological sequence, the nature of occupation and the use of space in the excavated area through time. Furthermore, through detailed integrated analysis of the different forms of evidence, assessment is also made of the representativity of the remains for interpretation, within different periods in the use of the excavated area, i.e. whether the archaeological evidence is representative of the excavated zone alone, or a much larger settlement area. Hence, the end goal of this book is to produce an integrated chronological interpretation of the character and nature of occupation in order to establish the limits of inference for wider comparative analysis and interpretation, which take place to a certain extent in Volume 3, and primarily in Volume 4.

This is achieved through a consideration of the excavation and recording strategies during the 1989 to 1991 campaign of fieldwork, followed by discussion of the approaches to post-excavation analysis and interpretation of the occupation sequence, in Chapter 2. Chapters 3 to 7 then discuss the integrated results in detail, within a chronological framework established through identification of periods within the stratigraphic sequence characterised by distinctive use of space; and by dating evidence, provided mainly by artefacts. Assessments of the representativity of the activities identified for the excavated area alone, or the wider settlement, are included within these chapters. Chapter 8 provides detailed consideration of the nature and interpretation of the mortuary remains of some of the inhabitants, recovered from the 1988 to 1991 excavations; namely, the graves discovered by Kevin Leahy in 1988, and the graves within and in association with one of the buildings on the settlement. The subsequent phases in the interpretation of the archaeological remains, in relation to the material-specific data (artefacts, industrial residues and biological remains), and interpretation of lifestyles and the wider importance of the evidence are then presented in Volumes 2, 3, and above all, in Volume 4.

2 The Excavations 1989–91, and Approaches to Post-Excavation Analysis

Christopher Loveluck, Matthew Canti and Andrew Payne

2.1 The excavations, 1989–1991 and approaches to recording

by Christopher Loveluck

Following the preliminary evaluations of 1988, two further trial trenches were excavated by the Humberside Archaeology Unit (now Humber Field Archaeology) to ascertain the nature of possible settlement remains, thought to be of 'Mid' Saxon date, to the north of the inhumation graves (see Figs 1.8, 1.9 and 2.2 below). These trial trenches uncovered parts of foundation trenches and post-holes for earth-fast timber buildings, together with occupation deposits and indications of the presence and preservation of a considerable artefact assemblage. As a result of the potential importance of the settlement and cemetery remains, both on a regional and national scale, English Heritage funded a two-year campaign of excavations to recover the maximum information possible from the Anglo-Saxon settlement remains; and the project also received financial support from British Steel and Clugston. The excavation team was supervised by David Tomlinson and David Atkinson, with guidance from Ben Whitwell, Kevin Leahy and David Evans; and the team members from this excavation phase are listed in the acknowledgements section of this volume.

Between 1989 and 1991, a two-dimensional surface area of 55 metres by 75 metres was opened up for excavation on the two sand spurs; part of the escarpment that they abutted; and also in the shallow valley, running into the centre of the excavated area, which ended in a hollow (Fig. 2.1). This excavation area was opened in stages during the two-year period as a precaution against damage to the site through illicit metal detecting. The focus of research extended around the trial trenches dug by the Humberside Archaeology Unit (Fig. 2.2). The overall surface area of the excavations was then divided into site zones/areas to best manage the excavation of the different types of structural remains and deposits in relation to topography and other factors which influenced preservation and recovery, such as natural erosion of the sand spurs and agricultural erosion on the western fringes of the site (Figs 2.2 and 2.3). The latter had occurred since the drainage of the Trent floodplain, by Cornelius Vermuyden and others, from the seventeenth century onwards, and also after enhancement of agricultural potential by flood warping (Gaunt, Chapter 1, this volume; Muir 2000, 49; Gaunt and Loveluck, Volume 4, Chapter 4).

The extension of the excavations eastward towards the site of All Saints' church was prevented as the eastern edge of the site adjoined the boundary of the cemetery associated with the ruined church. The latest burials in this churchyard dated from the eighteenth and nineteenth centuries, and disturbance of the ground within this comparatively recent burial area was not possible. Immediately beyond the church, the previously mentioned iron slag heaps from the former Normanby steel works stretched to the east and north-east. On the basis of aerial photographic evidence it is estimated that this area was covered by slag between 1924 and 1947 (Loveluck and McKenna 1999).

Recent trial excavation by Humber Field Archaeology, on behalf of north Lincolnshire Museums and Archaeology Service, revealed parts of the moated settlement, between 300 and 400 metres to the east of the church, which was formerly the manor house of North Conesby (Duggan, Fraser and Steedman 2001; Bradley 2005). The area between the church and the moated site was formerly known as 'Church field' when Snape recorded the name in 1778, and it is possible that this field may have held housing plots for the medieval settlement of North Conesby. At present, however, insufficient opportunity has presented itself for undertaking detailed survey and evaluation work immediately to the east of All Saints' church to confirm the existence of further archaeological remains, whether from the Anglo-Saxon or later periods.

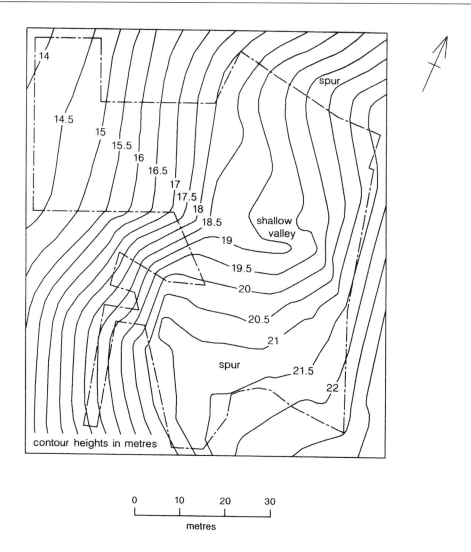

FIG. 2.1. *Contour map of the excavated area, 1989–1991, showing the sand spurs and the central shallow valley* (M. Frankland).

To a certain extent, work is hampered by the nature of the environment for excavation, with the presence of unstable slag heaps, heavy metals and ordnance, dating from 1939–45; and unfortunately, it is unknown to what extent any archaeological deposits on the escarpment were truncated when the ground was cleared prior to dumping iron slag.

The excavated settlement remains were both located upon, and sealed by blown sand; and the sealing deposits were up to two metres deep in places. Below this sand inundation, post-excavation analysis (see below) has identified evidence of six broad periods of settlement activity, with definable phases within them, dating from at least the early seventh century AD until the mid fourteenth/early fifteenth century. The overall stratigraphic sequence can be summarised as a series of phases of buildings and other structures, associated at different periods with refuse dumped around them in middens and yards, or with a central refuse zone in the shallow valley

that ran up into the centre of the excavated area (FIG. 2.4*). Several of the main structural phases were also separated by demolition and levelling dumps, and it is this superimposition that has resulted in the exceptional occupation sequence. The majority of the recovered finds, approximately 15,000 artefacts and hundreds of thousands of animal bone fragments (of which approximately 200,000 of the hand-collected bones were identifiable, not including the sieved assemblage), were found within these refuse, levelling and other occupation deposits. The high wood-ash content of a significant number of the dumps, their rapid build up, and the constant accretion of sand within them, formed a soil micro-environment which was chemically inert – the alkalinity of the wood-ash and sand accretion preventing acid leaching (Canti 1992, 18; Canti, below). It was this fortuitous burial environment that ensured the excellent preservation conditions for the artefact and vertebrate skeletal assemblages.

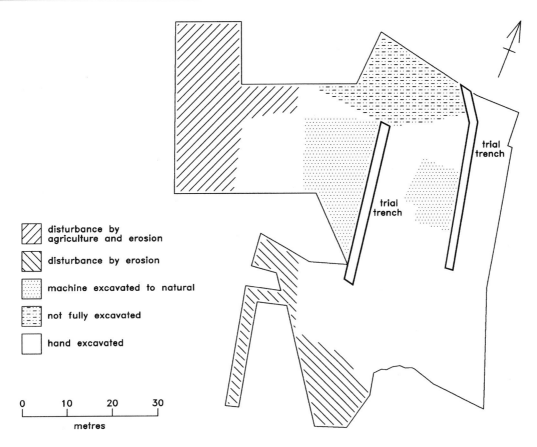

Fig. 2.2. Excavation methods in different parts of the site, and areas damaged by erosion or agriculture (M. Frankland).

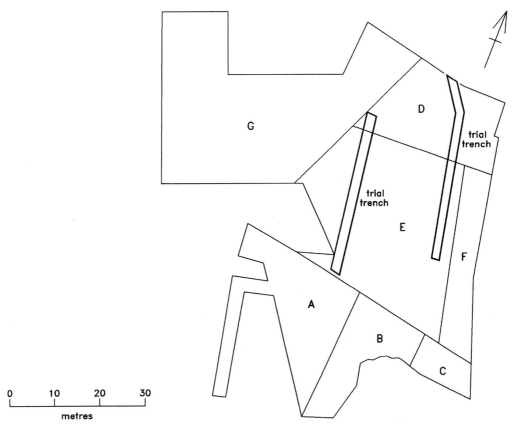

Fig. 2.3. Location of 'site areas' within the 1989–1991 excavation trench (M. Frankland).

Excavation, recording and sampling strategies within the defined intra-site areas were governed by the nature of the deposits present and the topography. Site areas A, B and C formed the southern edge of the excavation area (FIG. 2.3). They also constituted the southern and western edges of the southern spur (in areas A and B), and a working sand quarry edge (in areas B and C), which accounts for the irregular limit of the excavation in this area (FIG. 2.2). The contour plan (FIG. 2.1) shows this southern edge before the quarry had expanded to the edge of the excavated area. The central part of the site – areas E and F – comprised the hollow forming the end of the shallow valley (E) and a more gently upward sloping area of sand along the eastern edge of the site, next to the boundary enclosing the cemetery of All Saints' church (F). Area G represented a gently sloping area where the shallow valley opens out on to the lower land leading into the floodplain of the River Trent. Due to its gently sloping nature, area G had suffered erosion by natural slope erosion and also by ploughing (FIG. 2.2). Area D then formed the northern extremity of the excavated area, where the gradual southern slope of the second, and less pronounced spur began to rise from the shallow valley (FIG. 2.3).

The vast majority of the site was excavated by hand, following removal of the sand overburden by machine. Each stratigraphic unit or 'context' was excavated individually in stratigraphic order from the latest to earliest feature or deposit. Due to constraints of time and finance, however, small areas were excavated by machine. This time pressure was caused by the difficulties of excavating in a working sand quarry, and by the sheer scale of environmental sampling, artefact recovery, and associated three-dimensional recording of the locations of find-spots and sample points. The zones subjected to partial machine excavation were in the central part of the site, in areas G and E (FIG. 2.2). Area G contained a substantial ditch terminal, sealed by deposits described as 'dark soils' (see below). The ditch was sectioned by machine, and the fills (stratigraphic units) within it were given a single context number, with the exception of selected areas that were hand-cleaned and recorded in section. The contexts/stratigraphic units recorded in section were given individual numbers. The ditch terminal was also hand-excavated. Area E, containing the terminal of the shallow valley, had been the focus for repeated phases of construction, refuse dumping and levelling. The area excavated by machine in this zone overlay part of building 13 from Period 3, phase 3b (see Loveluck and Atkinson, Chapter 4, this volume). As a result, parts of building 13 and associated deposits were recorded in plan only.

In the early stages of the excavations, the exceptional nature of the deposits, their apparent 'Mid Saxon' date, their excellent state of preservation, and early hints of the unique vertical stratigraphic sequence from a rural settlement of this period, prompted the excavators to put

in place artefact, biological and geo-archaeological sampling and recovery procedures appropriate to the importance and scale of the remains encountered. For the artefacts, two recording procedures were followed. The first procedure provided a system to record artefacts and seemingly important pieces of industrial debris individually, as 'Recorded Finds' (RFs); and the second provided a system to record industrial debris and certain fragmentary artefacts as 'Bulk Finds'. The exact location of each RF was recorded in three dimensions, whereas the locations of artefact remains designated as 'bulk finds' were recorded on the basis of the general three-dimensional position of their associated context/stratigraphic unit.

Authorized metal-detecting in the location of the excavated site had also been one of the principal reasons for the rediscovery of the Anglo-Saxon settlement remains, following Riley's initial finds of 1933. Indeed, it was the legitimately collected and reported finds recovered by metal-detector that hinted at the potential wealth of the settlement. Subsequently, survey of spoil by metal detector during the course of the excavations provided further artefacts, primarily as unstratified finds. The key concern of this volume is the stratified settlement sequence and its associated artefact and biological remains. Nevertheless, key unstratified finds recovered by metal detector and other chance stray finds, such as the tool hoard and lead tanks, were also considered during the course of the research, mainly in volumes 2 and 4.

Turning to the 'environmental' data, the necessary sampling and recovery procedures were achieved through consultation with, and the active participation of the Environmental Archaeology Unit, University of York (funded by English Heritage), and advice from other Ancient Monuments Laboratory (English Heritage) specialists. A rigorous sampling approach was pursued for both hand-collected bones and sediment samples, following the methodology later published by the *Association for Environmental Archaeology Sampling and Recovery Work Group* (Hall 1995). All hand-collected bones were retained, and up to 1759 *General Biological Analysis* and *Bulk-sieved* (flotation) sediment samples were taken from deposits on the site, to provide comprehensive systematic coverage of the individual contexts. When large surface refuse/occupation deposits and pits were encountered extra sediment samples were also taken on a judgement basis, to assess the homogeneity or otherwise of their contents (see Dobney *et al.*, Volume 3). Selection of samples for geo-archaeological analysis was also made on a judgement basis with a view to examining the nature of refuse and ditch deposits, and to understand the preservation conditions and circumstances of archaeological site formation (see Canti, below).

The excavation programme finished in 1991, and it was clear that further remains dating from the Anglo-Saxon period were to be found in the vicinity of the excavated area, based on the fact that structural features continued under the eastern limit of the excavated area towards All Saints' church, and the recovery of stray finds. As a consequence, an area to the east and north of the excavations was designated as a Scheduled Ancient Monument in 1992. Following the emergency designation of the scheduled monument, magnetometer and resistivity surveys were undertaken in 1993 in the areas surrounding the former excavations, demonstrating the existence of further archaeological remains – especially to the east, although their character has yet to be proven (see Payne, below). Following the discovery of the Anglo-Saxon lead tanks and tool hoard, limited trial excavation and surface collection survey was also undertaken within the sand quarry, in 1994 and 1995, and some additional evidence of occupation deposits and post-holes of Anglo-Saxon date was identified. Further quarrying, 300 metres to the north, has also demonstrated beyond doubt the importance of the blown sand belt for the preservation of buried archaeological remains and landscapes, with the discovery of sealed Iron Age settlement deposits (North Lincolnshire Sites and Monuments Record; Loveluck and McKenna 1999). Previous stray finds and artefacts from the 1989–91 excavations also demonstrate Romano-British settlement somewhere in the immediate vicinity or even adjacent to the excavated area (Dudley 1931; Loveluck and Atkinson, Chapters 3 to 7, this volume).

2.2 Geoarchaeological studies at Flixborough-North Conesby: understanding the burial environment, taphonomy and preservation conditions
by Matthew Canti

The geo-archaeological studies undertaken on soils from the excavations at Flixborough were intended to address two general themes of inquiry. Firstly, the nature of the blown sand and its relationship to the exceptional preservation of bones in certain deposits; and secondly, the circumstances of the formation and the nature of the major refuse deposits located during the excavations. To this end, samples of the blown sand and refuse/occupation deposits were collected on a visit to the site during the course of the excavations. They were taken from different locations on and around the excavated area (see FIGS 2.5 and 2.6). Some deposits, which were shown to be important subsequently as a result of post-excavation analysis, were not selected. However, the samples still provide a generally representative range of refuse deposits from the excavated area.

2.2.1 The Blown Sand
The blown sand of the spurs on which the settlement remains were located is a key element of the archaeological story at Flixborough, since it forms the background to all the deposits and may, of itself, provide the basis for understanding the taphonomic conditions.

Particle-Size Analysis
Particle-size analyses of the five blown sand samples taken were carried out using sieves and a Sedigraph 5000ET (see FIG. 2.7). These curves are a standard representation of the full range of mineral particle-sizes found in each sample, and a discussion of interpretation methods can be found in Canti (1991). It is immediately apparent that the materials are almost identical, despite the vertical and lateral variations in the sampling points. They consist of extremely well-sorted sands with the bulk of material (steepest part of curve) between 100 and 300 μm.

Calcareous Mineralogy
Sieve fractions were regularly examined and tested for their particulate calcium carbonate ($CaCO_3$) content. This was carried out by two means. The coarser fractions down to 45 μm were submerged in hydrochloric acid (HCl) and viewed reacting under the microscope. For fractions down to 400 μm, it was possible to do rough identifications of the grain type reacting and these are recorded on FIG. 2.8. The finer fractions down to 20 μm were counted under polarising light, where calcite and calcareous materials are easily identified by their high birefringence and extreme variations in relief on stage rotation. Inherent differences in the two techniques were investigated in the 45 and 38 μm fractions of S3, but the errors were found to be only 2–3%.

Typical results for both shallow and deep samples are shown on FIG. 2.8. It can be seen that while deep (FIG. 2.8, upper) and shallow samples (FIG. 2.8, lower) both have increasing percentages of calcium carbonate below about 150 μm, only the deep samples show an increase above 150 μm up to the maximum grain size around 2 mm. The difference between the types of calcareous materials is also highly significant. The coarse distributions on FIG. 2.8 (upper) are made up of limestone, chalk calcareous sandstone, tufa etc. – clearly a detrital assemblage blown in with the original sand; the fine calcareous material in both shallow and deep sands, however, consists almost entirely of individual crystals. The latter are varied in shape but often consist of elongated or jagged grains, unlikely to survive a long phase of aeolian transport without wear. Two hypotheses can be put forward to explain this pattern of distribution below.

The calcareous materials are part of an even distribution that was diluted by addition of the quartz-dominated sand. This would imply two original sources for the aeolian material, and is untenable if the fine calcite is authigenic. With the coarse quartz grains (>200 μm), travel by atmospheric suspension is only possible under extreme wind conditions (Catt 1988) and they would typically travel more by saltation. The fine calcite could not have undergone such a process and can, at most, have undergone only a light phase of suspended transport, perhaps simultaneously with the saltation of the coarse particles. These complications weigh against the theory,

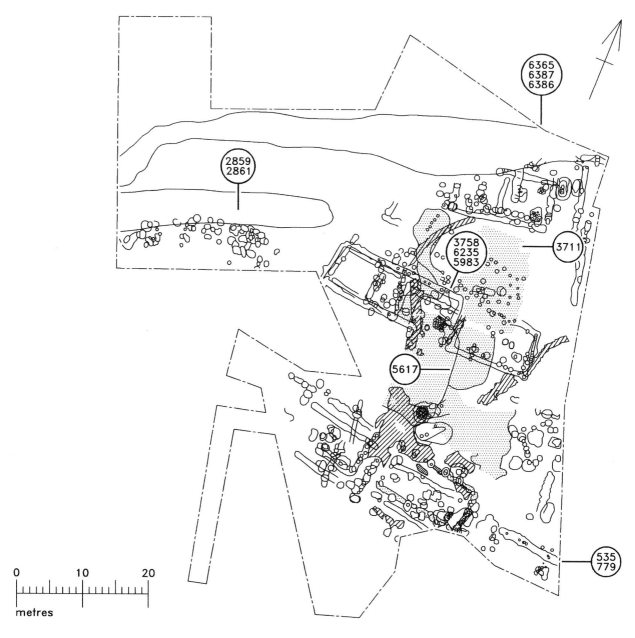

Fig. 2.5. *Schematic plan of the locations of the soil samples from the archaeological deposits (M. Canti and M. Frankland).*

but it has the merit of clearly explaining the bowl-shaped distribution having its nadir at the point of maximum grain percentage, i.e. 200–300 μm.

The second hypothesis is that the distribution of calcareous material is a function of dissolution dynamics. This hypothesis works well for the left-half of the distribution on FIG. 2.8 (upper). Here, detrital calcareous components are getting smaller due to dissolution and have almost disappeared around 300 μm. On FIG. 2.8 (lower), the detrital materials have completely dissolved, in keeping with their stratigraphic positions nearer the surface. The problem with this hypothesis lies in explaining the apparent growth of the fine calcite on the right-hand side of these diagrams. It is pertinent here to

note that the interstitial spaces between the sand grains (assuming perfectly packed 300 μm spheres) would offer a maximum size for crystal growth of about 120 μm, and indeed, no authigenic-type calcites were seen in the fractions above this size. Whether they truly grew *in situ* or not, their presence cannot pre-date, or be contemporaneous with, the leaching of the detrital material, since the fine grains would obviously dissolve first in the leaching environment.

Neither hypothesis is completely satisfactory. There may have been other factors at work, for example a difference in dissolution rates between the limestone, tufa etc. and the tighter structured crystals. The other main possibility is that the shifting nature of the sand put coarse

Sample/context number	Phase	Nature of material	pH	Location/Site grid reference
S1		Blown sand	7.6	Dune-bedded deposits in the quarry-trench to the W of the excavation. Probably more than 4 m down from the pre-excavation land surface.
S2		Blown sand	6.4	0.75 m depth (from surface) in the deep capping deposit on the east face of the excavation area.
S3		Blown sand	7.5	Dune-bedded deposits in the quarry-trench to the W of the excavation. Probably more than 4 m down from the pre-excavation land surface.
S4		Blown sand	6.6	Natural subsoil 0.6 m depth exposed in the quarry-trench to the west of the excavation.
S5		Blown sand	6.6	0.5 m depth in the deep pit around 100 m to the south of the excavation.
535	6iii	Dark Soil	6.8	96.85/107.25 at 22.63 m O.D.
779	6iii	Dark Soil/Occupation deposit	6.8	96.85/107.25 at 22.49 m O.D.
6365	6ii – 6iii	Dark Soil	7.3	93.43/107.25 at 20.12 m O.D.
6387	2–5b	Occupation deposit	7.8	93.43/107.25 at 19.87 m O.D.
6386	2–5b	Occupation deposit	6.8	93.43/107.25 at 19.61 m O.D.
3711	5a	Ash dump	8.2	88.65/153.27 at 19.45 m O.D.
5617	3bv	Bone dump	7.8	80.18/135.63 at 19.23 m O.D.
3758	4ii	Ash dump	7.5	80.08/147.15 at 18.46 m O.D.
5983	3biv	Ash dump	7.9	80.08/147.15 at 18.27 m O.D.
2859	4ii	Ditch fill	6.7	48.72/159.20 at 15.87 m O.D.
2861	2–4ii	Ditch base	7.4	48.40/158.96 at 15.23 m O.D.

FIG. 2.6. Number, location and pH of all the samples. Blown sand samples consisted of bagged material only; archaeological samples consisted of undisturbed Kubiena tins for micromorphology, each with a matching bulk sample. Locations can be found on FIG. 2.5 (M. Canti).

and fine materials out of phase on a micro-scale, the detail being lost in bulk sampling. The pH values (see FIG. 2.6) reflect accurately the broad concept of near-surface samples being more leached; those with no left-hand side to their calcareous distributions (FIG. 2.8 – lower) are more acid (*c*. pH 6.6), while those with coarse calcareous components (FIG. 2.8 – upper) are more alkaline (*c*. pH 7.6).

Summary

For the purposes of understanding the taphonomy within and around the excavated area at Flixborough, the sand can be seen as a weakly calcareous material, constantly undergoing leaching, but not yet having developed any significant acidity. The sand's accretion since the

fourteenth and fifteenth centuries means that a constant supply of calcium carbonate has been added to the top of the profile at regular intervals. This has arrived in the form of hard limestones, soft limestones including chalk and tufa, shell and calcareous sandstone. At some stage, interstitial calcite appears to have grown, but very local derivation of these crystals cannot be absolutely ruled out. It is these calcareous additions which prevented the acidification, and hence artefact and bone decay, that would otherwise be expected on such a coarse parent material.

2.2.2 The Archaeological Deposits

The range of archaeological deposits at Flixborough

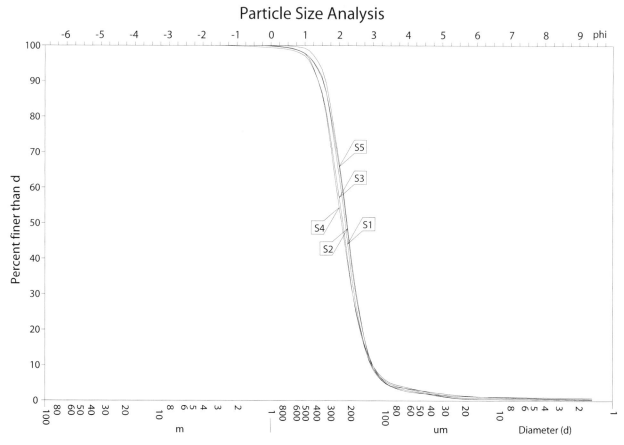

Fig. 2.7. Particle-size analyses of the blown sand samples (M. Canti).

includes purely man-made dumps through to semi-natural ditch fills. They have been studied using two techniques. Particle-size analysis was carried out to look at the relationship of these deposits to the blown sand, and to provide any additional information on the make-up of the bulk materials. Micromorphology was used to examine the details of the ash and occupation deposits. This involved impregnating undisturbed samples with resin, sectioning them down to 30 μm thickness, and examining them under a petrological microscope.

Particle-Size Analyses

The particle-size analyses of the deposits sampled are presented in bulk form on Fig. 2.9. This allows gross comparisons of the types of mineral background in the materials. It can be seen that all of the deposits are strongly influenced by a blown sand content – chiefly represented by the steep part of the curve around 200– 300 μm. The coarse ends (500 μm upwards) are rather variable due to stone, bone, mortar and slag mainly in stratigraphic units/contexts 5617, 3711, 3758 and 5983. At the fine end, the ash dumps (3711, 3758 and 5983) have all received a large proportion (approx. 20%) of fine silt (15–2 μm) from the ash itself; this is also true, to a lesser extent, of the occupation horizon 6387. This material is characteristic of plant ash, and comes from the heat-induced conversion of plant calcium oxalate

crystals (prisms and druses) to calcium carbonate pseudomorphs (Brochier 1983; Canti 2003). Many of these pseudomorphs are still visible in the relevant thin-sections. The soil on top of the Anglo-Saxon ditch (2859) and the uppermost dark soil layer (535) have received the least of the various human-made inputs, and their curves match the blown sand closely. What little variation there is in both 2859 and 535 appeared to consist chiefly of finely divided bone powder. This material was found in most of the fine sieve fractions (125–45 μm) of all samples, and dominated the finest grades (63 and 45 μm) in many.

Micromorphology

Only results of the more significant deposits/stratigraphic units are presented below.

2859 and 2861 – These are from the ditch on the north-west side of the site (see Loveluck and Atkinson, Chapters 3 to 5, this volume). 2859, the sealing soil is the most featureless of the samples taken. As was suggested by its particle size analysis, it contains no material other than blown sand and a weak humus content, not even the small amounts of charcoal typical elsewhere. On this evidence alone, it would seem that the final stabilisation of the ditch fill occurred prior to subsequent human activity. At the

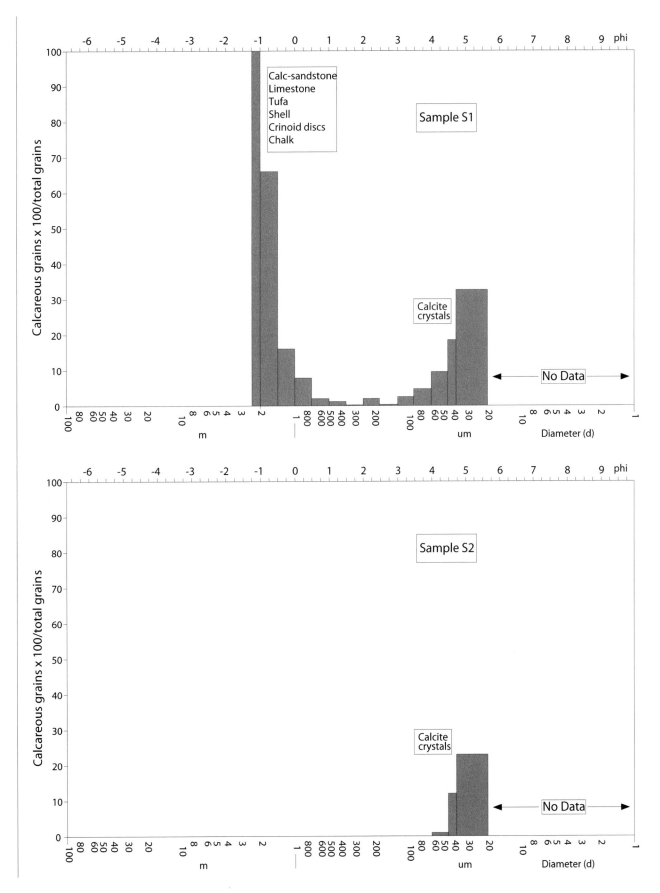

Fig. 2.8. Upper – Predominant types and percentages of calcareous grains from deep sand sample S1. Lower – Percentages of calcareous grains (all fresh sharp-edged calcite) from shallow sand sample S2 (M. Canti).

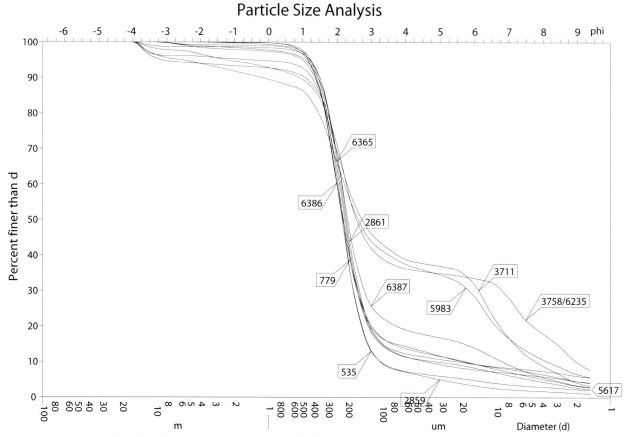

FIG. 2.9. *Particle-size analyses of all the archaeological deposits (M. Canti).*

base of the ditch fill (2861), the primary soil lining the sides is much richer. The basic fabric is non-calcareous sand, but many areas show individual grains with coatings of a clay-sized orange material. This has been found in patches in a number of slides, and a clue to its possible origin is to be found in a highly weathered bone fragment in 2861 (FIG. 2.10*).

The orange material can be seen covering most surfaces of the bone, even the most internal enlarged pores. It seems possible that the clay-sized aggregates are breakdown products of the bone, perhaps forming clays together with iron and silica in the soil water. The clay is more thickly deposited inside this bone than elsewhere on the slide, suggesting perhaps that it is fairly mobile, but is being protected from translocation by being contained in the remaining bone structure. Once the bone had completely gone, the clay would then be free to form the coatings found elsewhere. This view cannot be proven, however, because the bone fragment may have been blown in after a period of burial in nearby soils where it picked up translocating clay. It would also not be an explanation for all the mobile clay in the slide; there are other areas where clear examples of partially broken-down imported soil fragments can be found. However, the coatings produced by these fragments are typically associated with a large

proportion of silt grains, probably implying mudstone or alluvial sources for the aggregates.

On the bottom left of the slide, there is a large intact piece of bone, lightly-coated with the orange material. The proximity between the highly weathered and the intact fragments may be due to the relative porosity of the bone types, but an implication could be that this context is acidifying only patchily. Although there is a general lack of calcareous elements, the occasional decaying shell or tufa fragment can be found, supporting the view that it was calcareous until relatively recently.

Little has been preserved that could elucidate the use of this ditch. Macromorphologically, the dark staining appears to have 'soaked' into the surrounding sand suggesting that it was temporarily wet, but no micro-sedimentary structures have been preserved in the thin-section. The few fine fabric aggregates that do occur are not due to sedimentary sorting, but are lumps of local soil. Periods of bank collapse and refilling with sand appear to have occurred, alternating with dark bands suggestive more of dirty water than periods of soil development. If the sand was as erosive as it is today, little time would be available for plant establishment in such a ditch before it became refilled with sand.

6365, 6387 and 6386 – 6387 and 6386 are occupation deposits, and 6365 is the 'dark soil' overlying them. 6365 consists of sand with very few of the orange coatings discussed above. Of three large bone fragments present, only one is slightly weathered; again it is the larger pores that are weathering out, and again the coatings are beginning to develop. The pH is similar to 2861 at *c.* 7.5, and it is suggested that this context is at a similar stage of acidification. It is less advanced in this respect than its possible counterpart 535. It has been buried under a more clayey deposit in the cultivated area to the north-west of the dune (see FIG. 2.2) and will therefore have generally received a more alkaline throughput. Two large limestone/calcareous sandstone fragments are present in the slide along with a small amount of charcoal. 6387 has a partially weathered wood ash matrix denoting a status somewhere between the clean sands so far discussed and the ash dumps, as reflected in its particle-size analysis. Within this matrix there are many fragments of ceramic, charcoal, and limestone as well as a portion of bird's egg and decaying earthworm granules (calcareous excretions of *Lumbricidae*).

6386 is a similar layer to 6387 in most respects. There appears to be a higher sand to wood ash ratio in 6386, leading to its having a more regular blown sand-type of particle size curve. However, the thin-section barely reflects this difference, and all the same sorts of objects are found in the matrix. One unusual part is an area of fused wood or possibly grass ash on the left-hand side of the slide (FIG. 2.11*). This is typical of the high-temperature burning of plants (Folk and Hoops 1982; Robinson and Straker 1991), the glassy material arising from silica (in the form of sand or biogenic opal) being fluxed by alkaline salts from the plant ash.

It is interesting to note that neither 6386 nor 6387 contain any bone. This could be due to chance, but the excellent preservation associated with ash in other samples may suggest either a different use (e.g. industrial), or the systematic removal of the bone (e.g. by dogs?).

3711 – was an ash deposit possibly from ovens to its north. The matrix is extremely rich in calcium carbonate from the ash, along with charcoal, shell, sandstone, limestone, bone, and two pieces of shell-tempered pottery. All calcareous elements are near-perfect in their preservation due to the calcareous matrix and high pH (8.2). Bone is, therefore, almost pristine and has none of the orange clay adhering to its surfaces (FIG. 2.12*).

3758 – was designated as an ash dump from phase 4ii (see Loveluck and Atkinson, Chapters 4 and 5, this volume). Parts of the lower half of the slide (FIG. 2.13*) are rich in dark fused masses of ash and finely divided charcoal, while the upper half is dominated more by a pale calcareous ash matrix, although there is not a strong division. The ash matrix contains large amounts of charcoal, micritic calcareous aggregates, tufa, sandstone, earthworm granules, fused ash and shell fragments. The large central charcoal can be positively identified as oak (*Quercus* sp.) and some of the upper fragments probably are as well (Carruthers pers. comm.). Only small quantities of bone are present, and these show the same high degree of preservation as those in 3711.

5983 – from phase 3biv, also an ash dump, is considerably different to the others in that its contents are nearly all fused. The ashes are mixed with both burnt and unburnt soil, as well as plant material, ceramic and stone (FIG. 2.14*). Bone preservation is generally good, but some of the bone is burnt, making comparison with other slides problematic. Much (but not all) of the fused area has fine orange-clay coatings similar to those found on the weathering bone. Bone itself can still just be made out amongst the melted mass, but the extent of its proportions before heating cannot be assessed. The isotropy of the resultant glasses and the low birefringence of whole bone are too similar optically for any sure identification.

Summary
The results from the study of the archaeological deposits show the clear effect of wood ash in maintaining a high pH and thus promoting the preservation of calcareous components including bone. In this respect, both calcium carbonate (ash, limestone, chalk, tufa, earthworm granules, shell) and calcium phosphate (bone) are similarly affected by the soil water alkalinity. Phosphate itself has not been examined, since measuring its levels in soils consisting partly of bone powder, relative to the clean sand containing no collophane or other phosphatic components, would be pointless. There must be a bone-preserving effect amongst the lower stratigraphic layers receiving water that has picked up ions from the bone above; it will be less effective at high pH, however, because of the tendency of phosphate ions to form calcium phosphates and phosphate-carbonates under alkaline conditions (Limbrey 1975). The nature of the clay-sized coatings found on weathered bone is beyond the scope of this study, but would be a useful area for further research. Specifically, if it is the result of bone decay, then its presence as grain coatings in 2861 may represent the products of large amounts of bone now vanished. This could relate to the phenomenon of soil silhouettes (Keeley *et al.* 1977), where decaying bone appears to attract manganese from the surrounding soil.

2.2.3 Discussion and conclusions

The issue of the bone preservation at Flixborough can now be seen as a coincidental relationship between two factors – the wood ash itself, and the calcareous component of the blown sand. Constant accretion of the sand has meant that the residual calcium carbonate in the ash deposits has never had to undergo the acid leaching that would be expected on such a substrate if it were pure quartz. This has slowed down its removal, even in layers relatively close to the surface, and allowed pH values as high as 8.2 (though more typically in the 7–8 range) to be maintained. The sheer volume of ash is therefore another part of the equation, as is the unknown factor of the speed of deposition. This latter question is important for its implications on open-air pre-weathering of the bone, which would presumably act to hasten its breakdown. There is no evidence in any of the slides for lengthy surface exposure of the ash layers, although the deposits examined represent a small sample of the deposits excavated and artefact weathering does suggest longer surface exposure of ash deposits in some instances (see Loveluck and Atkinson, Chapters 3 to 7, this volume). Rainfall and wind would be expected to create sorted layers and micro-sedimentation features (e.g. crusts), which would survive burial as long as they were not disturbed by soil fauna.

Site staff reported minimal earthworm activity and limited disturbance from animal burrows. This would be unlikely to destroy all evidence of sedimentary effects, and it can reasonably be concluded that, in the sampled areas, the ash was laid down in deep layers rather than as slowly accumulating deposits (see Loveluck and Atkinson, Chapters 4, 5 and 6). How the bone fits in to this pattern depends rather on its origin, and the organisation of disposal. In certain cases, the large quantities might have necessitated deliberate emplacement below the surface. Burial in what appear, occasionally, to have been very hot ashes (especially 5983) would also have discouraged scavenging animals, at least for some of the time.

The peculiarities of the refuse dumps examined here have provided a snapshot of taphonomic conditions where leaching has been reduced to a minimum. Thus, we are effectively viewing an archaeological site where preservation conditions, at least in some aspects, are more typical of a far shorter period of burial. In the absence of the sand, much of the detail would have been lost to acidity and reduced to a series of mainly charcoal layers.

2.3 Attempts to establish an idea of the overall settlement area: geophysical surveys at Flixborough-North Conesby, 1993 to 1997

by Andrew Payne

In 1993 the Ancient Monuments Laboratory undertook a series of limited trial geophysical surveys at Flixborough to test the potential of non-intrusive methods for tracing the eastern and northern continuation of the Anglo-Saxon settlement, beyond the area of the 1989–91 archaeological excavations. If effective it was hoped that geophysical investigation of the immediate environs of the excavation

could help determine the excavated proportion of the site and allow the accuracy of the boundary of the scheduled area to be assessed. It was anticipated that the physical nature of the archaeological features adjacent to the excavated area, combined with their potentially deep burial beneath more than a metre of wind-blown sand, would present challenging conditions for geophysical methods and restrict their effectiveness, accounting for the hesitancy with which geophysical survey was initially applied to the site.

When the site was scheduled in 1992, definition of the scheduled area (FIG. 2.15) was largely based on information already available from excavation. Geophysical survey was not included in the original scheduling process. After the site had been scheduled, there still remained a need to establish with greater certainty the full extent of the settlement activity at Flixborough in order to place the excavated remains in a wider context, inform the future management of the site, and to help secure the archaeological deposits from further disturbance in the future.

It had not been possible to uncover the full extent of settlement activity during the two year excavation programme. Foundations of buildings clearly continued underneath the eastern edge of the area excavated during 1989–91 (into Area 1 of the geophysical survey: see FIG. 2.17), while pits and gullies containing Mid to Late Saxon ceramics were also encountered in 1994 and 1995 on the gentle southern slope of the spur (see FIGS 2.15 and 2.17). These discoveries demonstrated that the Anglo-Saxon settlement area continued to the east and south of the main excavated site, probably encompassing the cemetery found in 1988 (also of presumed Mid to Late Saxon date: FIG. 2.17, area 3).

The pasture field north of the excavation (Area 2 of the geophysical survey: see FIG. 2.17) contains a spring which could have served as a water source for the settlement (Whitwell *pers comm* 1991). A further indication that settlement may have extended to the north of the excavated remains, was a scatter of Mid to Late Saxon pottery collected during fieldwalking in 1991, downslope of the north field. Cropmark features are also visible in the field where it slopes up to the limestone plateau (the Lincoln Edge: see area 5 on FIGS 2.15 and 2.17). These may be linked to settlement, although they could also be natural features associated with bands of ironstone that outcrop in the area. These are shown on a similar alignment to the earthwork and cropmark features on the geology mapping (British Geological Survey 1983). Another possibility is that archaeological features, present in the field to the north of the excavation (especially those higher up the slope near the 40m contour line), could be connected with the later abandoned medieval settlement of North Conesby, located approximately 100m further east up the escarpment from the Mid to Late Saxon remains. This presents a problem when assigning geophysical anomalies at Flixborough to

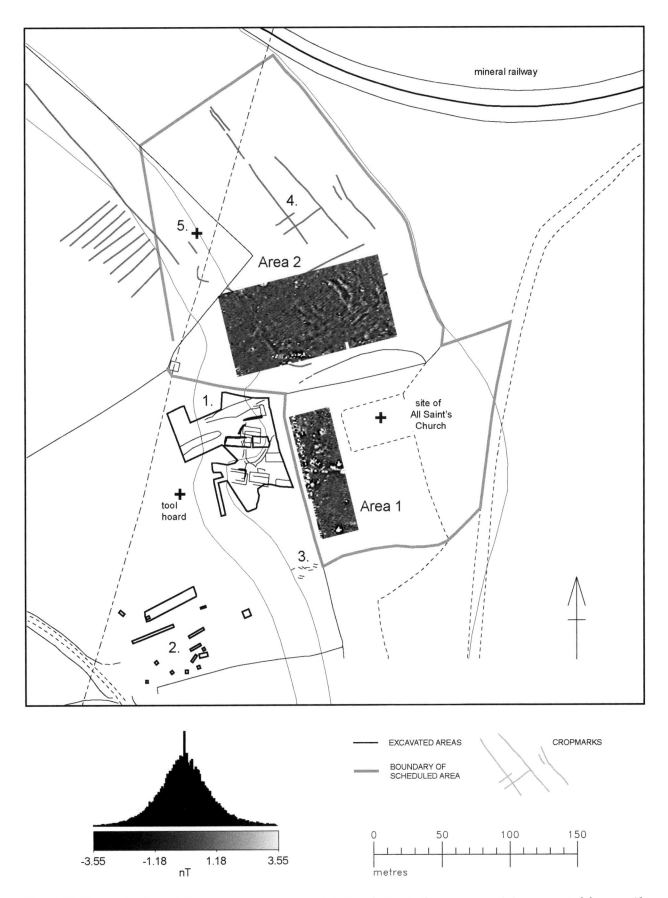

FIG. 2.15. Greyscale plots of the magnetometer survey data in relation to the areas containing excavated features (1, 2 and 3), cropmarks (4) and the evidence from fieldwalking (5) (A. Payne).

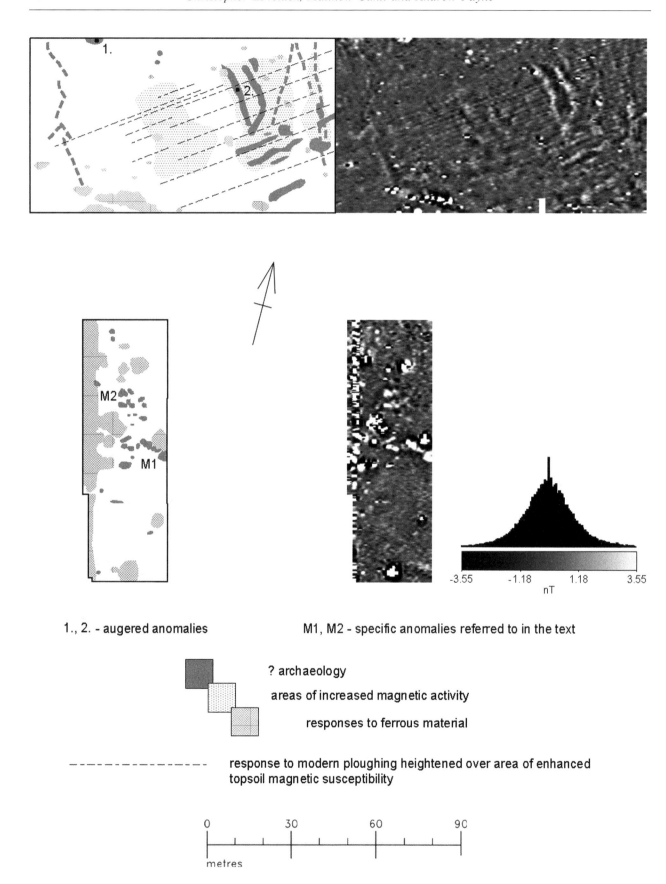

1., 2. - augered anomalies   M1, M2 - specific anomalies referred to in the text

? archaeology

areas of increased magnetic activity

responses to ferrous material

– – – – – – – – – – – – –   response to modern ploughing heightened over area of enhanced
topsoil magnetic susceptibility

FIG. 2.16. Larger-scale greyscale plots of the magnetometer data and detailed interpretation of the magnetometer data without underlying mapping (A. Payne).

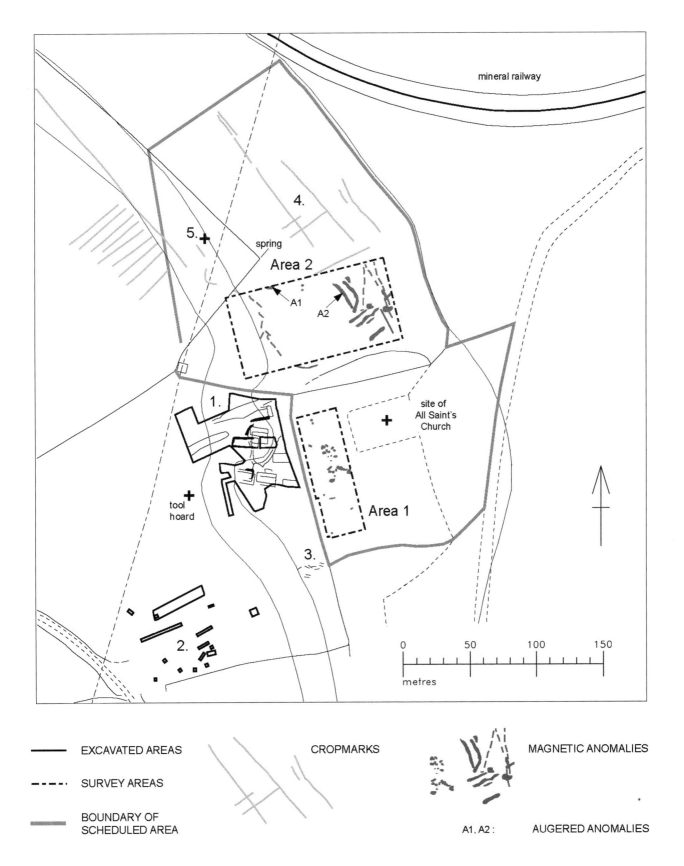

mineral railway

4.

5.

spring

Area 2

A1

A2

1.

tool
hoard

3.

2.

site of
All Saint's
Church

Area 1

0   50   100   150

metres

———— EXCAVATED AREAS

– – – – SURVEY AREAS

———— BOUNDARY OF
SCHEDULED AREA

CROPMARKS

MAGNETIC ANOMALIES

A1, A2 :   AUGERED ANOMALIES

F IG. 2.17. *Map-based interpretation of the magnetic anomalies of possible archaeological significance relative to the excavated features (nos 1 to 3 on the plan), the cropmarks (4), and the evidence from fieldwalking (5). This also shows the positions of auger holes A1 and A2 (A. Payne).*

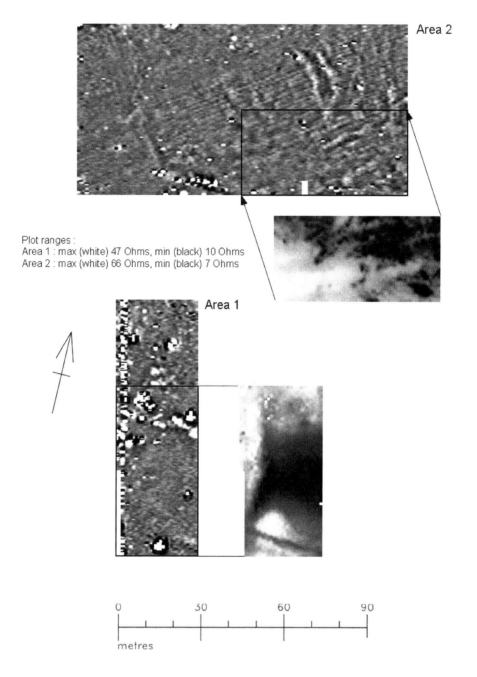

Plot ranges :
Area 1 : max (white) 47 Ohms, min (black) 10 Ohms
Area 2 : max (white) 66 Ohms, min (black) 7 Ohms

FIG. 2.18. *Plots of earth resistance data shown in relation to magnetic data for Survey Areas 1 and 2 – greyscale plots of both data-sets (A. Payne).*

a particular period of activity, as the site represents a multi-period landscape of which the known Mid to Late Saxon remains are only one component (see Loveluck above).

2.3.1 Methods

Survey areas

Since the primary aim of the geophysical survey was to attempt to trace the extent of the known monument as far

as was practical, survey was concentrated in the two pasture fields immediately east and north of the excavations (survey areas 1 and 2) where the evidence suggested potential for further settlement remains (see FIGS 2.15 and 2.17). Further quarrying west, south and south-west of the excavated area prevented any attempt to trace the continuation of settlement in these directions. Survey coverage to the east of the main excavation (in Area 1) was also restricted by impenetrable vegetation, covering graves, and the presence of the standing remains of the later medieval church and its successors, limiting the area that could be surveyed in support of tracing the eastern continuation of settlement activity from the excavated site.

Survey techniques

A magnetometer survey combined with more limited magnetic susceptibility (MS) and resistivity survey was carried out. All three surveys were based on a grid consisting of 30m squares with a north-south axis aligned parallel to the eastern limit of the main area of excavation (see Figs 2.15, 2.17, and 2.19).

Magnetometer survey was carried out intially in Areas 1 and 2, as this technique is the most useful ground-based prospecting method for the rapid evaluation of the archaeological content of a landscape (Clark 1996). Magnetometers respond to local modification of the geomagnetic field by magnetic iron oxides in archaeological features, either due to the thermoremanent effect (Aitken 1974) in fired structures, or the magnetic susceptibility (MS) contrast between the silting of features and the subsoil into which they are cut. The general naturally higher magnetism of the topsoil is enhanced by activities associated with human occupation, especially burning (Le Borgne 1960), and when this becomes incorporated in the fills of ditches, detectable magnetic anomalies occur. Direct magnetic susceptibility measurement, in contrast to magnetometer measurement, is used to detect zones of generalised magnetic enhancement of the topsoil linked to a past human presence on a site. It is mostly used for the broad definition of areas of former occupation or industrial activity (often as a precursor to magnetometer survey), or to support the interpretation of magnetometer data. Because the MS of the topsoil influences the ability of the magnetometer to detect earth-filled features, the magnetic susceptibility may provide an insight into the variation of magnetometer response over a site, particularly where the drift geology is variable. One disadvantage of MS is that it is substantially influenced by natural factors, notably soil parent material (which affects the overall iron content of the soil and the quantities of magnetic minerals present) and pedogenic processes such as gleying. Thus, areas of enhancement may arise from human activity (e.g. burning) or natural factors, and therefore caution has to be exercised in interpreting MS surveys.

The fluxgate magnetometers employed for the survey are generally capable of detecting a wide range of buried archaeological features including silted-up ditches and pits, walls constructed from materials with contrasting magnetism to the surrounding soil, fired-clay structures and deposits of burnt material. However, in the case of Flixborough, because the archaeological features are known from excavation to be sealed beneath up to 2m of sand, only the most strongly magnetised features (normally industrial-type features such as kilns and furnaces) would be expected to produce clearly defined

anomalies at the surface. Oven and hearth-type structures were uncovered during the excavations, particularly in Period 5, Phase 5a of the occupation sequence, in Area D of the excavation (see Loveluck and Atkinson, Chapter 6, this volume), and if susceptible to detection by remote methods, their distribution beyond the area of excavation would effectively indicate the wider extent of settlement (albeit without adding significant further detail to the settlement plan).

By analogy to Clark's (1992) work on archaeological remains sealed by a similar depth of alluvium, the sand deposits sealing the archaeological features at Flixborough should allow the detection of industrial structures/features subjected to high temperature at 2–3m in depth. Whereas most ditches and pits, and especially post-holes and bedding trenches of former timber structures, would be at the margins of detectability. For a fluxgate gradiometer, a 100 nano-tesla (nT) anomaly when under 2m of alluvium will only give a 2 nT anomaly at the surface with normal instrument detector heights, while a 5 nT ditch under the same depth of alluvium would be in the sub nano-tesla range (*c.* 0.3 nT), below the normal noise level threshold of the instrument. The same conditions might also be expected to apply to features sealed beneath a deep deposit of wind-blown sand. It is also important to note that the foundation trenches and sockets of the timber buildings excavated at Flixborough were cut into sand, and filled with the same material. Due to this lack of a physical contrast between the features and surrounding deposits, the remains of further buried buildings would be unlikely to be detectable by geophysical means unless the foundation trenches were filled in with heavily burnt material, even without the considerable depth of burial.

Resistivity survey was applied only selectively to sample the response from the site. The reasons for this are various. In their specific burial environment, the features present at Flixborough are less susceptible to detection by resistivity than with magnetic techniques. Resistivity also responds to a more restricted range of features than magnetometry, and, because of the relative slowness of the method, it is less suitable for evaluating large areas. The technique is most powerful as a method of detecting and defining masonry building foundations and other stone structures such as rubble spreads and road surfaces (the electrical resistance of the ground varies according to soil moisture content, and the presence of relatively impermeable masonry will cause an increase at that location). Even if substantial stone structures were present in the Mid to Late Saxon period at Flixborough (which on the basis of excavation seems unlikely), resistivity survey is generally not well suited to the detection of such features when buried in well-drained sandy deposits because of insufficient moisture contrast. The limited use of resistivity was also conditioned by time constraints and the slow mode of operation of the technique with a RM 15 resistivity meter, which pre-

30   Christopher Loveluck, Matthew Canti and Andrew Payne

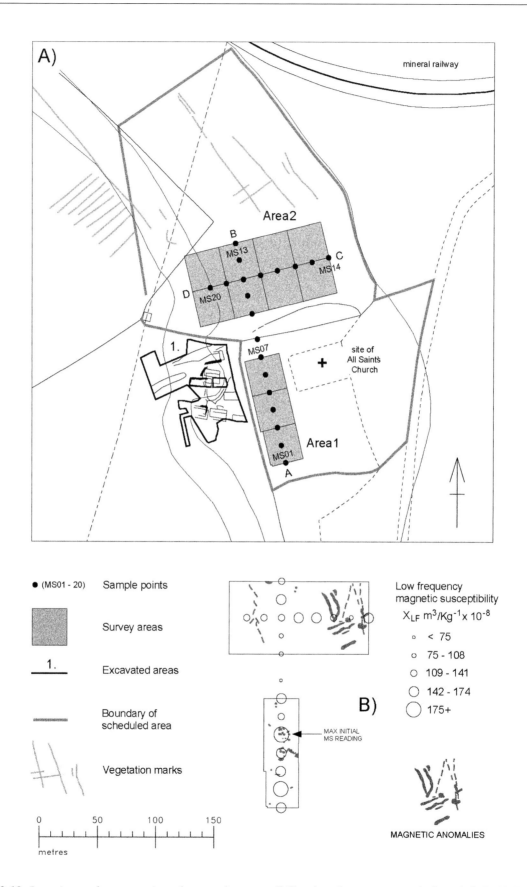

FIG. 2.19. Location and presentation of magnetic susceptibility data from transects A–B and C–D (A. Payne).

vented larger-scale resistivity coverage in the time available.

2.3.2 Survey procedure

Magnetometry
Geoscan FM36 fluxgate gradiometers were carried along successive 30m traverses spaced at 1.0m intervals and orientated north-south. The magnetometer signal (sensitive to changes of a tenth of a nano-tesla) was sampled at 0.25m intervals along each traverse, generating 120 recorded measurements per traverse line. The data are presented in the form of greyscale images in FIGS 2.15, 2.16 and 2.18, having first undergone processing to eliminate the effects of instrument drift and to reduce extreme values in the data, caused by superficial iron objects. No further processing or enhancement of the data was considered necessary. Interpretations of the magnetic data are supplied in FIGS 2.16 and 2.17.

Magnetic susceptibility (MS)
Samples of topsoil were collected at 15m intervals along a south-north transect across Areas 1 and 2 and an east-west transect across Area 2 (see the two traverses on FIG. 2.19A). The resulting 20 samples were transported to the laboratory and subsequently dried, ground to a uniform fine particle size, sieved through a 2.8mm mesh and weighed. Mass specific (100g) low frequency (χ_{LF}) MS values were then obtained from each of the prepared samples using a Bartington MS1 magnetic susceptibility meter and MS2B laboratory sensor. The resulting data are presented on FIG. 2.19B, in the form of proportional circles superimposed on the site plan.

Resistivity
Four 30m squares (two in Area 1 and two in Area 2) were surveyed with the Geoscan RM15 resistivity meter using the Twin Electrode configuration and a mobile probe separation of 0.5m. The data were collected at a 1.0m reading density (1.0m intervals along traverses spaced 1.0m apart). The location of the earth resistance surveys relative to the magnetometer coverage and the resulting data are presented in FIG. 2.18.

Soil augering tests
Following the identification of a number of anomalies of potential archaeological interest in the 1993 magnetometer survey, a selected number of anomalies in Area 2 (**A1** and **A2** on FIG. 2.17) was investigated further by soil auger in July 1997, as part of the post-excavation analysis programme (Loveluck 1996). The aim of this exercise was to determine the origin of the anomalies and confirm their interpretation as archaeological features.

The positions of the individual anomalies were first relocated by visually scanning the instrument panel of a magnetometer for anomalous readings. A Dutch auger was then used to extract a series of soil samples at 20cm intervals from a vertical profile through the anomaly source (or feature) until subsoil was reached. Mass-specific magnetic susceptibility measurements were then obtained in the laboratory for the modern topsoil (sealing the anomaly source), the feature composition or fill, and the natural subsoil beneath it. Control samples were also collected from adjacent areas where the magnetic field was undisturbed and the ground was therefore more typical of the normal soil profile for the site. These samples enabled estimation of the depth to which archaeological features were cut into the subsoil and the depth of the archaeological horizon. Examination of the samples and the MS readings from the anomaly sources enabled the nature of these features to be interpreted with a higher degree of confidence than from the magnetometer data alone. The susceptibility data from the augered samples are presented in FIG. 2.20.

2.3.3 Results

Area 1 – eastern side of excavation
i) Magnetometry
The readings from parts of this area were marred by intense magnetic disturbance from modern features, including a concrete-reinforced post (possibly quarrying rights or graveyard boundary marker) in the south of the area, and traces of a former metallic fence-line immediately east of the present boundary. Fortunately, the modern disturbance did not prevent the detection of a number of other anomalous responses of distinctly different character, which are potentially of archaeological origin. These include what might loosely be termed an alignment of positive magnetic anomalies (M1 on FIG. 2.16) in the centre of the survey (running approximately north-west to south-east, and continuing beyond the eastern limit of coverage); and a second group of positive anomalies (M2; FIG. 2.16) arranged in a roughly square setting situated further to the north. The most likely explanation for these anomalies is that they represent hearths, ovens or other burnt features associated with further remains of the Mid to Late Saxon settlement. They share a similar alignment with the ovens from Period 5 of the occupation sequence (see Loveluck and Atkinson, Chapter 6, this volume). The anomalies also lie immediately beyond the main concentration of buildings uncovered by excavation, and coincide with the maximum topsoil magnetic susceptibility values recorded from the site (χ_{LF} values of 171 and 194 m^3/Kg^{-1} × 10^{-8}; see FIG. 2.20B).

Although no obvious actual foundations of buildings were detected continuing beyond the eastern limit of excavation, the survey data from Area 1 do provide some limited support for an extension of the settlement into the undisturbed area between the excavation and the site of All Saints' Church. This additional area would represent an increase of the known extent of settlement by approximately thirty to forty percent.

ii) Resistivity survey
The resistivity data from Area A (FIG. 2.19) bear little

Anomaly 1

Borehole 1	K$_{LF}$	Mass (g)	χ_{LF}
00–20cm	235	206.0	114.08
30–40cm	223	279.7	79.73
40–60cm	592	224.4	263.81
60–80cm subsoil	34	235.6	14.43

Borehole 2			
00–20cm	198	188.6	104.98
20–40cm	217	245.4	88.43
40–60cm transition to subsoil	104	291.9	35.63
60–80cm subsoil	23	196.3	11.72

Anomaly 2

Borehole 1	K$_{LF}$	Mass (g)	χ_{LF}
00–20cm	259	201.3	128.66
20–40cm	332	211.8	156.75
40–60cm	201	233.5	86.08
60–80cm	148	202.9	72.94
80–100cm transition to subsoil	94	198.9	47.26

Borehole 2			
00–20cm	363	205.5	176.64
20–40cm transition to subsoil	82	221.2	37.07
40cm	41	203.7	20.13

F*IG. 2.20. The results of the magnetic susceptibility samples from auger holes 1 and 2 (A. Payne).*

relation to the magnetometer results and mainly reflect geological and topographical variation which, in turn, has influenced drainage and local soil moisture conditions. The mound of wind-blown sand sealing the excavated deposits is visible as an area of high resistance and appears to terminate fairly abruptly approximately 10m north of the boundary fence. Beyond this there is a transition to low resistance, suggesting moister ground conditions and a change to soils with a higher clay content. Towards the southern edge of the survey a series of topographical features – including a sunken trackway leading down the side of the escarpment – have been detected as a group of high and low resistance anomalies. The trackway is probably of medieval origin (associated with the site of North Conesby to the north-east), but it is noticeable that it shares a similar alignment to the long axes of the excavated Mid to Late Saxon building remains, immediately to the north-west. It is even possible that this feature represents a boundary on the south side of the settlement, as contemporary cemetery remains are known to lie 20 to 30m beyond it to the south-west.

Area 2 – pasture field to the north of the excavation
i) Magnetometer survey
Generally speaking, there are few anomalous responses in the south and western part of this area, suggesting that it is unlikely that the Mid to Late Saxon settlement continued directly north of the later medieval ditch present near the northern limit of excavation (see Loveluck and Atkinson, Chapter 7, this volume). However, remains of former timber structures in the form of

shallow and narrow foundation trenches and post-holes, without associated burnt features, might not easily be identified by the magnetometer in this area, and therefore the lack of evidence for a northerly continuation cannot be conclusive.

A number of isolated, positive magnetic anomalies of similar magnitude (10–15 nano-tesla (nT)) to those mapped in Area 1 are present near the far northern extremity of the survey coverage in Area 2, separated from the excavated area by some 75m. One of these anomalies was examined in more detail by carrying out a series of MS measurements on a column of soil samples extracted from an auger bore-hole through the source feature (**A1** on FIGS 2.16 and 2.17; see Section 2.4). The anomaly was found to have originated from a layer of burnt material (approximately 0.2m thick and 0.4m from the surface) with a very high magnetic susceptibility (263 compared to adjacent topsoil values of 104.98 and 114.08, and subsoil values of 11.72 and 14.43 – χ_{LF} values in units of m^3/Kg^{-1} × 10^{-8}). These attributes are suggestive of an oven or hearth. Two other closely juxtaposed, positive magnetic anomalies of similar magnitude, lying 23m to the east, may indicate similar features.

Higher up the slope towards the eastern boundary of the scheduled area, a series of anomalies on an identical alignment to the cropmark features (see FIG. 2.17), may represent cultivation terraces, enclosures, or field systems associated with the medieval settlement of North Conesby which lies immediately to the south. Small-scale opencast quarrying (for exploiting the local Ironstone) is another possible explanation for these linear anomalies.

Although sharing a similar alignment to banding in the local geological strata, a geological explanation for the anomalies is less likely on the basis of evidence obtained by augering. An auger profile through one of the linear features in 1997 (**A2**, Figs 2.16 and 2.17) showed the feature to have the characteristics of a ditch or trench with a magnetically enhanced fill (with MS values decreasing vertically with depth down through the fill – 156.75, 86.08, 72.94 m³/Kg⁻¹ × 10⁻⁸, from 0.2 to 0.8m below the ground surface at 20cm intervals). The feature was cut to a depth of approximately 0.5m into the subsoil, and overlain by approximately 30cm of topsoil. The subsoil in Area 2 typically lay at a depth of 40cm from the surface, but where the linear feature was cut into the subsoil, natural was not reached until 1.00m down the profile. The auger borehole data from Area 2 is summarised in Fig. 2.20.

ii) Resistivity
The survey coverage in this area is unfortunately too limited in extent to allow meaningful interpretation, but a steep rise in the resistance towards the south and western limits of the survey area is suggestive of a geological change from clayey to sandy or stonier deposits. The results may therefore partially indicate the northerly extent of the wind-blown sand deposits that seal the Mid to Late Saxon remains further to the south. Partly as a result of the extreme variation in resistance across such a small area, no anomalies of obvious archaeological significance can be discerned in the resistivity data from Area 2.

Magnetic susceptibility (MS) 1997
The average χ_{LF} (low frequency mass specific) MS value for the topsoil across the whole of the surveyed area in Fields 1 and 2 is 139.1 m³/Kg⁻¹ × 10⁻⁸ derived from 20 samples. The maximum and minimum values are 194 and 73 (units as above). The values for the topsoil from the augered set of samples show a similar range (104.98 – 176.64 m³/Kg⁻¹ × 10⁻⁸ from four samples) to the samples obtained from the two transects (A–B and C–D; see Fig. 2.18). The highest values (in the 170s to 190s) recorded along the N–S transect occur in the region of sample points 2–5 – the area containing the highest concentration of possible archaeological anomalies, adjacent to the main excavated area. The peak values on the E–W transect in Area 2 (in the 160s) occur at sample points 17–18 (see Fig. 2.19) in the area bracketed by the two groups of augered anomalies (**A3** and **A4** on Fig. 2.17). Values for the subsoil in Area 2 range from 11.72 to 47.26 (four samples) exhibiting a clear contrast with the topsoil readings, and the readings obtained from the samples of the augered features. Any similar features elsewhere on the site should, therefore, be easily detectable by magnetometer survey. An anomalously high value of 263.81 was obtained from **A1**, borehole 1 (see Fig. 2.20) at a depth of 40–60cm, presumably from an archaeological context. The high MS value of this sample is

comparable with, but at the lower end of the range, of the MS values obtained from samples of excavated oven and hearth material, investigated for industrial residues by David Starley (see Volume 2).

High frequency (χ_{HF}) MS measurements are generally very similar resulting in low frequency dependency ($\%\chi_{fd}$) values. A selection of four of the samples from Flixborough exhibit a fractional conversion (initial reading expressed as a % of the final reading (χ_{Max}) after heat treatment) of around 10% on average. This is a measure of the extent to which the potential susceptibility has been achieved in the original soil before simulated heating in reducing and then oxidizing conditions in the laboratory (Clark 1996). Because of the small number of samples and the localised nature of the area sampled it is not possible to attach any significance to this data, but the measurements are nevertheless quoted here for the record. The variability of χ_{Max} values (751 – 2625 χ_{LF} m³/Kg⁻¹ × 10⁻⁸) probably reflects variable geology (with different concentrations of naturally occurring iron) at Flixborough as suggested by the resistivity data.

2.3.4 Conclusions

Although far from conclusive, magnetometer survey at Flixborough has shown sufficient promise to merit further extension in the field north of the excavation, to trace the northward extent of the anomalies encountered there. Despite the evidence from augering, the archaeological significance of the anomalies mapped in Area 2 remains unproven and there is as yet no direct relationship between them and the excavated settlement remains. Further intrusive investigation will be required to advance understanding of these features and determine if they are contemporary with the excavated deposits to the south. Resistivity survey has been found to be less useful, except for mapping the possible lateral extent of the sand deposits that protect the Anglo-Saxon archaeology.

The area directly east of the excavation presents a considerable challenge for any further non-destructive investigation, in part due to the nature of the terrain, but also because of the depth and nature of the archaeological deposits. However, some assumptions on the effectiveness of geophysical techniques on the site have been challenged by the moderately useful results obtained from Area 1. More sophisticated techniques, capable of providing greater information on the vertical dimension, have yet to be tried because they were less well developed and had been less widely adopted in 1993 than they are now. The use of electrical imaging to produce a resistivity pseudo-section of the remaining area east of the excavation might be a useful approach to adopt, if only for mapping the distribution of blown sand across the scheduled area. It is possible that ground-penetrating radar (GPR) may have a similar role for detecting the presence of, and tracing the remaining extent of the Anglo-Saxon occupation horizon, within the sand deposits, although the detection of individual features of the Mid to Late Saxon complex with this technique is probably over-optimistic, given the limitations of the site conditions.

2.4 The post-excavation analysis methodology

by Christopher Loveluck

2.4.1 Approaches to post-excavation analysis and interpretation in this volume

Following the end of the excavation in 1991, preliminary conservation of the artefact assemblage, and the geophysical surveys of 1993, the nature and the importance of the remains were assessed over a two-year period, with a view to gaining the maximum academic understanding of the remains through their integrated analysis and interpretation (Loveluck 1996). As a consequence, the programme of research culminating in the four Flixborough volumes was set in motion in 1997, funded by English Heritage. The specific aim of the post-excavation project was to establish the lifestyles of the inhabitants of the settlement throughout its occupational history, when made possible by the presence of appropriate archaeological deposits. Furthermore, by integrating information from the structural, artefact and biological evidence, it was also hoped to investigate the possibility of changes in lifestyles, and social phenomena associated with them through time.

In order to establish the character of lifestyles, and to enable comparative analysis and interpretation of wider research themes, two tasks had to be completed. First, a site-wide chronology had to be established; and secondly, study of discard patterns of artefacts and bones, and their condition, needed to be achieved to arrive at an understanding of site formation processes, and hence come to a conclusion on the representativity of data for interpretation. Without such critical analyses of the deposits and their contents, it would not be possible to come to an interpretation of whether the remains were representative of the settlement as a whole or only part of it, at different periods in the occupation sequence. These tasks constitute the primary level of interpretation of the Flixborough settlement evidence, and due to the scale of the task – integrating the evidence from thousands of stratigraphic units/contexts, thousands of artefacts, and hundreds of thousands of animal bones – its realisation is the purpose of the entire first volume of the publication series.

The formation of the site-wide chronology, analysis of the changing material culture profiles through time, and assessment of the scale of interpretation possible from the archaeological remains was conducted between 1997 and 1999. The long duration of this stage in the analysis reflected the scale and complexity of the exercise. The first stage was the formation of the relative stratigraphic sequence and provisional site chronology, undertaken by Chris Loveluck, David Atkinson, Jane Young and Peter

Didsbury. This entailed production of Harris matrices, and spot-dating of stratigraphic units/contexts on the basis of chronological evidence from pottery, coinage, and other artefacts thought to have diagnostically datable stylistic features (see Archaeological Data Service archive). Hence, a provisional phasing of the occupation sequence was produced.

During this process of translation from the excavation recording to the post-excavation analysis stage of the research, the initial interpretative and vague, colour-related labels for deposits in the excavation record were not necessarily followed for purposes of interpretation, although the context/stratigraphic unit numbers remained the same and the original site record was not altered, to facilitate re-assessment by future archaeologists. The lack of adherence to some of the interpretative labels assigned during excavation was the consequence of a desire not to be sent along particular trajectories of interpretation, on the basis of subjectively perceived deposit characters from the excavation stage of the research (Jones 2002, 57–61; Loveluck 2005, 91). Interpretation of the nature of deposits rests on the analysis of their contents. Consequently, deposits described as *occupation deposits*, *dumps* and *dark soils* in the excavation records in Chapters 3 to 7 below, and in the forthcoming British Archaeological Data Service archive, reflect their primary description and interpretation at the moment of discovery. It will be apparent from the analysis of their contents in following chapters that many of these deposit labels describe stratigraphic units of nearly identical character, i.e. they are refuse deposits, and at the level of interpretation of the remains the descriptive labels assigned during the excavation are almost meaningless (Loveluck 2005, 91). In reality, the use of the descriptive terminology assigned to deposits at Flixborough during excavation reflects only initial perceptions of their scale. For example, *occupation deposits* tend to be smaller refuse deposits than *dumps*.

The results of the provisional phasing exercise were then sent to all researchers working on the artefact and animal bone assemblages. On the basis of the provisional phasing, the artefact specialists undertook their detailed artefact identifications, including analysis of conditions of preservation and states of fragmentation. Similarly, the vertebrate remains (bones) research team began to undertake their detailed species identification, quantification, and assessment of preservation conditions and states of fragmentation. The results of these detailed identification and preservation assessments from the researchers working on individual categories of material were then used by Chris Loveluck and David Atkinson to produce the final site phasing and periodisation, once all indications of deposit reworking, movement, artefact residuality and intrusivity had been assessed. The final interpretation of site chronology was then fed back to the material-specific researchers and research teams, to enable them to finalise the chronological scope of their analyses. The subsequent integration of all the forms of evidence, within the defined chronological framework of the occupation sequence, then allowed the analysis of the representativity of discard practices within the excavated area, for purposes of interpretation of the lifestyles of the inhabitants through time.

2.4.2 Factors influencing construction of the site-wide chronology

The chronology of the Flixborough settlement sequence was established, as described above, by reflexive and integrated analysis of the vertical and horizontal strati-graphic relationships of structural evidence and refuse deposits, in conjunction with analysis of datable chronological indicators found within them. The evidence for attributing calendar-based date ranges to the relative chronology of the stratigraphic sequence was provided mainly by pottery, coinage, dress accessories with diagnostic stylistic decoration, certain glass vessels, and to a lesser extent by archaeomagnetic dates from fired-clay oven and hearth bases. Some assessment and estimation was also made concerning the longevity of structures built on the site, on the basis of their architectural features and limited charred timber remains; and also on an awareness of the hostile nature of the calcareous windblown sand geology, which was subject to acid leaching in the absence of deposits ameliorating its effects (see Canti, above).

An exceptional feature of the Flixborough remains is the relative abundance of datable material amongst the artefact assemblages. Certain periods in the occupation sequence, however, provided far more datable material than others: for example, artefacts dated to the eighth and ninth centuries are very numerous; and due to their abundance and the extent of refuse re-organisation in most periods, they are often the most numerous artefacts in later phases as well. Consequently, great care has to be taken in attributing smaller quantities of artefact remains from other periods their appropriate significance. This is particularly the case with the structural and depositional remains from Period 6 (see Chapter 7), which contained small quantities of material datable to the tenth century, alongside the largest buildings and some of the largest animal bone refuse deposits from the settlement's history. A uniform expectation of equivalent quantities of datable material in different periods might have led to the assumption that there was a diminution of settlement activity on the basis of datable artefacts – yet the structural, depositional and vertical stratigraphic data demonstrate that such an assumption would be false. Consequently, the account and interpretation of the history of occupation within the settlement area in following chapters relies on the integrated analysis of all the different forms of evidence, and is not dispro-portionately led by archaeological visibility factors relating to certain types of artefact, such as coinage and dress accessories.

Different forms of chronological indicator within the sequence also have different values for providing information on the temporal evolution of the site, and on the nature and derivation of deposits. The most valuable chronological indicator at Flixborough is provided by over 5,000 sherds of Anglo-Saxon and contemporary continental pottery, in addition to smaller numbers of Iron Age, Romano-British, and later Medieval sherds (Young and Didsbury contributions, Chapters 3 to 7, this volume; Young, Vince, Blinkhorn and Didsbury, Volume 2). The size of this pottery assemblage is currently exceptionally large for an Anglo-Saxon settlement in Lincolnshire, particularly from the Mid Saxon period, and this relates directly to the nature of the deposits and the preservation conditions provided by large quantities of wood ash. The extent to which the collection of Anglo-Saxon pottery is exceptional can be assessed by comparison with other contemporary sites in the East Midlands of England (Vince and Young, and Blinkhorn, Volume 2). Indeed, it is as a consequence of the work of Alan Vince and Jane Young that the Anglo-Saxon pottery is such a useful chronological indicator. Within the East Midlands Anglo-Saxon pottery project, they examined all the Anglo-Saxon pottery types from settlement and cemetery contexts, between the Humber estuary, the Trent valley and the Fens (Vince and Young, Volume 2). This has provided a chronological framework of broad calendar-based date ranges for the pottery types, supported by more closely dated fixed points gained from other artefact studies, for the Early to Late Anglo-Saxon periods. As pottery is the most consistently discarded form of artefact, despite quantities fluctuating in different periods, it provides the basis for the dating of the occupation sequence at Flixborough.

The chronology based on the vertical stratigraphic relationships, and the relatively broad dating bands provided by the pottery, is augmented by artefact forms whose dates of manufacture are more closely attributable, although they were discarded less often: for example, coinage, dress accessories, and other diagnostically datable forms of artefact – often imported luxuries. Unfortunately, the fact that many of these artefacts were luxuries of high intrinsic value had the effect of keeping them in contemporary use for extended periods of time, so their value for purposes of site chronology can be diminished. Added to this, artefacts such as coins are small, compact, and hence easily transported when their primary deposition contexts are disturbed. Therefore, indications of the nature of deposits as a whole, with all their artefact components, had to be assessed before giving chronological or other significance to particular objects. Fortunately, however, the unusually large quantity of broadly, or specifically datable artefacts at Flixborough rendered it possible, in conjunction with the exceptional vertical stratigraphic sequence, to produce a relatively detailed picture of the temporal development of the settlement within the excavated area.

Period	Date range	Phase	Date range	Key structures, features and deposits
Period 1	Seventh Century	Phase 1a	Seventh Century	Building 16, hearth 5114, Refuse deposit 4807
		Phase 1b	Mid-Late Seventh Century	Buildings 18 and 19, 'Floor/sub-floor' deposit 3323, External refuse ('yard') deposits 3194, 3347 and 1649
Period 2	Late Seventh to Early Eighth Century			Buildings 6a, 17, 20 and 21a, Ditch 446?, 'Soakaway' gullies 970/3967 and 10235, 'Floor/sub-floor' deposits 4769, 3281, 3336, 3346, 4950, External refuse deposits 4784 and 4866
Period 3	Early Eighth to Early Ninth Century	Phase 3a	Early-Mid Eighth Century	Buildings 1a, 6b, 11, 17, 21b, Graves 1960, 2231/2, 3580, 3706, 3878 and 4010, Ditch 446, 'Soakaway' gulley 11144, Gravel 'hardstanding' 484, External refuse deposits 4323, 5314, and 5369
		Phase 3b	Mid Eighth-Early Ninth Century	
		Phase 3bi		Buildings 1b, 2, 5, 8, 13, 22, and 23, Ditch 446/50
		Phase 3bii		Buildings 1b, 2, 5, 8, 13, 22 and 23 and 40, Ditch 446/50, External refuse deposits 6464, 6465, 7276, 7546, 10399 and 11699
		Phase 3biii		Buildings 1b, 2, 5, 8, 22 and 23, Rectangular pits 12296 and 12210, Ditch 446/50, Demolition and Refuse deposits 7153,7220, 8200, 11663 and 12925
		Phase 3biv		Buildings 1b, 2, 5, 8, 9, 22 and 23, Ditch 446/50, Pit 6709, External refuse deposits 5653, 5983 and 6039
		Phase 3bv		Buildings 1b, 2, 5, 8, 9, 22 and 23, Ditch 446/50, External refuse deposits 5617, 6040, 6136, 6235, 6304 and 6305
Period 4	Early to Mid Ninth Century	Phase 4i	Early-Mid Ninth Century	Buildings 3, 10a, 15, 24, 25, 35 and 39, Ditch 50, Isolated hearth base 668, Paths 3085 and 2448
		Phase 4ii	Mid Ninth Century	Buildings, 3, 10b and 15 (for part of the phase), External refuse deposits 3256, 3758, 5503, 5856 and 6885, Ditch Fills 51, 3107, 10772
Period 5	Mid to Late Ninth to Early Tenth Century	Phase 5a	Mid-Late Ninth Century	Buildings 26, 27, 28, 29, 36/37 and 38, Gravel path-ways 4040, 5245, 3237, 6393, 11008 and 12242, Ovens 6486, 6488, 7288, 7364, 8635 and 8686, Oven sweepings refuse deposit 3711, External refuse deposits 5860, 5885, 6312, 6491, 6886, 8787, 11412 and 11442
		Phase 5b	Late Ninth-Early Tenth Century	Buildings 4, 14, 30/31, 36, 27?, 28?, 38?, Isolated Hearth Base 850, External refuse deposits 1727, 1728, 2518, 2562, 2776, 3081, 5553, 6472, 6490 and 6803
Period 6	Early Tenth to Early Eleventh Century	Phase 6i	Early-Mid Tenth Century	Buildings 7, 12, 32, 33?, 34, External refuse deposits 1680 and 2488, Pits 7076 and 7089
		Phase 6ii	Mid Tenth Century	Buildings 32?, 33, 34, Gullies 8460, 1758 and 5322, Pit 77, External refuse deposits 3255, 3610, 3891, 5281, 6499, 6797 and 7280
		Phase 6iii	Mid Tenth-Early Eleventh Century	Refuse deposit 6300, 'Dark Soil' refuse deposits 176, 636, 1145, 1147, 1154, 1155, 1167, 1168, 1170, 1173, 1182, 1183, 1186, 1243, 1244, 1246, 1269, 1270, 1280, 1282, 1283, 1284, 1285, 1286, 1287, 1288, 1289, 1307, 1427, 1439, 1440, 1449, 1450, 1451, 1452, 1453, 1454, 1455, 1456, 1457, 1458, 1459, 1460, 1461, 1462, 1464, 1465, 1479, 1480, 1587, 1588, 1831, 1832, 1833, 1834, 1835, 1836, 1837, 1838, 1839, 1840, 1841, 1888, 1889, 1890, 1891, 1892, 1893, 2024, 7817, 10393, 10394
Period 7	Twelfth to Fifteenth Centuries			Ditch 85/6362, Oven 1342, Pit 1699, Building foundation? 1313

FIG. 2.21. Summary of the occupation sequence and site chronology by period and phase (C. Loveluck).

The chronological periodisation, based on strati-graphic relationships and artefact dating was further supported by more limited indications of the duration of the standing 'lifetime' of buildings on individual plots. These were assessed on the basis of the analysis of the

building foundation 'footprints' and the charred timber remains (Darrah, Volume 4, Chapter 3), and by analogy to exceptional eighth- and ninth-century timber fragments placed within similar sand foundations from the Varde district of Ribe Amt, in Denmark (Frandsen 1999, 42–

50; Loveluck, Volume 4, Chapter 3). The artefact evidence, presented in succeeding chapters suggests that buildings stood, on average, for a period of between 25 and 50 years. This suggested longevity for wooden standing buildings, constructed in sand, is supported by dendro-chronological dates derived from oak piles for a raised trackway at Varde. There, oak piles driven into sand, felled in AD 761, were repaired and replaced between AD 785 and 791 (Frandsen 1999, 50). The buildings from Flixborough were also constructed in oak, and the artefact evidence suggests a similar longevity for standing buildings as the replacement witnessed at Varde. Such an assumption, however, has not driven the construction of the phasing at Flixborough. The vertical stratigraphic sequence has been chronologically fixed, above all, by artefact chronologies. Nevertheless, the absolute chronological corroboration for replacement of wooden structures at Varde, in identical soil conditions, provides an extra supporting dimension to the artefact generated chronology from Flixborough.

Within the context of abundant dating indicators, the absolute chronological ranges provided by the archaeo-magnetic dating of fired-clay oven and hearth bases, gave a broader chronological span for these structural remains than can be suggested from artefact-derived evidence (Linford and Linford 1994; see Archaeological Data Service – ADS – Archive). Nevertheless, their contribution is important for having provided chronological date ranges independent of typological analysis. Radiocarbon dating of carbonised wood remains was also considered in detail. However, consideration of the deposition contexts of potential samples suggested that the dating information they could provide would not give more significant information for the interpretation of site chronology than was already available through the artefact remains (Bayliss 1994; Bayliss pers comm). All the best potential samples were recovered from deposits which possessed significant elements of residual, re-worked material. Adding to this potentially re-deposited nature, the likelihood that fragments of structural timber could have been re-used from significantly earlier periods limited the potential value of radiocarbon date ranges for dating deposits. Furthermore, the complicating factor of the source of the wood from within a tree trunk, and the tree's age when felled, also cautioned against a potentially spurious reliance on absolute radiocarbon dates. Consequently, the analysis of the chronological development and character of the Anglo-Saxon occupation sequence at Flixborough relied overwhelmingly on artefact-led chronologies, not on radiometric chronologies.

2.4.3 Depositional patterns of artefacts and faunal remains, site taphonomy and establishing limits of inference from the data

Interpretation of the settlement remains, relating to themes such as the agricultural economy, craft-working, exchange, and problems of defining settlement character etc., is of necessity viewed through the filter of site taphonomy and discernible patterns in the discard of artefacts and faunal remains. The undertaking of the thematic social analysis presented in Volume 4 depended on the extent to which deposits and their contents could be shown to be representative of the settlement as a whole, or the excavated area alone. Furthermore, analysis of changing trends through time could be achieved only through establishment of the existence of like deposits in different periods of the occupation sequence. Assessment of the parameters of interpretation possible in different periods of occupation rested on a range of factors. These comprised the refuse-disposal strategies used; the extent of artefact residuality and re-deposition (Brown 1994, 3–7; Lucas 2001, 149–152); survival factors relating to particular types of evidence: for example, artefact fragmentation and animal bone taphonomy (Lee-Lyman 1994; Ervynck 1999, 129–133); and the presence of intact occupation surfaces, within or in association with structures, e.g. floors within buildings.

Varied organisation of refuse disposal in different periods of occupation had a great impact on our ability to associate specific activities with particular parts of the excavated area. The reworking of earlier refuse material as disposal strategies changed also resulted in a high degree of residuality of eighth- and ninth-century artefacts throughout the settlement's occupational history. In most cases, the identification of any patterning in the finds profiles related to the association of large refuse dump deposits with neighbouring buildings. It is the analysis of what Michael Schiffer has called *waste streams* (Schiffer 1987, 66–68), associated with different refuse discard strategies, that have provided the key to understanding the human agency associated with rubbish accumulation at Flixborough, thereby enabling the interpretation of the social practices of inhabitants reflected in those rubbish deposits (Bourdieu 1994, 22–23; Hill 1995).

As will become evident, a contrast exists in our ability to draw conclusions relating to social practices in different periods due to changes in *waste streams*, i.e. demonstrable changes in the origins of components of the refuse. For example, floor deposits and external yard deposits were found in association with buildings in Periods 1 and 2, dated to between the mid to late seventh century and early eighth century (see Chapter 3 below), but the floors were kept relatively clean and very few finds were recovered from the yards. As a result, the majority of the finds from the seventh-century phases were found in the fills of post-holes, and in comparison with other periods of occupation the numbers of finds are small (although large in comparison with most other Anglo-Saxon rural settlements). Whereas for much of the eighth, ninth and tenth centuries, refuse was collected and dumped in the central part of the site. Artefact residuality and fragmentation studies suggest that during these three latter centuries both heavily reworked and 'pristine', undisturbed refuse deposits were dumped in this central area. Presence of debris from activities for which there was no trace in the excavated area also showed importation of material from other parts of the settlement. The pristine and fragmented artefacts, and the identifiable imported components within the refuse from the eighth to late tenth centuries, suggest focussed use of a designated refuse zone for the settlement. Therefore, the extent to which trends from the seventh century can be compared to those from the eighth, ninth and tenth centuries demand critical consideration of the different depositional circumstances (Chapters 3 to 7 below; Loveluck, Volume 4, Chapter 2).

The chapters which follow present an interpretation of the occupational history within the area excavated from 1989–91, for the period between the mid to late seventh century and the fourteenth century. As already stated, the defined periods of settlement activity are differentiated on the basis of similar use of space within the excavated area, and by the various indicators of the chronology of that particular use of space. Within the narratives, stratigraphic and structural evidence is presented for each period, combined with an integrated analysis of the evidence provided by artefacts, industrial residues and biological remains. Hence, the reasoning behind the interpretation of the structural and spatial character of each period of occupation is apparent, and so too is the

reasoning behind the interpretation of the longevity of each period, based on the full range of chronological indicators discussed earlier in this chapter. The character and condition of key artefacts, industrial residues and biological remains are also discussed in relation to their varied depositional circumstances, in order to enable an assessment of the representativity of the recovered finds assemblages for interpretation. Due to the huge quantity of finds, it has not been possible to present and discuss every individual artefact, animal bone and industrial residue encountered in the following chapters. The narratives present the most important, and a very significant proportion of all the finds, integrated within the stratigraphic and structural sequence of activity for each period. Nevertheless, the presented and interpreted data reflect analysis of all the different sets of data, even though not all are presented (see ADS archive for a total, phased presentation of the finds assemblages, and Volume 2 for all individual material and artefact-specific reports). The overall result of this integrated analysis is an interpretation of the occupation sequence at Flixborough, on which all the thematic discussions, presented in Volumes 3 and 4, are based. A summary of the defined site chronology by period is presented on p.36, alongside information on the occurrence of the main structural remains and key deposits by phase (FIG. 2.21).

3   Periods 1 and 2: The Seventh Century

Christopher Loveluck and David Atkinson

with contributions by Jane Young and Peter Didsbury

3.1 Introduction

Prior to the arrival of Mid Saxon Maxey-type pottery wares on the Anglo-Saxon settlement, during the late seventh or early eighth centuries (coinciding with the onset of Period 2 on the site), there were two phases of partly superimposed buildings beneath the structures of that period. These building phases, defined as belonging to Period 1 of the occupation sequence, were associated with late fourth-century Romano-British pottery vessels; local Early Anglo-Saxon hand-made wares; and a spout from an oxidised vessel, which may be a contemporary import from the Continent. In the later of these two building phases (1b) from Period 1, Maxey-type pottery sherds were present in the fills of the post-holes, following the demolition of the buildings. Given that the foundations of buildings 16 (FIG. 3.1) and 18 (FIG. 3.2) were partly covered by building 20 in Period 2, and that building 17 – also from Period 2 – was possibly juxtaposed over building 19 (FIG. 3.6), it is likely that loosely organised building plots were laid out in Period 1, sometime in the seventh century.

On the basis that this probably represents continuity in the use of space, it is logical to suggest that the two building phases existing prior to the arrival of the first Maxey-type wares reflect continuity of occupation in the excavated area from before the late seventh century. The longevity of the first two phases of buildings in the occupation sequence is difficult to ascertain, on the basis of the artefacts retrieved from their filled-in foundations, and from associated yard deposits. However, consideration of their earth-fast construction and comparative data on the lifespan of wooden structures in identical soil conditions (on the basis of dendrochronology), would suggest a tentative span of use of between twenty-five and fifty years – probably closer to the shorter end of the scale (Frandsen 1999, 50; Darrah, Volume 4, Chapter 3). It is suggested, therefore, that the two building phases

from Period 1 should be tentatively dated to the seventh, and mid to late seventh centuries respectively, and that they represent the western periphery of a possible Early Anglo-Saxon settlement focus – perhaps extending to the south-east of the excavated area. Residual fifth- and predominantly sixth-century dress accessories, recovered from later periods of the occupation sequence, and earlier discoveries in the immediate vicinity certainly demonstrate the existence of a larger settlement and cemetery zone from the Early Anglo-Saxon period (Hines, Volume 2; Rogers, Volume 2; Volume 4, FIG. 2.21; Dudley 1931, 44).

3.2 Phase 1a – seventh century

The earlier of the two structural phases within Period 1 comprised a single building – building 16, constructed on an approximate south-west to north-east alignment (FIG. 3.1; FIG. 3.3), which cut an earlier refuse deposit (4807). An external stone hearth (5114) was located to the north-west of the building (FIG. 3.4). The building was rectangular and had earth-fast post-hole foundations, which showed no signs of an entrance, although it is assumed that a single, or a pair of entrances, were located in the centre of the long walls of the building. In size, the structure was approximately 11m in length and 6m in width, on the basis of the foundations. The fills of post-holes 4409 and 4629 each contained a sherd of two late fourth-century Romano-British lid-seated jars – vessels 1 and 2 respectively (Didsbury, Volume 2, Chapter 14), and a probably intrusive sherd of Maxey-type ware was retrieved from the fill of post-hole 4582. The latter could have subsided into the fill of the earlier feature, or it could have become incorporated during considerable truncation of features in this area, from the construction of at least seven subsequent buildings. In addition to the pottery, post-hole 4888 also yielded a possible fired-clay

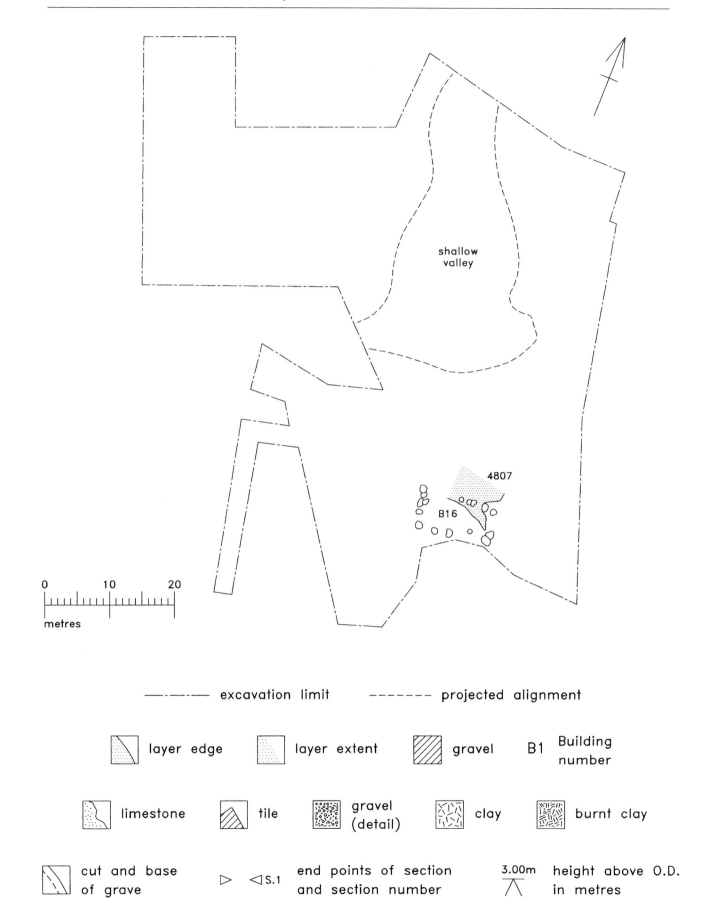

FIG. 3.1. Plan – Period 1, phase 1a, seventh century, plus convention key (M. Frankland).

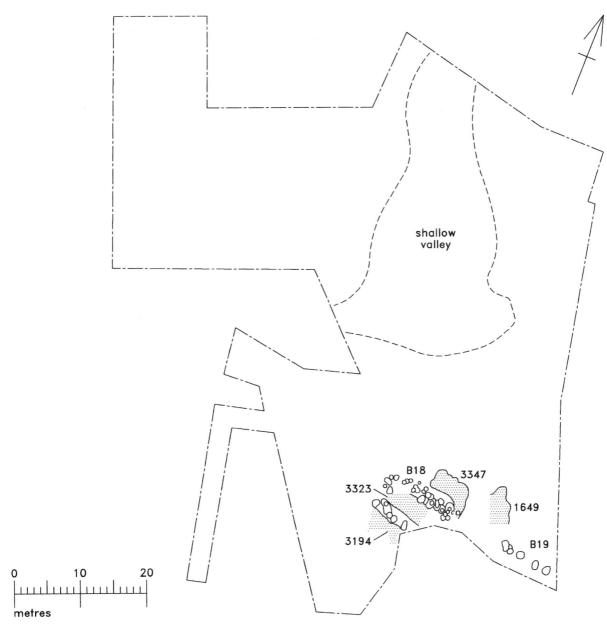

FIG. 3.2. Plan – Period 1, phase 1b, mid to late seventh century (M. Frankland).

mould fragment (RF 14389 from 4889; Wastling, Volume 2, Chapter 11). The occupation deposit 4807 contained two further small sherds of the Late Roman lid-seated jar – vessel 1, providing an indication of the post-depositional disturbance and movement of fragments of this vessel. The sherd from post-hole 4409 could have become incorporated into its fill on the construction or demolition of building 16. Two other pits also contained a further late Roman sherd, and a very worn piece of an Anglo-Saxon hand-made vessel.

3.3 Phase 1b – mid to late seventh century

Building 16 was succeeded by building 18, which was

partly superimposed over the earlier structure, on a more west-north-west to east-north-east alignment; and a further structure, building 19, was constructed to its east on broadly the same alignment (FIG. 3.2). The short walls – with no signs of entrances – faced the prevailing wind from the Trent floodplain, the marshes of Thorne moors, and the Humber estuary.

Building 18 is particularly interesting due to the survival of occupation deposits, both within and outside the structure (FIG. 3.2). The building itself was broadly rectangular, although the south-east corner had been lost due to quarrying. It possessed post-hole foundations for an earth-fast superstructure (FIG. 3.5). In terms of dimensions, the building was approximately 10m long

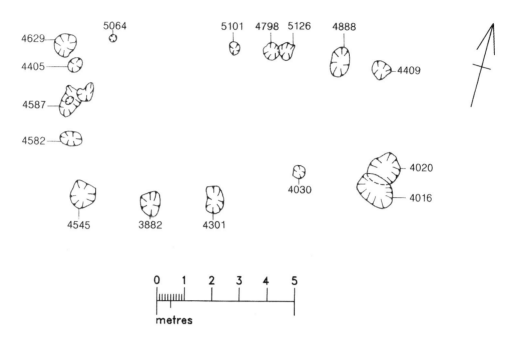

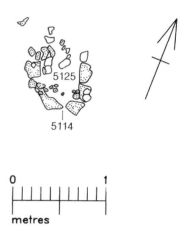

FIG. 3.3. Plan of building 16 (R. Smith).

and 5.50m wide. Inside, a broadly rectangular occupation deposit of darker-coloured sand (3323) occurred, which could represent a floor deposit or a collection of refuse beneath a raised floor. The latter possibility may be more likely, since the deposit followed the building outline but was very clean, with no discarded pottery present. The relative sterility of the deposit, apart from a very small quantity of iron-working slag (Starley, Volume 2, Chapter 10), could also reflect the intentional act of keeping the interior of the house devoid of refuse. What can be termed external 'yard' deposits, where refuse accumulated, also followed the exterior of the post-holes forming the long walls of the building (deposits 3194 and 3347 respectively; FIG. 3.2). Indeed 3347 also curved around the corner of the short wall at the building's north-eastern end. The apparent gap between the post-holes of the building and these yard middens, running the length of the long walls, is likely to reflect the 'eaves-drip' of the roof – probably of thatch, considering the settlement's location on the edge of the Trent valley and Humber wetlands. The heavily truncated sections of this building are presented with those of building 16 in the ADS archive.

Bearing in mind the very partial nature of the recovered element of building 19, it is not appropriate to give exact estimates of the dimensions of the structure, although it was probably of equivalent size to building 18. The line of post-holes reflects its northern long wall; and a refuse deposit (1649) was located to its north-west (FIG. 3.2).

A range of finds was recovered from the fills of the post-holes in buildings 18 and 19, as well as from the yard deposits 3347 and 3194. The material from the post-

FIG. 3.4. Plan of hearth 5114 (R. Smith).

holes is likely to have been incorporated into the voids of the building foundations on their demolition. Eleven sherds of pottery were recovered from the fills of features associated with building 18. These included a sherd of an Early Anglo-Saxon hand-made pot (vessel 16) in post-hole 3665; and the spout of an imported, oxidised ware pitcher (DR345), from post-hole 3914, probably dating from the late seventh century (Vince, Volume 2, Chapter 12). A further sherd of the Late Roman jar (vessel 2) was also recovered from post-hole 4629. These fragments were accompanied by eight sherds of Maxey-type pottery, in fabrics A, B and U – all northern Maxey fabrics (Young, Volume 2, Chapter 12). Two sherds from vessel 3a, in fabric U, were recovered in separate post-holes – 3667 and 4492 respectively. The latter vessel was a

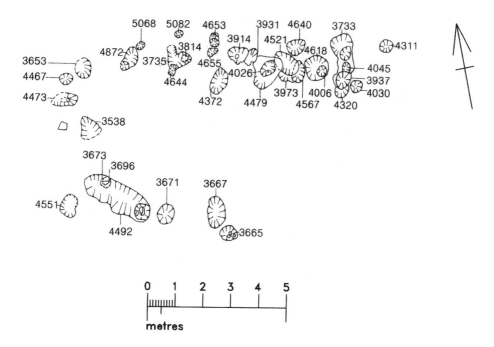

Fig. 3.5. Plan of building 18 (R. Smith).

medium-sized bowl with a flat-topped rim and slightly curved sides (type VIi), and represents the earliest known profile of a Maxey-type vessel from the site (Young, Volume 2, Chapter 12). The surface of the bowl seems to have been brushed to mask the shell temper, and parts of an identical vessel (3b) were found in later deposits. Sherds from two other vessels were jars, one of type IIb. The span of time when building 18 was standing, therefore, seems to have straddled the arrival of Maxey-type pottery wares at the settlement, currently suggested to have been between the late seventh and early eighth centuries. Other finds from the fills of the post-holes include fragments of lava quern from the Eifel region of Germany (RF 3295).

The post-hole fills of building 19, although heavily truncated by later buildings, also yielded a sherd of Maxey-type ware in fabric B, and a small, very abraded sherd, possibly of Ipswich ware. The latter sherd may well have been incorporated from a later phase by subsidence and the fore-mentioned truncation of features. Such subsidence into earlier earth-cut features is amply demonstrated in relation to post-hole 2230 from building 19. The skull and several vertebrae, thought to have originated from an extended inhumation of a child, probably from phase 3a, had slumped into the fill of this post-hole (Mays, this volume, Chapter 8). An iron spike from a heckle or wool-comb, for fibre preparation in textile production, was also found in this feature. Small quantities of iron-working slag and some vitrified hearth lining were also found in the fill (1134) of post-hole 1133.

The open surfaces of the external refuse or yard deposits, outside the buildings, yielded 13 sherds of pottery (weighing 100g). These included one Romano-British sherd and a tiny fragment of an Early Anglo-Saxon, hand-made local pot. The remainder were Maxey-type sherds, many of them sooted, reflecting cooking or secondary uses. Jane Young has also noted signs of the leaching of the shell-temper on three of the Maxey sherds, suggesting exposure to acid leaching, within the mixed sand and refuse. Deposit 3347 contained a sherd of a late fourth-century, Roman lid-seated jar – vessel 1, showing the continued re-working of material discarded in the immediate area. In this case, 3347 directly overlay deposit 4807 (phase 1a) which also contained a sherd from vessel 1. The yard deposit 3194 also produced small quantities of undiagnostic iron-working slag and vitrified hearth lining, as had post-hole 1133 of building 19. A deposit, 3348, possibly associated with building 18, also yielded a reticella-decorated glass bead (RF 3562; Evison, Volume 2, Chapter 2). In a typology of 1977, this type of bead was given a date range between AD 790 and 990, and it is possible that the object was incorporated into the spread 3348 during demolition and truncation of earlier deposits on the same building plot as building 18 (which saw at least six, and probably seven buildings between Periods 1 and 5). Alternatively, the dating associated with the typology may need amendment (Callmer 1977).

3.4 Period 2 – late seventh to early eighth century

The period of the occupation sequence dated to between the late seventh and early eighth centuries, defined as

Period 2, saw both elements of continuity and significant change in the organisation of the excavated area, in terms of buildings, drainage and boundary features (FIG. 3.6). Buildings 18 and 19 had been demolished and were replaced by three buildings – 6, 20 and 17, aligned on variations between approximate west to east, and west-south-west to east-north-east axes. On the opposite, and lower side of the shallow valley, building 21 was constructed – representing the earliest structure in that part of the excavated area.

A far more difficult matter to interpret is the date at which a ditch (446/2842) was dug in the western sector of the site (FIG. 3.6). This probable boundary feature was created running in a relatively straight line towards the

floodplain of the River Trent, to the west. There are no grounds in the physical evidence to suggest that it formed a boundary of the settlement, as has been suggested previously (Whitwell 1991, 246–247). Instead, the ditch seems to follow the lines of existing contours, stretching from the floodplain along relatively flat land, ending at the edge of the shallow valley, to the west of the zone of buildings (see FIG. 2.2, this volume). The most certain chronological point that can be made about the ditch is that it had been completely filled in by the middle decades of the ninth century (see Chapter 5, this volume). It cut two earlier features, namely an occupation deposit (75) and a post-hole (451). The latter contained only a sherd of Early Anglo-Saxon chaff-tempered ware. Spread 75,

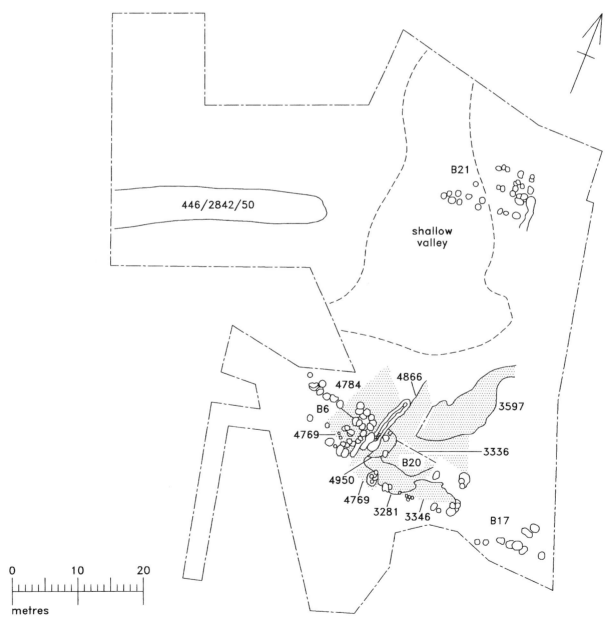

FIG. 3.6. *Plan – Period 2, late seventh to early eighth centuries (M. Frankland).*

however, contained a sherd of Maxey-type ware in type B fabric, and a sherd of wheel-made, grey-burnished ware (vessel 42), imported from northern France or the Low Countries, and which could date from the seventh or eighth centuries (Vince, Volume 2, Chapter 12). If the Maxey-type sherd was discarded at a point contemporary with the first arrival of this pottery on the site, then the ditch may have been dug in the late seventh or early eighth centuries. Yet, it is equally possible that the ditch was created as a feature at any time in the eighth century. Within its period of use, it was recut once (cut 50, Figs 5.13 and 5.14, this volume), prior to its intentional filling in the mid ninth century.

Like all the buildings from the earlier seventh-century structural phases, all of the buildings from Period 2, with one exception, were constructed within earth-fast post-hole foundations. Buildings 20 and 17 also covered part of the sites of buildings 18 and 19, having been built slightly to the north of them (Fig. 3.6). Building 20 was broadly rectangular, 13m by 6m in size, with large post-holes at its corners (see sections on the ADS archive), and smaller more ephemeral post-holes, located mainly along its long walls (Fig. 3.7). The plan of building 17 was more partial, and so estimation of the dimensions of the overall structure is inappropriate.

The most interesting structures from this period are buildings 6 and 21, both located either side of the central shallow valley, on newly defined building plots; and each building had two structural phases, extending over Period

2 and phase 3a (Figs 3.6 and 4.1). From the plans of these buildings (Fig. 3.8), it is difficult to tell which of the structural phases was constructed first. Both are represented by indications of two rectangular post-hole outlines. The location, however, of two purposely created gullies or 'soakaway' features (970/3967 for building 6 and 10235 for building 21), and the location of a possible door in the eastern end wall of building 6, hint at the order of construction. 'Soakaway' 970/3967 was created with a squared-off collection point, at the middle of the east short wall during one of the phases of building 6. The gulley, which was partly stone-lined to aid run off, then ran down the slope into the central area of the site (Fig. 3.9). One of the phases of building 6, possessed a possible doorway, which if contemporary with the gulley, would have opened out straight on to it, and would have acted as a barrier against access to building 20 and its successor, building 1a, to the east. Consequently, it is most likely that both the phases of buildings 6 and 21, which appear to be immediately adjacent to the 'soakaway' gullies, represent the secondary phases of these buildings (6b and 21b), constructed at a time when the soakaway gullies had been filled in. Whereas, the gullies make more sense as features contemporary with the earlier phases of the buildings (6a and 21a), as they would have been slightly further away from the structures and would have been more appropriate for drainage of water from hipped roofs. The secondary phases of these buildings were probably constructed after the gullies were

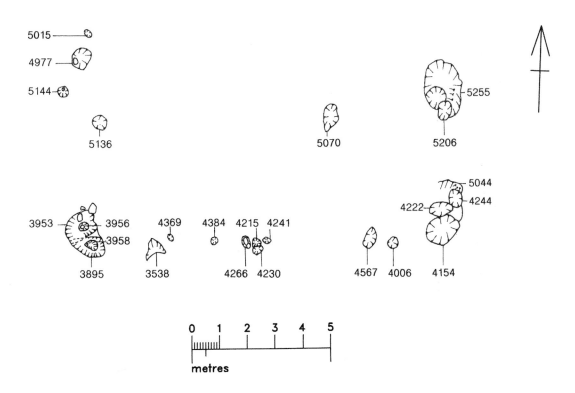

Fig. 3.7. Plan of building 20 (R. Smith).

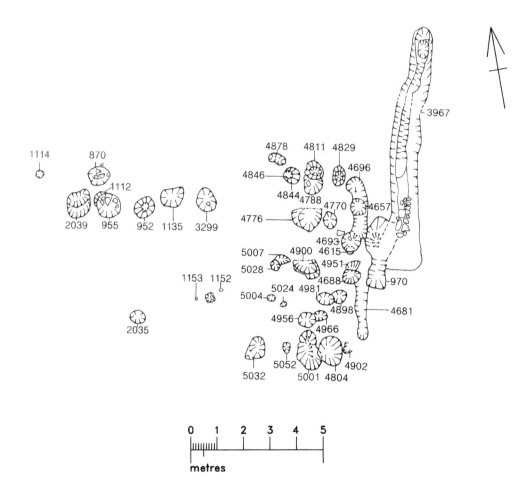

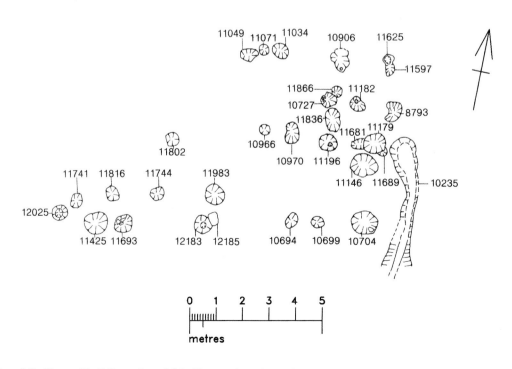

FIG. 3.8. Plan of buildings 6 and 21. Upper plan shows building 6; the lower building 21 (R. Smith).

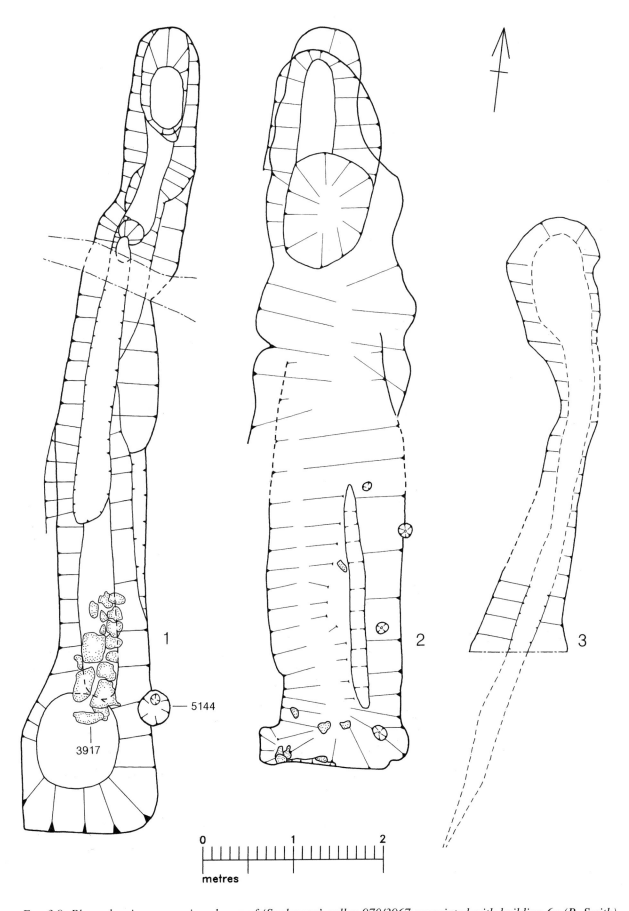

FIG. 3.9. *Plans showing successive phases of 'Soakaway' gulley 970/3967 associated with building 6a (R. Smith).*

filled with gravel, in the south of the site, and sand in the north, during phase 3a.

The plans of both phases of buildings 6 and 21 have suffered the loss of the western ends of the buildings, due to erosion of the sand spur in the case of building 6; and later disturbance by successive buildings, and a twelfth-century ditch, in the case of building 21 (see FIG. 2.3, this volume). It is not, therefore, possible to give the precise lengths of these buildings, but they were at least 11m long and between 6 and 6.5m wide. The second phase of building 6, probably built between the early and mid eighth century, is also notable for its combination of earth-fast foundation styles, having both post-holes and a foundation trench (FIG. 3.8). The foundation trench 4681, which forms the eastern end of the building, also possessed post-hole foundations cut into it, and two post-holes marking the place of a possible door, in the middle of the wall.

Preserved occupation deposits, in the form of possible floor and yard/midden material, were found in association with the buildings in the central, southern part of the excavated area. A potential floor deposit (4769) mirrored the interior of the north-east corner of the earlier phase of building 6, and an external surface deposit between the latter structure and building 20 was also given the same context/stratigraphic unit number during excavation. A further series of deposits reflect refuse which collected within or beneath the floor of building 20 (3281, 3336, 3346, 4950 – FIG. 3.6). In addition, deposits 4784 and 4866 probably represent external refuse accumulations, outside buildings 6 and 20. Taken together, these deposits contained 17 sherds of pottery, representing a maximum of ten vessels. One of the sherds came from the late fourth-century, lid-seated jar – vessel 1; and another came from vessel 2, fragments of which were re-worked in refuse deposits in this immediate area from phase 1a. Three other later Romano-British vessels are also represented, amongst an otherwise Maxey-type ware pottery assemblage; and animal bones formed the other main find component within the deposits, in relatively small numbers compared to later periods. Like some of the pottery sherds from phase 1b, some of the shell-tempered Maxey-type pottery showed signs of the leaching of the temper, reflecting the hostile soil environment. Other artefacts found within or beneath the floor of building 20 included a spindle whorl (RF 4001) from 3336/3346; and a pair of shears (RF 3587) and a needle (RF 12059) were recovered nearby. Metalworking debris, in the form of undiagnostic pieces of iron-working slag, was also found in two of these deposits (3281 and 3336) in small quantities.

Likewise, the post-hole fills of the buildings also contained a varied, although small range of artefacts. The post-holes of building 20 contained only three sherds of pottery, from two vessels – both of them from the Roman period. Both phases of building 6 taken together

yielded 41 sherds of pottery, from a similar number of vessels. All but one of the features that yielded pottery seem to be part of the earlier phase of the building, which had post-hole foundations only. Again it seems probable that the incorporation of most of the pottery fragments occurred during the demolition process; many were burnt, coated in soot, and chemically leached. Three of the sherds were Romano-British, in date, and two came from an Early Saxon chaff-tempered (ECHAF) ware bowl – vessel 62. Several sherds of sandstone-tempered vessel 4 were recovered (Young, Volume 2, Chapter 12); and the remainder of the sherds were Maxey-type wares, including an example of a new fabric – type E, from the fill of 3299. Other finds from the filled-in post-holes of building 6 include two fragments of an imported, clear glass bowl (RF 5000) with yellow trails, from post-hole 5001 (Evison, Volume 2, Chapter 2; FIG. 3.10*). 'Soakaway' 970/3967, associated with the earlier phase of building 6, contained seven late Roman pottery sherds, and a fragment of a Maxey-type jar or bowl (fabric B). Again one of the Roman pottery sherds came from the late fourth-century jar – vessel 2, reflecting the localised re-working and the water transport of material in the 'soakaway'. Other finds in the fills of the gulley included annular loom weight fragments (Walton Rogers, Volume 2, Chapter 9) and imported lava quern fragments, together with significant quantities of bones from small birds and fish (Dobney, Jaques and Barrett, Volume 3), presumably carried in suspension from building 6.

The post-holes and soakaway of building 21 yielded finds of pottery, and a fired-clay fragment, possibly associated with non-ferrous metalworking (RF14352). A group of 38 sherds was recovered from the fills of the post-holes of the building, and the sherds from all but two seem to relate to the probable later phase of the building, standing in phase 3a, and demolished sometime in the mid eighth century. Hence, the finds from the post-holes are discussed in the next section. The pottery fragments from the 'soakaway' (10235), however, can be attributed to Period 2, and comprise two small fragments (weighing 4g): one sherd was from a Maxey-type vessel in fabric B; and the other was from a local Mid Saxon, shell-tempered ware. The fragment of fired clay (RF 14352), possibly associated with non-ferrous metal-working, was also found in the fill of 10235 (Wastling, Volume 2, Chapter 11). A well-preserved, single-bladed, woodworking axe-head (RF 12107) was also recovered from an occupation deposit adjacent to building 21 (FIG. 3.11*). The axe-head also retained mineralised remains of a handle of beech wood (Ottaway, Volume 2, Chapter 7; Jones *et al.*, Volume 2, Chapter 7). Like buildings 6b and 21b, building 17 may also have remained standing through the first half of the eighth century; and consequently, the finds recovered are discussed within the context of those from early to mid eighth-century contexts/stratigraphic units.

4 Period 3: Early Eighth to Early Ninth Century

Christopher Loveluck and David Atkinson

with contributions by Jane Young and Peter Didsbury

4.1 Introduction

The third broadly defined period within the excavated occupation sequence is composed of two main structural phases – 3a and 3b, spanning most of the eighth century and possibly extending into the early ninth century. The earlier of these phases saw the maintenance and further development of the building plots, inherited from the early eighth century. There were, however, significant alterations in phase 3a to the structural character and use of space in the southern central zone of the site, on the plot and in the vicinity of the former building 20. Subsequently, sometime in the middle of the eighth century, all of the buildings seem to have been replaced, or renovated, and the central shallow valley became a focus for systematic refuse dumping, possibly as a communal refuse area for the settlement as a whole (phase 3b). Consequently, from the middle of the eighth century, the quantities of discarded artefact and faunal remains increased dramatically.

4.2 Phase 3a – early to mid eighth century

The major change in the structural character and use of space in the excavated area during the first half of the eighth century involved the use of the central, shallow valley for structures, and the construction of a large rectangular building – building 1a, in the south of the site (Fig. 4.1). This large new building partially overlay building 20, but was constructed on a more east to west alignment. It possessed a unique structural character in relation to the other building remains from Flixborough, having had a gravel foundation underlying its entire 'footprint' (Fig. 4.2; Fig. 4.3*). This probably formed the foundation base for a structure based on a wooden sill (see Darrah, Volume 4, Chapter 3). A shallow foundation trench (4137) in the southern long wall, and several deep post-holes in the eastern short wall, also suggest the possibility of an earlier, earth-fast phase to building 1a.

In both phases, there appear to have been post-holes, either supporting the wall, or the sill-based structure, particularly at the eastern end of the building – the sections of the sill-base and the post-holes are presented within the ADS archive. In its phase with the gravel sill-foundation, building 1a appears to have been divided into two halves internally, defined by gravel patches and post-holes. The eastern half also possessed a large, broadly rectangular, fired-clay hearth base (3418). In size, the structure was 14m long by 6m wide, and the two subdivisions were approximately 6.5m long in the east, and 7m long in the west, with the central division taking the remaining space.

Within the building, four human inhumation graves had been cut through the floors or through parts of the gravel foundation for the sill-based structure (Fig. 4.2). Two additional burials were interred outside the building. One, grave 3877, containing skeleton RF 3878, was located immediately to the south of the building (Fig. 4.2). The other lay to its east, a skull (RF 2231/2), which had slumped into the fill of a post-hole (2230) of former building 19 (see Geake and Mays, Chapter 8, this volume). All the burials, both within and outside the building, were interred on east-west alignments. Those within the building were buried along the long walls of the structure, one within its eastern, and three within its western halves. The two graves within the southern corner of the western half of the building contained an adult female in grave 3581 (RF 3580), buried in association with a peri-natal foetus (grave 3703; RF 3706), possibly reflecting the death of both in childbirth (Fig. 4.4; Mays, Chapter 8, this volume). Fig. 4.5* shows the female skeleton RF 3580 placed in her grave within the interior line of the gravel wall foundation. This wall foundation was later re-built and overlay the filled-in grave, when large limestone slabs for an interrupted sill were placed on top of it, during the construction of building 1b in phase 3b (see below: Loveluck and Darrah, Volume 4, Chapter 3). The third grave, in the west of the building,

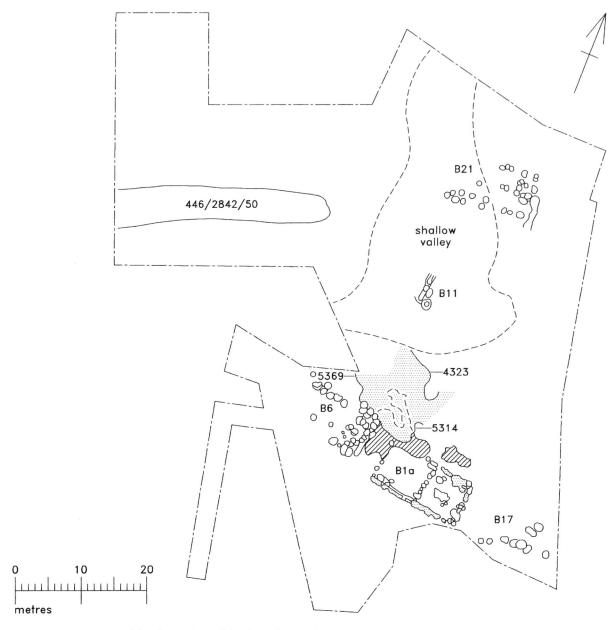

FIG. 4.1. Plan – Period 3, phase 3a, early to mid eighth century (M. Frankland).

and housing the skeleton of a juvenile (RF 4010), was placed at the junction of the northern long wall and the internal division of the building (FIG. 4.2). Both this burial and the adult female were buried as extended inhumations (FIG. 4.4). In contrast, the fourth burial, interred in the north-east corner of the building, was placed in a flexed manner (RF 1960). FIG. 4.4 shows the grave, which had been cut through the sill foundation (1731), and the filled-in grave was then partly overlain by the limestone slabs of the phase 3b-interrupted sill, for building 1b. The burial (RF 3878), interred outside the building, to the south, was also laid out in a flexed manner (FIG. 4.4).

At the same time as the construction of building 1a, its gravel foundation base (484) was extended to fill in the former soakaway 970/3967 from Period 2, and to

provide an area of 'hardstanding', between building 1a and a newly rebuilt version of building 6 (building 6b). The latter now possibly possessed a door in its eastern end, opening on to this gravel spread, facing building 1a. A similar filling in of the soakaway 10235, and its possible successor 11144, can also be suggested for building 21b, which was probably rebuilt at a similar period to building 6b, contemporary to the construction of building 1a. This was followed slightly later by the formation of the selective burial focus in and around the latter building. The relationship between this burial focus and the cemetery, partly excavated in 1988 by Kevin Leahy, is a matter of conjecture. They may reflect differentiated burial locations according to social rank within the settlement, with certain elements of the

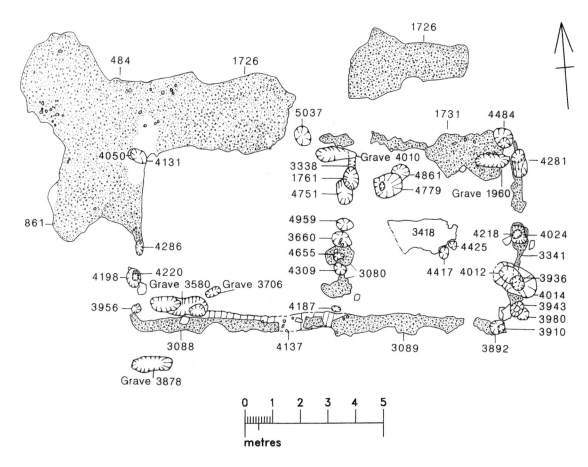

FIG. 4.2. Plan of building 1a (R. Smith).

population being buried in a building used as a mortuary chapel (Geake, Chapter 8, this volume; Loveluck, Volume 4, Chapters 3 and 9).

The major change in the use of space, however, is exemplified by the utilisation of the central part of the site for structures, following the filling in of the 'soakaway' gullies, and hence the end of organised drainage into the shallow valley. Although difficult to place within the occupation sequence, part of a foundation trench which appears to represent the west end of a building was uncovered, underlying a yard deposit of building 13, from phase 3b. The fills of these foundations yielded several sherds of Maxey-type ware. Consequently, it can be assumed that the building was demolished after the early eighth century, when the production of this pottery had certainly begun. At the same time, the existence of a building in the central valley during Period 2, when the 'soakaways' were draining into it, would seem illogical. Therefore, this structure, described as building 11, was probably constructed during the first half of the eighth century, before the construction of building 13. Building 11 was one of the earliest buildings on the site constructed by setting posts or planks within a foundation trench, together with building 6b, also from phase 3a. The plan is too partial, however, to estimate

the dimensions of the structure (FIG. 4.6; sections of the building foundations are presented in the ADS archive). A series of post-holes also provides ephemeral hints of a possible building, which stood to the south-west of building 11, although it did not overly the plot of the latter building (FIG. 4.1).

Building 17 also seems to have remained standing during phase 3a, prior to its demolition and replacement by building 2, in the middle of the eighth century. Furthermore, as already discussed above, the creation of the ditch (446) could have taken place at any time after the late seventh century, and before the middle of the ninth century. However, the indications that it was re-cut at least once (cut 50), suggest a feature of some longevity by the latter period.

The finds from phase 3a provided an interesting assemblage of artefacts associated with the buildings, in addition to a range of artefact and faunal remains from dumps 4323, 5314 and 5369 (FIG. 4.1). Unlike the refuse deposits of Period 2, which were located on both sides around buildings 6 and 20, the refuse of phase 3a was tipped mainly to the north, down the slope of the spur, into the shallow valley. This more organised refuse disposal – although still adjacent to the buildings – provided a larger number of finds than similar deposits

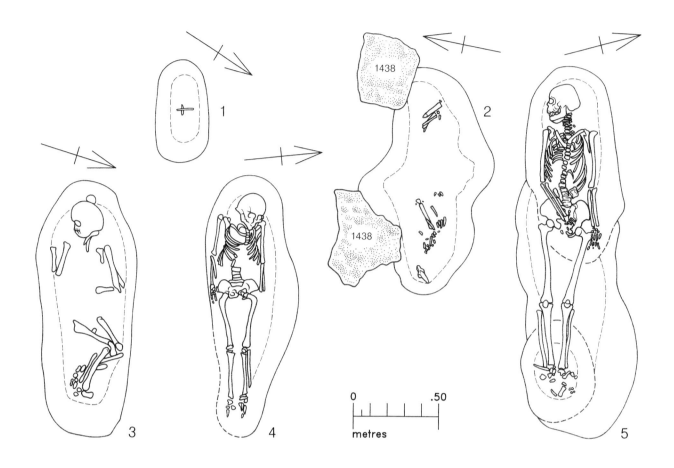

Fig. 4.4. Plan of graves sited in association with building 1a.
1. Grave 3706. 2. Grave 1960. 3. Grave 3878. 4. Grave 4010. 5. Grave 3580. (M. Frankland).

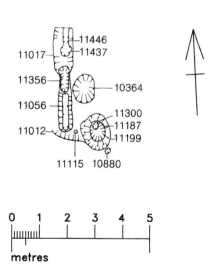

Fig. 4.6. Plan of building 11 (R. Smith).

from Periods 1 and 2 on the site. They produced significant quantities of animal bones, in addition to 18 sherds of pottery from dumps 5314 and 5369. These included fragments of four vessels of hand-made, Mid Saxon quartz-tempered fabrics, together with sherds of sandstone-tempered pottery – including a piece of vessel 4, possibly linking the refuse with building 6, which yielded other sherds of vessel 4 (Young, Volume 2). A Maxey-type sherd (fabric E) and a Romano-British sherd made up the remainder of the pottery assemblage. Both dumps also contained unfired-clay loom weight fragments, and 5314 also yielded an iron clench bolt (RF 5194).

Building 1a provided a group of 17 sherds of pottery from the features associated with it, from a maximum of 12 vessels. Three fragments were from the late Roman period, including a piece of the lid-seated jar, vessel 1, reflecting the constant rebuilding on this plot from the early seventh century. The gravel sill foundation-'hardstanding' (484) also yielded a small sherd of black-burnished ware, imported from the Continent (Vince, Volume 2, Chapter 12). The remaining pottery vessels represented were Maxey-types and the forms present included a type IIb jar, and a medium-sized type VII bowl. Three of the vessels were also covered in soot and several were chemically leached. Other finds included two fragments of imported glass vessels (RFs 3543 and 3544), found adjacent to hearth 3418; a fragment of imported lava quern from the gravel of 484; and two iron spikes for fibre preparation, in textile manufacture from the grave fill associated with the adult female RF 3580.

The finds associated with the post-holes of building 6 were discussed in relation with those from Period 2, since most of the finds came from post-holes associated with the earlier phase of the building (6a). Yet, the opposite is true for building 21. The finds associated with this building came from the fills of post-holes, associated with its secondary phase, with the exception of the already discussed finds from 'soakaway' 10235. Only pottery was found within the post-holes, and the possible secondary 'soakaway' 11144. Thirty-eight sherds were recovered, the majority of which were from Maxey-type vessels, in fabric B. The condition of the sherds was variable, with weights of individual fragments ranging from 0.5g to 47g, and the larger unabraded sherds could represent material contemporary with the building, or its demolition. A range of jars and a bowl are represented. Furthermore, none of the fragments was leached and less than 50 percent were covered in soot. Post-hole 10835 also yielded a sherd of an imported white-ware product, from the Vorgebirge region of the Rhineland, known as Walberberg ware (Tischler 1952; Böhner 1955; Hodges 1981, 83–84). Twelve sherds of this ware – all adjoining fragments from the same shouldered jar (vessel 13) were re-worked throughout the occupation sequence at Flixborough (Vince, Volume 2, Chapter 12). It was made in the seventh century, and its earliest deposition context is the fill of 10835, from the early to mid eighth century.

Building 17, like the other buildings in the south of the excavated area, in both Period 2 and phase 3a, yielded a combination of pottery sherds, glass vessel fragments and weaving equipment. Ten sherds of pottery were recovered from the post-holes, mainly Maxey-type wares, in a range of jar and bowl forms; in addition to a residual Roman sherd. A fragment of a glass vessel (RF 2553), imported from the Continent was also recovered, in addition to a bone pin-beater, for weaving, from the fill of post-hole 2355 (Walton Rogers, Volume 2, Chapter 9). Building 11, in the centre of the site, also yielded seven very small sherds of Maxey-type ware (weighing 11g), probably incorporated during demolition of the building. All showed signs of the leaching of the shell temper.

4.3 Phase 3b – mid eighth to early ninth century

During the middle decades of the eighth century, all the buildings of phase 3a were completely replaced with the exception of building 1a, which was extensively renovated without any reference to the graves within or outside the

building. The extent of the replacement of buildings with the onset of this phase seems to reflect an organised rebuilding event, accompanied by the more intensive use of the shallow valley, both for structures and organised refuse disposal. The extent of the re-organisation of the central part of the site during this period was considerable. For the purpose of clarity in data presentation and discussion, the depositional sequence has been broken down into sub-phases. Consequently, after describing the main buildings which seem to stand for the whole of the time span, between the mid to late eighth and early ninth centuries, the depositional and building events in the central shallow valley are defined within the sub-phases 3bii to 3bv.

Considering the main buildings constructed at the beginning of the phase as a starting point, all of the structures seem to represent large buildings of between 13m and 14m in length, and between 6.5m and 7m in width. A range of foundation styles was exhibited: most buildings were constructed within continuous foundation trenches, but post-hole foundations, and interrupted-sill and post-hole foundations were also used. The majority of the buildings were also positioned to broadly respect most of the building plots of the earlier eighth century, with significant additions (Fig. 4.7).

Building 1b seems to be a direct rebuild of its predecessor (building 1a), in terms of its direct super-imposition on to the 'foot-print' of the earlier structure. Other than this direct physical relationship, however, the differences between the two buildings outweigh their similarities. Building 1a was demolished prior to the reuse of parts of the gravel sill-foundation for its successor. The new building was constructed seemingly using an interrupted-sill technique, reflected by large limestone slabs, laid in part on the gravel, and part on sand. They were spaced between major opposing post-holes in the long walls of the building (Fig. 4.8; Loveluck and Darrah, Volume 4, Chapter 3). A large line of post-holes beyond the former eastern end of building 1a reflects the new eastern wall of building 1b, and hence a larger structure than 1a. It would appear to have been a structure with dimensions of 15m by between 6.8 and 7m. Two entrances in the centre of the northern and southern long walls are also suggested, between post-holes 3969 and 3358 in the north, and between 3326 and 3478 in the south. The interior of the building was also organised very differently from its predecessor. The former central division was demolished, and a fired-clay hearth base (1982) was constructed over the line of the former dividing wall or screen (Figs 4.8 and 4.9*). There is also no sign of an awareness of the graves in the immediate vicinity, as the limestone slab sill-foundation 1438 immediately overlay the fill of burial 1960 (Fig. 4.4).

Either side of the above structure, buildings 2 and 5 were constructed, on an approximate west-south-west to east-south-east alignment, although they were set slightly further south than building 1b. Their identical alignment,

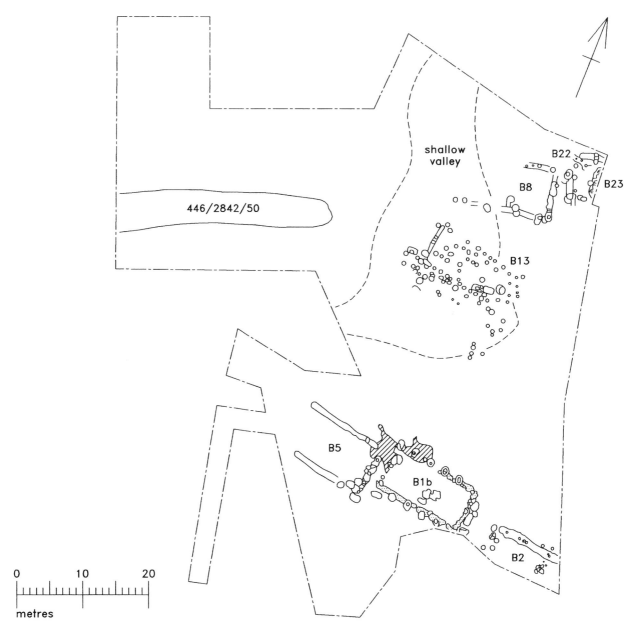

FIG. 4.7. Plan – Period 3, phase 3b, mid eighth to early ninth centuries (M. Frankland).

constructional techniques and positioning with reference to the latter building, suggest that they may have been built at the same time, following the demolition of buildings 6 and 17 (FIG. 4.7). The extent of the super-imposition on these plots is illustrated with reference to buildings 5 and 6 (and 3, from Period 4) in FIG. 4.10*, which shows the foundations sited at slightly offset angles from each other.

Both buildings 2 and 5 were constructed within continuous foundation trench long walls, with some post-holes, but mainly limestone bases for posts. The short walls were either represented by individual post-holes, as in the case of building 2, or by a separate foundation trench with post-holes cut into its base, in the case of

building 5 (FIG. 4.11). The extent to which the plans of both buildings are recoverable has been influenced by erosion of the sand spur, and sand quarrying. The western end of building 5 was lost due to slope erosion, although it is still possible to say that the rectangular structure was at least 13m in length and 7m in width. Building 2, in contrast had suffered the fate of most of the buildings in the south-eastern corner of the site, in that only its north-eastern corner was recovered. The remainder had been quarried away to the south, and the eastern end was beyond the excavated area. Consequently, although it is not possible to give an accurate estimate of its original size, the similarities with building 5 might hint at its dimensions. Building 2 also possessed an additional

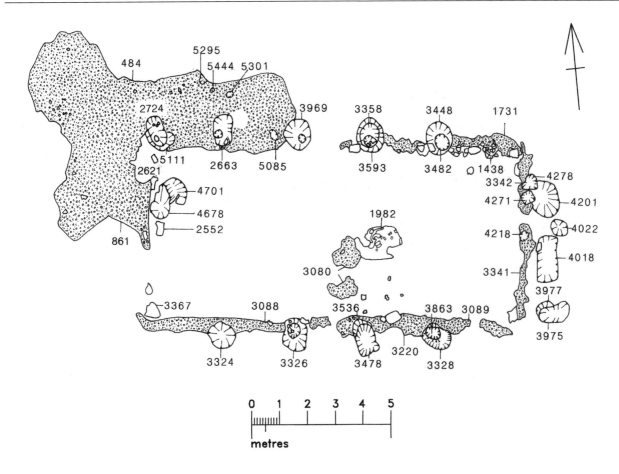

FIG. 4.8. Plan of building 1b (R. Smith).

feature, in the form of a fired-clay hearth base, seemingly located in the central part of the building, like the example in building 1b (FIG. 4.11).

On the opposite side of the shallow valley, building 8 was constructed on a south-west to north-east alignment, on the same broad plot as building 21, although not directly superimposed over it (FIG. 4.7). Due to later truncation of its foundations by further buildings and by a twelfth-century ditch, it is not possible to comment on a complete plan of this building. Nevertheless, it is possible to say that it was constructed by setting earth-fast posts or timbers within continuous foundation trenches. There are also traces of a possible internal division that split a smaller eastern section from the rest of the building (FIG. 4.12). Building 8 was just under 15m long and was 6m wide.

To the east of building 8, parts of at least two further structures were uncovered, designated as buildings 22 and 23. Of the latter collections of features, building 22 appears to be parts of at least two buildings, represented by small foundation trenches and post-holes which could not be given coherent form, due to their partial plans and proximity to the edge of the excavation (FIG. 4.12). Building 23, however, provided much more interesting information on constructional techniques, despite the fact

that only the western edge of the building was uncovered. The excavated portion appears to represent a small ancillary structure, constructed using a continuous trench foundation and combinations of post-holes, limestone or ironstone pads as bases for certain posts, and stone packing (FIG. 4.13).

The final building for consideration with those which appear to have been constructed at the beginning of phase 3b is building 13, which later formed a focus for refuse disposal, before being completely demolished and buried under further refuse. Unlike the other structures from this phase, building 13 was an earth-fast construction based within post-hole foundations. Unfortunately, its full plan was only uncovered late in the excavations by machine; and as a consequence, sections of many of the post-holes were not drawn (see FIG. 2.2, this volume). Nevertheless, the recovery of the complete plan of the building allows for some consideration of the character of the structure. In terms of location, building 13 was sited on a previously unused plot on the northern side of the shallow valley, running up the centre of the excavated area (FIG. 4.7). The main features of its foundations can be summarised as two sets of double lines of relatively small post-holes, forming the north and south walls, with similar single lines of post-holes forming the shorter east

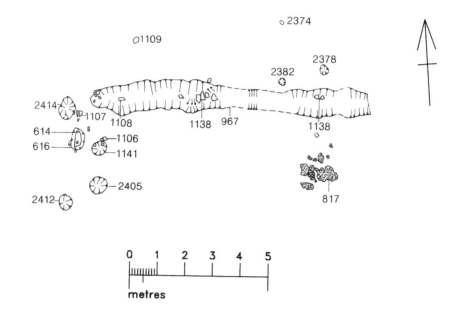

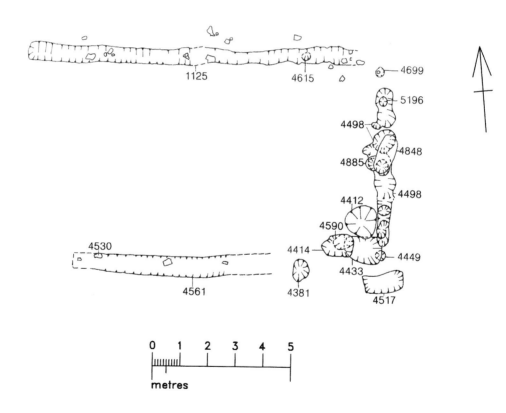

Fig. 4.11. Plans of buildings 2 and 5. Upper plan shows building 2, the lower building 5 (R. Smith).

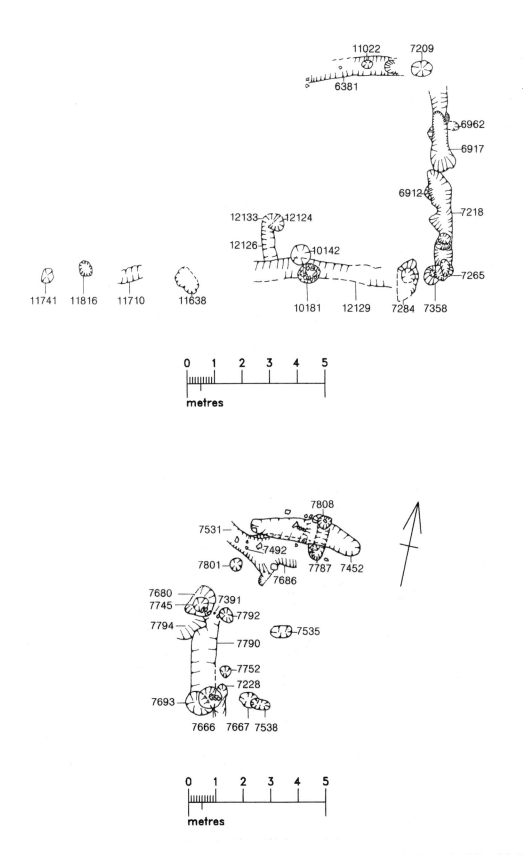

FIG. 4.12. *Plans of buildings 8 and 22. The upper plan shows building 8, the lower building 22 (R. Smith).*

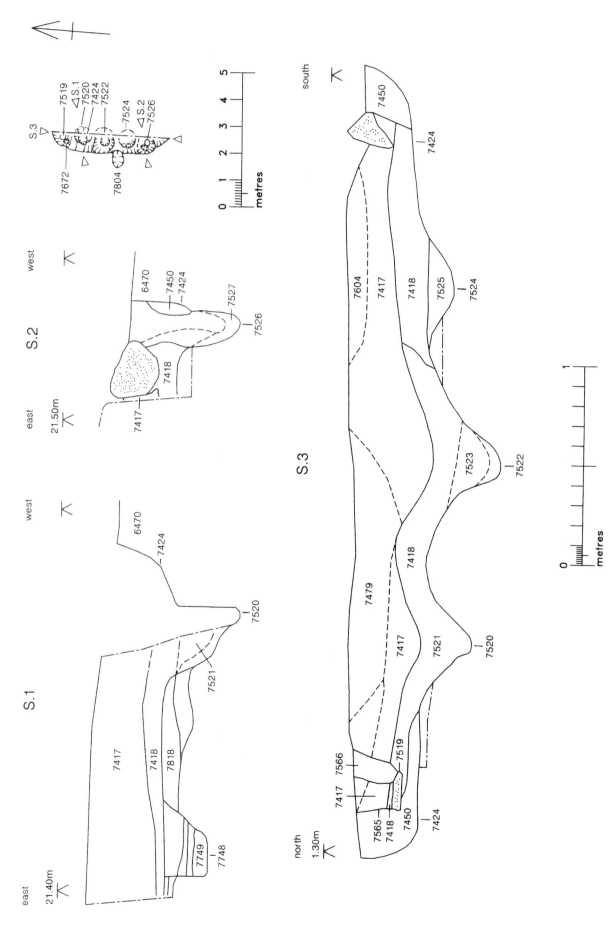

FIG. 4.13. Plan (far right on the figure) and sections of building 23 (R. Smith, M. Frankland).

and west end walls (FIG. 4.14). The external post-holes could possibly have had a role as foundations for raking timbers, to assist in roof support. The main roof-supporting role, however, is more probably reflected by the line of large post-holes running down the central long axis of the building. The longer north and south walls also appear to reflect a slightly bowed structure. An entrance may also be indicated in the centre of the southern wall, in the aperture defined between the small post-holes 10822 and 10674, and the larger post-holes immediately to the north of them, recorded as part of 12221 (FIG. 4.14). In terms of alignment, the building was constructed on an east – west axis, and was approximately 14m long and 6.5m wide, at its extremities.

Building 13 also possessed a group of post-holes at its western end, which may or may not be associated with the building. The thin foundation trench 11851, however, with its internal small post-holes does seem to represent the western end of the building (FIG. 4.14). The difference between the west end and its eastern counterpart is probably explained by the fact that 11851 was hand-excavated, whereas post alignment 12222 was recorded in plan only. To the south of the building, a series of other small post-holes, for example, 12435, 12434, 12433

and 12440, may represent a fence line, organising the use of space around certain parts of the structure (Loveluck, Volume 4, Chapter 3).

The finds found in association with the buildings described above are discussed in the following sections, relating to the phase in which they were demolished. The majority of the artefact remains came from the fills of sand-cut features – foundation trenches and post-holes. Indeed, when it is possible to tell, nearly all of the finds came from the fills of former trenches and post-holes, once the buildings had been demolished. As most of the buildings discussed above seem to have remained standing for the length of phase 3b, it is not possible to identify the temporal derivation of any artefacts in the fills of their foundations, within that period. Since the material filling the former foundations must have been placed, or have become incorporated within them on demolition, the finds from the buildings are discussed with those of the latest sub-phase – 3bv, giving a *terminus post quem* for their deposition. This latest period in the activities of phase 3b seems to correspond with a series of events involving spatial re-organisation and demolition, within the excavated area.

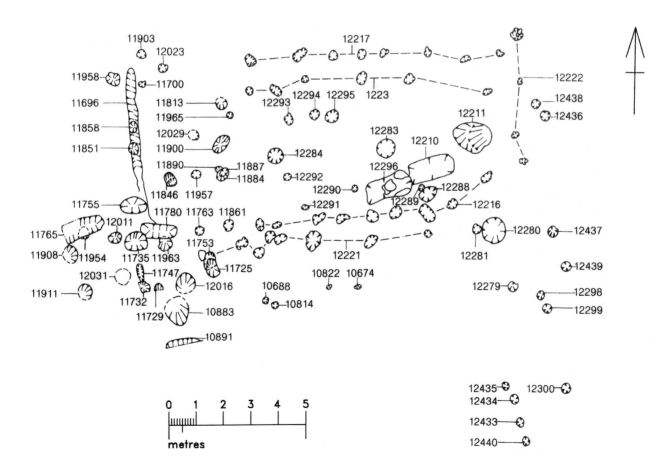

FIG. 4.14. Plan of building 13 (R. Smith).

Sub-phase 3bii

Subsequent to the construction of the buildings already discussed, the area immediately outside the south and west ends of building 13, to the west of the possible fence line, became a focus for organised refuse dumping. These refuse deposits formed a sort of yard of middens around building 13, and more occupation debris was spread to the west of the building, in the form of deposits 7276 and 7546 (FIG. 4.15). In turn, partial foundation trenches and post-holes of another structure (possible building 40) were cut through 7276 and 7546.

The refuse deposits around building 13 produced a large number of finds relating to textile production, non-ferrous metalworking, and iron-working. In addition, a small group of eight pottery sherds was recovered

(weighing 139g), consisting of two Romano-British fragments, including a piece of Samian ware – the first early Roman pottery from the sequence (Didsbury, Volume 2, Chapter 14); a single sherd of a sandstone-tempered Anglo-Saxon pot (vessel 92), paralleled at Fishergate (Young, Volume 2, Chapter 12; Mainman 1993); and five completely leached sherds of Maxey-type ware. The leaching reflects chemical weathering within the relatively shallow deposits. Iron-working slag and cinder were recovered in a series of fragments within deposit 6465 (weighing a total of 500g). In the same deposit, between 50 and 100 clay loom weights were recovered (including 55 recorded finds), weighing 2,900g (Walton Rogers, Volume 2, Chapter 9), together with 17 small fragments of fired-clay moulds, and one from a

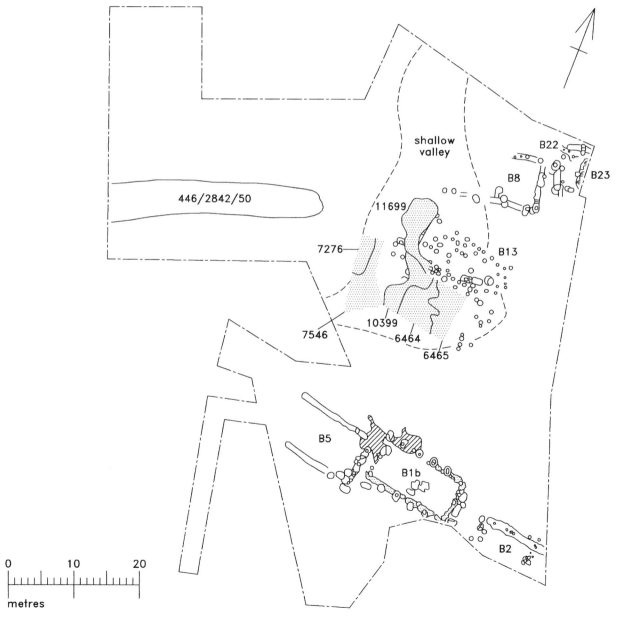

FIG. 4.15. Plan – Period 3, phase 3bii, mid eighth to early ninth centuries (M. Frankland).

crucible, for the casting of non-ferrous metal artefacts (Wastling, Volume 2, Chapter 11). The extremely fragmented state of the moulds suggests that they had been extensively re-worked in other refuse contexts, and that they were subsequently transported to their final site of deposition around building 13. The occurrence of Samian ware, the first early Roman pottery encountered, may also reflect deposit movement into the excavated area from unexcavated parts of the settlement. Deposits 10399 and 11699 also yielded small quantities of undiagnostic iron-working slag and furnace lining (Starley, Volume 2, Chapter 10); and 11699 and 7546 also provided a small number of loom weight fragments. Relatively small quantities of animal bones were also recovered, in comparison to the massive deposition of bones witnessed later in the occupation sequence.

Sub-phase 3biii

Following the use of the areas around building 13 for tipping refuse, both the latter structure and building 40, to its west, were demolished. During this demolition event, pottery from four vessels was incorporated into the fills of its post-hole foundations, comprising three sherds from a Maxey-type vessel, and two unidentifiable Romano-British pottery fragments. A fragment of a stone quern (RF 12986) was also recovered from the western end of the building, during excavation by machine. After the demolition of the building, the area of its former plot was cut by two large, flat-bottomed rectangular pits, which contained large quantities of charcoal – features 12296 and 12210 respectively (Fig. 4.14). Their function is uncertain.

The area of building 13 was then covered by what appears to be a combination of demolition and iron-working debris – deposit 12925. This contained large quantities of burnt daub, in small pieces; a hearth bottom associated with iron smithing, and a small amount of iron-working slag (Fig. 4.16). Further to its east, a series of demolition and refuse dumps covered the former area of building 40 and the western end of building 13: namely deposits 11663, 8200, 7220 and 7153. The earliest of these deposits – 11663 – probably the western extension of 12925, also contained a fragment of a hearth bottom associated with iron smithing, some cinder, and significant quantities of burnt daub (Starley, Volume 2, Chapter 10). No pottery was recovered from either 12925 or 11663.

Subsequent to this probable demolition phase in the valley, the area was used for further refuse dumping, extending out from the south-eastern corner of building 8. Indeed, the line of the large deposit 8200 mirrors the corner of the latter building (Fig. 4.16). The proximity to the building seems to reflect continuity of the practice of dumping refuse outside buildings, witnessed in earlier periods, although the highly re-worked mould fragments from 6465, also suggest the possibility of transport of refuse into the shallow valley in the mid to late eighth

century. Dump 8200 also contained the earliest stratified coin from the Flixborough settlement sequence – RF 10299 – a series E 'porcupine' sceat, from the Rhine mouth area of Frisia, probably minted between AD 700 and 730 (Archibald, Volume 2, Chapter 13). Several loom weight fragments were also retrieved from this deposit. Refuse deposits 7220 and 7153 then covered 8200 in successive episodes of dumping. The former deposit contained an iron spike from a heckle or wool comb, together with a small number of loom weight fragments. Likewise, 7153 contained a further small collection of loom weight fragments, pieces of imported, Eifel lava querns (RFs 7221 and 13927), iron-working slag, and a piece of roasted iron ore.

Deposits 8200, 7220 and 7153 also contained a small group of pottery, consisting of 15 sherds. Two were late Roman in date, including a piece of lid-seated jar vessel 1. This reflects an origin for some of the material from the southern building plots, especially the area of buildings 5 and 1b. Sherds of eight Maxey-type, medium-sized jars and bowls were also recovered, six of the vessels having internal sooting. Another Maxey-type vessel was a large triangular-lugged jar (type 1b in fabric B – vessel 79). Dump 7220 also produced the earliest undoubted, stratified sherd of Ipswich ware from the settlement, in the form of a pitcher (Blinkhorn, Volume 2, Chapter 12). The earliest sherd of the hand-made, greensand-tempered (ESGS) pot – vessel 21 – was also recovered from this deposit. Fragments of vessel 21 were subsequently found in 19 other deposits throughout the occupation sequence.

Sub-phase 3biv

After the activities of phase 3biii, the organisation of space within the central shallow valley was altered again, probably between the late eighth and early ninth centuries. Building 9 was constructed on an approximate east to west alignment, over the western refuse deposits of phase 3biii (Fig. 4.17; Fig. 4.18). The foundation trenches of this building cut through both 7220 (3biii) and 7546 (3bii), as can be clearly seen in the section shown in Fig. 4.19 – 5977 is a cut of one of the foundation trenches of building 9. Although the plan of the building is partial, due to the extent of disturbance by later structural features, it is possible to estimate that it was at least 9m long and 5.5m wide. Immediately beyond the eastern end of the building, the central part of the site was used for organised refuse disposal, in the form of three major dumps – deposits 5653, 5983 and 6039.

The main components of these refuse deposits were sherds of pottery, animal bones and loom weight fragments, in addition to smaller numbers of other finds. A total of 32 pottery sherds (weighing 345g) was recovered from these dumps, representing a maximum of 17 vessels. One vessel was Romano-British, and seven were made in Mid Saxon sandstone and quartz-tempered fabrics. One of the sandstone-tempered sherds from vessel 4 (in 5983) joins with another sherd of the same vessel,

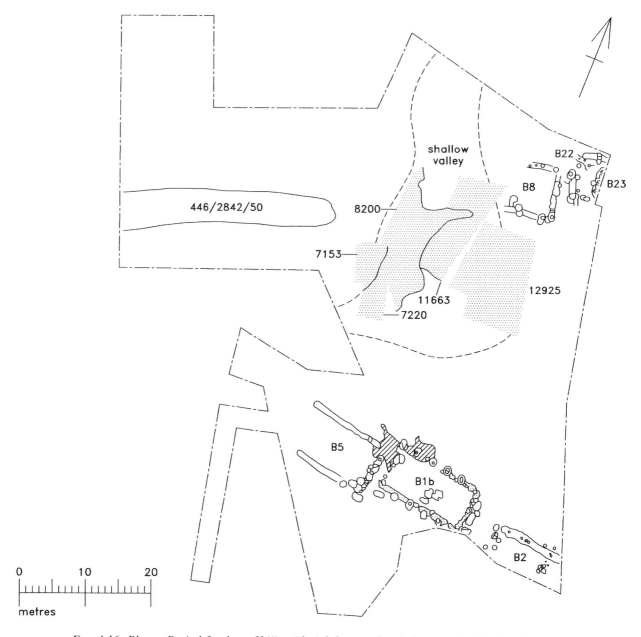

Fig. 4.16. Plan – Period 3, phase 3biii, mid eighth to early ninth centuries (M. Frankland).

found in one of the post-hole fills of building 6, suggesting that a component of the refuse came from the south of the site. At the same time, three sherds of the imported Walberberg jar (vessel 13) from these dumps might also reflect the dumping of refuse from the north of the site, where the first of its sherds was discovered, in a phase 3a context/stratigraphic unit. Only seven Maxey-type vessels are represented, including the first appearance of two pots with wheel-thrown rims (type IV vessels), in fabrics E and U. The first sherd of 'Early Lincolnshire Fine-shelled ware' (ELFS) also appeared in this phase, although it may represent a transition between a fine-shelled Maxey-type fabric and the true Early Lincolnshire Fine-shelled ware, found more commonly in ninth-

century deposits. Overall, the pottery assemblage from these dumps reflects a shift from Maxey-type wares to hand-made sandstone- and quartz-tempered wares (Young, Volume 2, Chapter 12).

Alongside the pottery, a significant number of unfired-clay loom weights and loom weight fragments were also recovered, particularly from 5893 (705g), in addition to pieces of Eifel lava querns and a fragment of window glass (RF 10205). The last find was the earliest occurrence of window glass within the Flixborough deposits (Cramp, Volume 2, Chapter 4). Metalworking evidence was also recovered in the form of a fired-clay mould fragment (RF 14418) from deposit 5653, for non-ferrous metal casting; and large fragments of hearth

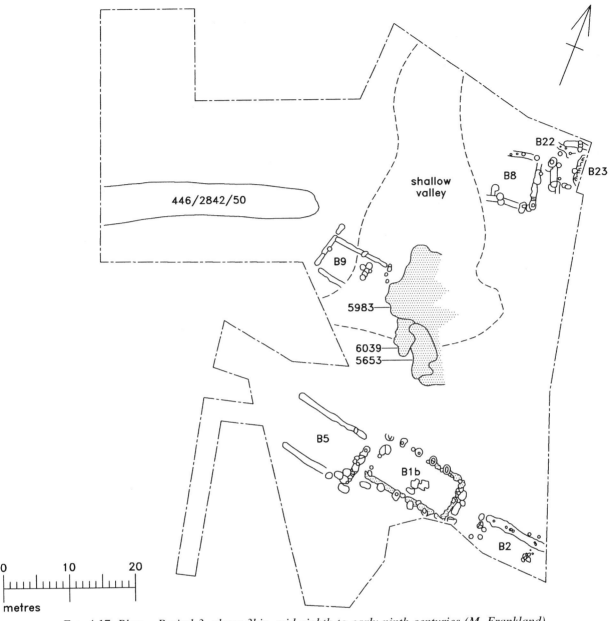

FIG. 4.17. Plan – Period 3, phase 3biv, mid eighth to early ninth centuries (M. Frankland).

bottoms, from iron smithing were also found in both 5653 and 5983. As with the moulds from 6465, in phase 3bii, there is no evidence of non-ferrous metalworking within the excavated area. The mould fragment and the iron-working debris are most likely to reflect deposit transport from other parts of the settlement, into a communal refuse zone.

Sub-phase 3bv

The final events of phase 3b can be summarised by the continued dumping of material within the central area of the site, which may well have been contemporary with the demolition of most, if not all of the buildings, prior to the re-planning of Period 4. Again, as with the 3biv refuse

dumps, the finds from the deposits of this sub-phase consisted of pottery, animal bones, and craft-working debris; although new artefact types, not previously deposited also appeared – as they did in the fills of the foundations of the demolished buildings.

The refuse dumps of this time extended over a larger area than those of preceding periods, consisting of six major deposits – 5617, 6040, 6136, 6235, 6304 and 6305 (FIG. 4.20). As a group, although mainly from 5617 and 6235, they yielded 55 sherds of pottery (weighing 1148g) from a maximum of 40 vessels. Fragments of three Romano-British vessels were recovered, including one from the fourth-century, lid-seated jar vessel 2, again indicating that a component of the refuse probably

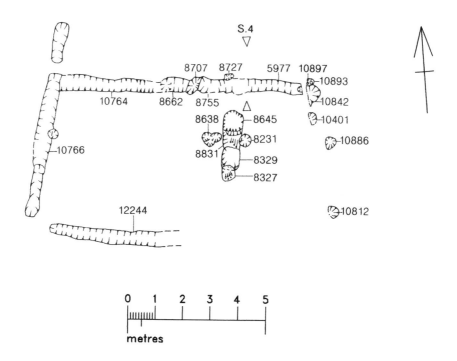

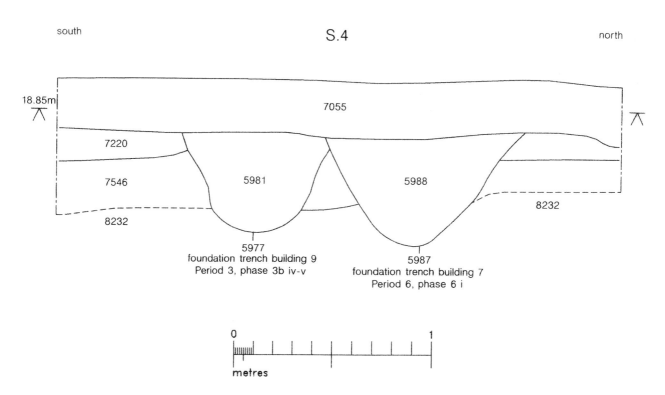

FIG. 4.18. Plan of building 9 (R. Smith).

FIG. 4.19. Section drawing showing the foundation trenches of buildings 9 and 7, cutting through deposits 7220 and 7546 (M. Frankland).

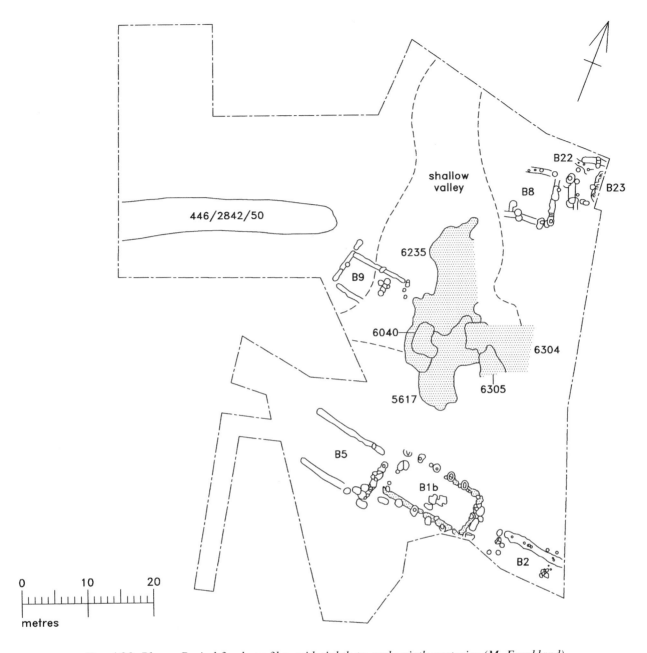

Fɪɢ. 4.20. Plan – Period 3, phase 3bv, mid eighth to early ninth centuries (M. Frankland).

originated from the excavated southern building plots. Sherds from five hand-made sandstone- or quartz-tempered vessels and one chaff-tempered pot were also found, including a further six sherds of sandstone-tempered vessel 21, from 5617, 6235 and 6304. The earliest appearance of this vessel was in the 3biii refuse deposit 7220, and its absence from other contemporary 3biii deposits and earlier deposits, in the vicinity of the buildings, suggests that it had been used and broken outside the excavated area. Subsequently it was transported, re-deposited and re-worked, within the central refuse zone. Cross-joining sherds from vessels also found in other deposits included examples from vessels 4 and 6. Fragments of the former vessel had previously been found

within deposits associated with the demolition of building 6b (phase 3a). A further sherd from the Walberberg jar vessel 13, from dump 5617, also reflected the further re-working of sherds of this vessel, the earliest of which had been deposited in post-hole 10835, from building 21b (phase 3a). Other vessels represented were all Maxey-types, with the exception of two unidentifiable sherds.

The refuse deposits from the end of phase 3b also contain further evidence for textile manufacture, iron-working and non-ferrous metalworking, like those from phases 3bii, 3biii and 3biv. Although overall, the dumps of 3bv contained fewer mould fragments than phase 3bii. Large fragments of hearth bottoms for iron smithing were found in 5617 and 6235; whilst iron-working slag was found in all the dumps, with the exception of 6304 and 6305. Copper alloy melt was also recovered from 5617, and two probable mould fragments (RFs 10350/10351) were found in 6304. Another mould fragment was also found in pit 6709 (Wastling, Volume 2, Chapter 11), amongst a fill (6710) consisting mainly of animal bones. Small quantities of loom weight fragments were recovered from 5617, 6235 and 6304, although a much larger quantity was yielded by 6136, with a combined weight of 3,234g – including 51 recorded finds (Walton Rogers, Volume 2, Chapter 9). A pair of shears (RF 10348) came from 6304; and iron spikes for fibre preparation came from 5617 and 6235. The other main component of the finds assemblage, in addition to the craft-working evidence, was animal bone, as was the case in the 3biv dumps.

The dumps from 3bv, however, also contained forms of material culture that had not previously been discarded. These included a gilded copper alloy stylus (RF 11568) from 6235 and an iron stylus (RF 10349) from 6304 (Pestell, Volume 2, Chapter 3). Others included a decorated hooked tag (RF 6439) from 5617, the second stratified dress accessory from the sequence, which was not a pin – the other being a buckle (RF 5535) from a deposit dating from between Period 1 and Period 2. Further finds were also recovered that suggest the existence of a stained-glass window, within a building – or former building – on the site. To augment the piece of window glass from dump 5983 (3biv), two pieces of lead window came (RFs 6186 and 10138), for holding stained glass within a window, were also found in refuse dumps 6136 and 6235 (Cramp, Volume 2, Chapter 4). Other finds included two clench bolts and further fragments of Eifel lava quern stones.

Alongside, the finds profiles from the dumps of 3biv and especially 3bv, the artefacts recovered from the filled-in foundations of the demolished buildings from phase 3bv also reflect similarities with certain material from the refuse.

The fills of the foundations of demolished building 1b yielded a small amount of pottery, only 13 sherds from 10 vessels. Six of the vessels represented were Romano-British, and four were of Maxey-types. In addition to the pottery, a range of other finds of a domestic and more specialised nature was also recovered. These included four fragments of bone and antler combs from post-hole 4701, as well as a copper-alloy stylus (RF 4762) from the top of the fill of the same feature (FIG. 4.21*). It is possible that this could represent subsidence into the fill of the former post-hole in the succeeding period. Other finds included an exquisite bone spoon, with a carved lyre-shaped handle (RF 4135) from an occupation or demolition deposit (2722) associated with the building (FIG. 4.22*). Likewise, a finely carved bone pin-beater (RF 3577; Walton Rogers, Volume 2, Chapter 9; Volume 4, FIG. 6.1) and fragments of Eifel querns were also recovered from probable demolition deposits of building

1b–3541 and 3349. The former of these two deposits also contained a piece of iron-working slag, suggesting an imported derivation for some of the material from a different part of the site, since no iron-working is reflected in the area of the building when it was standing, or after it was demolished.

The fills of the foundation trenches of buildings 2 and 5 also yielded a range of pottery sherds and other finds. Only ceramics were recovered from building 2, comprising an assemblage of 28 sherds, including large fragments (weighing 215g in total). Four of the vessels represented were Romano-British, and a range of Maxey-type ware jars and bowls, in fabrics B and U, formed the Anglo-Saxon component. Fragments from eight of the latter vessels were covered in soot, following cooking or possible re-use as lamps, and a small number of the sherds were leached, indicating exposure to chemical weathering prior to final incorporation in the former foundations of building 2. The pottery assemblage from the deposits filling post-holes from building 5 was much smaller than its contemporary building on the other side of building 1b, comprising only six sherds, from two Maxey-type and three Roman vessels. One of the latter vessel fragments, however, came from the late fourth-century jar, vessel 1, reflecting an element of continued disturbance of earlier material on this building plot from Period 1 onwards. A double-sided, composite bone comb was also recovered from post-hole 773 (fill 463) of building 5, with further bone comb teeth (RFs 763 and 7640) probably reflecting its incorporation and probable fragmentation within refuse, prior to deposition in this post-hole. Other finds from the fill of the same feature (773) included a possible though doubtful iron stylus (RF 465), and a bone pin-beater or needle fragment (RF 766).

On the northern building plots beyond the shallow valley, the fills of features associated with building 8 yielded 11 sherds of pottery (weighing 224g), consisting mainly of Maxey-type vessels, but also several pieces of a hand-made Anglo-Saxon pot (vessel 33), paralleled with vessels from phases 3a–b at Fishergate, in York (Mainman 1993, fig. 243; 2436). This was the first occurrence of fragments from this vessel in the Flixborough occupation sequence, reflecting the entry and breakage of the vessel sometime between the mid eighth and early ninth centuries. Pieces of vessel 33 were subsequently re-worked in deposits within the excavated area, on the same building plot, and in Period 5 dumps (context 5885) and Period 6 dumps (context 3891), reflecting the local derivation for some of their refuse. The post-hole 11710 also produced a sherd of an Iron Age pot (vessel 20; Didsbury, Volume 2, Chapter 14). Again this represents the first piece of this vessel from the settlement sequence, probably reflecting the moving of refuse from other parts of the settlement into the excavated area, also suggested by the first appearance of early Roman pottery in phase 3b. Fragments of loom weights and imported lava querns were also found in occupation deposit 6383, within building 8. Only a single Maxey-type sherd came from the features associated with buildings 22 and 23.

In the central shallow valley, the fills of the foundation trenches of building 9, immediately to the west of the major dumps of phases 3biv and 3bv, yielded slightly greater quantities of artefacts than their counterparts to the north and south. This was probably due to the incorporation of material from the nearby refuse heaps during the demolition of the building. Pottery finds were very limited. Only a Maxey-type sherd was recovered from foundation trench 5977. Two fragments of an imported glass drinking vessel (RFs 8717 and 8723; Fig. 4.23*), cobalt blue in colour with white trail decoration, were also found in a post-hole (8708) set within foundation trench 5977. A double-sided bone comb fragment was also recovered from the fill of foundation trench 10764. In addition, a small number of loom weights were also found in the foundation fills, reflecting potential derivation from the dumps as much as possible weaving in the former building

5 Period 4: Early to Mid Ninth Century

Christopher Loveluck and David Atkinson

with contributions by Jane Young and Peter Didsbury

5.1 Introduction

During the early decades of the ninth century, the layout of the settlement within the excavated area underwent significant alteration, with the complete rebuilding of all the structures on some of the already-established building plots, and the construction of new buildings in the central and northern zones of the site. Three lines of buildings were thus created for the only time in the occupation sequence, on variations of approximate east-west alignments. During the middle decades of the ninth century, however, the settlement structures appear to have been systematically levelled and filled. Vast quantities of artefacts, animal bones and industrial debris were deposited in dumps in the central area of the shallow valley and in the ditch. The latter feature was completely filled by the end of this period. The structural and depositional sequence in Period 4 is examined within two defined sub-phases: the first relates to the re-planning of the site and deposits associated with it, between the early and mid ninth century, designated phase 4i; whilst the demolition and depositional phase is described as phase 4ii. This use of Latin numerical labelling follows the method used to designate the sequence of accumulation of refuse deposits for phase 3b, as a contrast to the alphabetical labelling which denotes structural sub-phases within particular periods.

5.2 Phase 4i – early to mid ninth century

Sometime between the early and mid ninth century, the buildings of phase 3b were demolished and the layout of the excavated area was altered (probably represented by phase 3bv). Certain buildings to the north and south of the shallow valley were replaced, and new buildings were constructed overlying part of the former building 9 and the refuse dumps, and in the area to the west of former building 8 (FIGS 4.20 and 5.1).

On the higher ground of the sand spur, in the south of the site, buildings 1b, 5 and 2 were replaced on the same general plots, but offset to the north and south of the preceding building 'footprints'. Building 5 was replaced by building 3, constructed by setting a post or shaped-timber superstructure within a continuous foundation trench. The western end of the building had been lost due to erosion, as with the earlier buildings 6 and 5 in this area. It is still possible, however, to state that the structure was 7m wide and 9m in length to the point where the foundations were destroyed (FIG. 5.2). Occupation within the building was also at ground level, and a fired-clay hearth base (466) survived towards the centre of the building, with associated occupation deposits within and around it.

To the east of building 3, the former building 1b had been replaced by building 10a, also constructed using continuous foundation trenches like building 3, but with a different method of supporting the above-ground structure. In fact, the features within the foundation trenches could reflect two structural phases for the building. The shallow foundation trenches had been heavily truncated by later activity, but it is possible to identify limestone post-pads and the remains of a charred timber sill, which also probably served as a pad, rather than a sill proper (Loveluck and Darrah, Volume 4, Chapter 3). FIG. 5.3 shows the plan of the building with the stone post-pads and the fragmentary, charred timber sill, together with the sections of the foundation trenches. The sections clearly show that the trenches were dug first, and these may have provided the foundations for the first phase of the building. Subsequently, however, the trenches appear to have been partly filled, and the post-pads and sill were laid within them, presumably as the base for a replacement of the building. The eastern end of building 10a has been truncated to the point of its disappearance, and the south-eastern corner had been quarried away, but it is possible to estimate that it was at

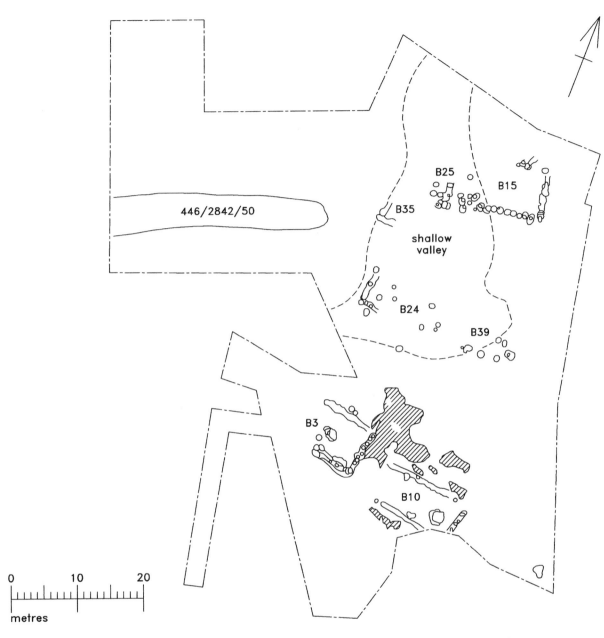

FIG. 5.1. Plan – Period 4, phase 4i, early to mid ninth century (M. Frankland).

least 13m long and 6m wide. Like building 3, it also possessed an internal hearth base (1964) made of fired clay and stone, although located in the centre of the eastern end of the building. Contemporary gravel paths (3085 and 2448, FIG. 5.3) also led up to central points of the long walls, suggesting the existence of two doors in these locations.

A further replacement for building 10a is also suggested by a line of substantial post-holes beyond the line of the northern long wall (FIG. 5.1), although an equivalent set of foundations could not be found contemporary with these features to the south. Traces of a building to the east of building 10a were also lacking, but

the presence of a fired-clay and stone hearth base (668) suggests that a contemporary building did stand on this plot (FIG. 5.1). The absence of cut foundations may be accounted for by their shallowness and complete truncation.

To the north of the shallow valley, the former building 8 was replaced by two buildings – numbers 15 and 25; and indications of a third building in this area were also suggested by the gravel foundation, designated 'building 35' (FIG. 5.1). Building 15 was constructed using post-hole foundations for its long walls, some of which had the remains of limestone and ironstone post-pads and packing within them (FIG. 5.4; see ADS archive for

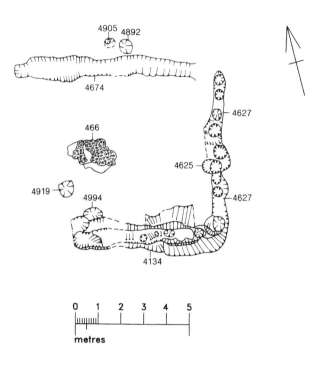

0 1   2   3   4   5
metres

FIG. 5.2. Plan of building 3 (R. Smith).

sections). Due to their uncovering during the evaluation stage of the excavations, it is unclear whether foundation trenches 6917 and 7218 were associated with building 8 or building 15. The building from Period 4 appears to have been slightly wider but shorter than most of the earlier buildings on the site, a trait also reflected in some other buildings from the early to middle decades of the ninth century. For example, building 15 was between 11 and 12m in length, and between 7 and 7.5m in width – a similar width to building 3. Despite the few wider buildings, however, the buildings from Period 4 were smaller than their eighth-century predecessors.

The remains of buildings 25 and 35 both represent partial plans of these structures. Building 25 appears to reflect two phases of construction on the same plot (FIG. 5.5), with foundations for a post-hole wall located immediately to the south of the corner of another building, which was constructed with post-holes set within a foundation trench. The post-holes to the south of the foundation trench do not appear to represent raking timbers for the roof support of a single building; hence, two construction phases are suggested. As already mentioned, building 35 is reflected only by the corner foundations of a structure built on a gravel sill base. Nothing constructive can be said about the dimensions of either building.

Within the central area of the site, two small buildings

were constructed on an east to west alignment, constituting a third line of buildings to complement those to the north and south. These structures, buildings 24 and 39, were constructed using a combination of post-hole and continuous trench foundations (FIG. 5.1), overlying earlier refuse deposits and part of the area occupied by building 9, in phases 3biv–v. Building 39 was built in the eastern half of the site and is represented by two lines of post-holes, possibly for the support of the roof of the structure, alongside a fired-clay hearth in its eastern end (FIG. 5.6). Building 24, in contrast was constructed using a combination of post-holes in foundation trenches, and post-holes. In many respects, the plans of these buildings are extremely partial due to the intensity of use, and the extent of the re-modelling of deposits in the central zone of the excavated area. The selected sections from the foundation trenches and post-holes of this building demonstrate the degree of cutting and truncation and the subsequent use of this area, reflected primarily in the Period 6 deposits (FIG. 5.6).

The finds associated with the period when all these buildings were standing are relatively few, which may well reflect the keeping of this area clean as a residential zone. The vast quantities of finds from this period were recovered primarily from dumped material covering the area of the demolished buildings 24 and 39, and from the filling of the ditch, in phase 4ii. Nevertheless, occupation deposits, possibly reflecting floor surfaces and limited middens, within and outside certain buildings do give some hints of the character of occupation. A fragment of a glass vessel was found in association with hearth 466 and its ash deposit 467, within building 3; and an iron stylus (RF 4316) was found in occupation deposit 1773, adjacent to the gravel 'hardstanding' 484/861 (FIG. 5.1). The keeping of the residential zone relatively clean, with limited middens, would also have resulted in the uppermost dumps from Period 3 (phase 3bv especially) forming the 'activity surface' for phase 4i, with the expectation of churning of the sandy deposits and the incorporation of artefacts discarded in Period 4. This could account for the first stylus, a window glass fragment and two lead cames being recovered from the surface of the 3bv dumps, and their exceptional nature set against the other artifact discard patterns from Period 3 (see Loveluck, Volume 4, Chapter 2).

A sherd of the imported Walberberg pottery vessel 13 was also found in a deposit (2720) within building 3. The occurrence of a sherd of this vessel on this southern plot reflects the movement of material from the north or central parts of the site southward, during the early to mid ninth century. Sherds of the latter vessel had previously only been found on the northern building plots, and within refuse dumps from phase 3b. A fragment from a glass vessel (RF 3287) was also found in a deposit within building 10a, but it may have been a relic of the demolition of building 1b. Craft-working debris within phase 4i deposits was also limited, although this is a

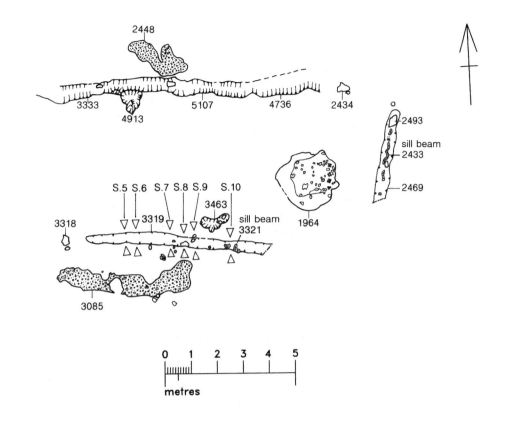

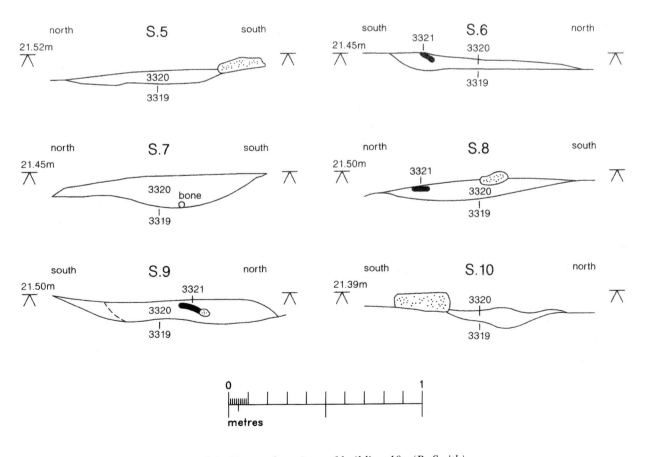

FIG. 5.3. *Plan and sections of building 10a (R. Smith).*

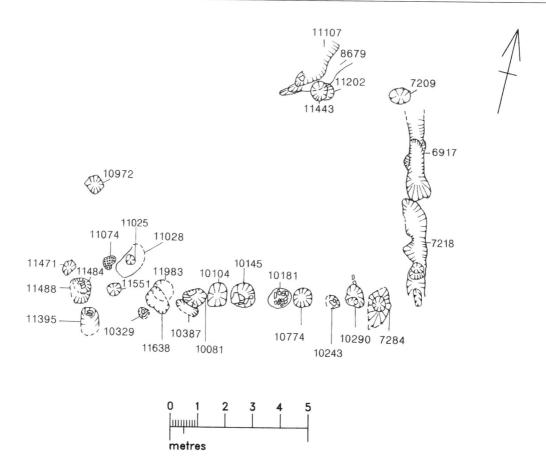

FIG. 5.4. Plan of building 15 (R. Smith).

reflection of the character and limited nature of the refuse deposits from this phase. During the middle decades of the ninth century, however, material dating predominantly from the end of the eighth to the mid ninth centuries was deposited in huge quantities, reflecting activities both within and outside the excavated area, during Period 4 as a whole.

5.3 Phase 4ii – mid ninth century

The middle decades of the ninth century saw a major change in the use of space within the excavated area. Sometime between the early and mid ninth century, the small buildings constructed in the shallow valley (buildings 24 and 39) were demolished, and both the central zone of the site and the ditch became foci for vast refuse dumping (FIG. 5.7). These deposits incorporated an exceptional range of dress accessories, glass vessel fragments, coins, iron and other tools, and craft-working debris. It is uncertain whether these dumping actions were associated with the wholesale levelling of the site, prior to re-organisation and re-planning. The demolition cuts for building 3, however, contained a new type of pottery, in the form of Early Lincolnshire Fine-shelled

ware, which also made its first appearance in the ditch fills and the central dumps from phase 4ii. Hence, even if the site was not cleared at the same time, its total re-organisation could have taken place within a relatively short time period.

At least two stages are suggested in the creation of the refuse dumps and the demolition of the buildings. Buildings 24 and 39 were demolished first, prior to the movement of refuse from the surrounding buildings, and possibly from other parts of the settlement, into the central zone of the excavated area. The buildings either side of the shallow valley may have remained in use at this time. Further refuse, containing material that appeared for the first time in the occupation sequence, was cast into the ditch. This probably reflects refuse transported into the area from an un-excavated part of the settlement. Subsequently, by the end of this phase the ditch had been completely filled, with coins of Æthelberht of Wessex (AD 858–865) present in its uppermost fill, and all the buildings had been demolished. All but one of the building plots that had influenced the organisation of the settlement, to differing extents, since the first half of the eighth century were abandoned.

Taking the structures and deposits in their probable

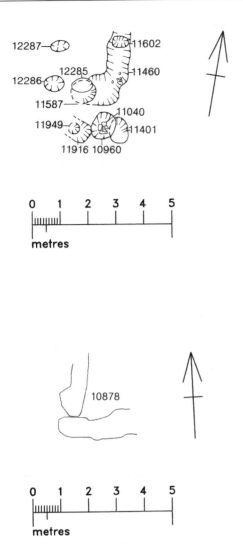

12287
11602
12285
12286
11460
11587
11040
11949
11401
11916 10960

0 1 2 3 4 5

metres

10878

0 1 2 3 4 5

metres

FIG. 5.5. Plans of buildings 25 and 35. The upper plan shows building 25, the lower building 35 (R. Smith).

order of demolition or accumulation, the foundations of buildings 24 and 39 yielded small collections of both pottery and craft-working debris, all of which could have been derived from the refuse material which sealed them. Building 24 produced 14 sherds, all in Maxey-type fragments, including two medium-sized jars. The post-holes of building 39 also produced several Maxey-type pottery sherds, and a fragment of the hand-made greensand vessel 21. Pieces of this vessel were also found in the underlying dumps from phase 3bv, and it probably arrived in post-hole 6324 during the construction of building 39, in the subsequent phase (Period 4). A small number of loom weight fragments were also found in the features of building 24, and an iron heckle/wool comb tooth or needle fragment was recovered from post-hole 6324, from building 39.

Following the demolition of these buildings, a series of large refuse dumps, with abundant wood-ash and vast

quantities of unburnt artefacts and animal bones, were created in the central shallow valley (see Volumes 2, 3 and 4). It was the highly alkaline wood-ash within these deposits that has chemically shielded the bulk of the artefacts and animal bones from this and earlier phases, by reducing the effects of the acid leaching of the otherwise calcareous sand, thus promoting their excellent state of preservation (Canti, Chapter 2, this volume). This advantageous burial environment for artefact survival is reflected in the very extensive recovery of mineral-preserved organic remains on so many knives and tools from within the Flixborough occupation sequence (Edwards, Watson, and Walton Rogers, Volume 2, Chapter 9). The main deposits forming this central refuse zone comprised dumps 3758, 6885, 5503, 5856, and to a lesser extent 3256 (FIG. 5.7).

The range of pottery found within these dumps exhibits the same traits, and it therefore makes sense to detail the assemblage together prior to examination of the differences between the deposits, expressed in their other artefact constituents. Together, the dumps yielded a large group of 345 sherds, recovered almost entirely from 3758 and 5503. Fragments from only three Maxey-type vessels came from deposit 6885; and similarly, pieces from only two vessels came from context 5856 – including another sherd from the greensand vessel 21. The majority of the pottery sherds were of Maxey-type wares, mainly in fabric B, although a significant number (approximately 18%) were in Fabric E.

The pottery assemblage from these dumps also shows that a new type of pottery, Early Lincolnshire Fine-shelled ware, was well in use by this phase (with 27 sherds present). This probably reflects an early to mid ninth-century date for its production and arrival at Flixborough. All of the form and rim types, however, are dissimilar to those found in ninth-century deposits on the settlement sites at Flaxengate (Adams Gilmour 1988) and Hungate (Vince and Young forthcoming) in Lincoln. Nor do the Flixborough vessel fragments readily parallel the examples found at Goltho (Coppack 1987). Instead the forms and rim types are more similar to those found on Maxey-type Fabric E and Fabric U vessels, during this phase (Young, Volume 2, Chapter 12).

The specific forms of 26 Maxey-type and Early Lincolnshire Fine-shelled ware vessels could be determined; and two Ipswich ware sherds were present, together with a small number of other vessels. These included 34 sherds from the greensand-tempered vessel 21; a single sherd of the imported Walberg jar – vessel 13 from 3758; and eight sherds from a single imported whiteware vessel (DR351) – also from 3758, with possible traces of red-painted decoration, and a likely derivation from northern France (Vince, Volume 2, Chapter 12). The sherds from the greensand and Walberg vessels, 21 and 13, reflect the re-working of pieces of these pots from deposits of the early to mid eighth century within the excavated area; and therefore indicate the local and

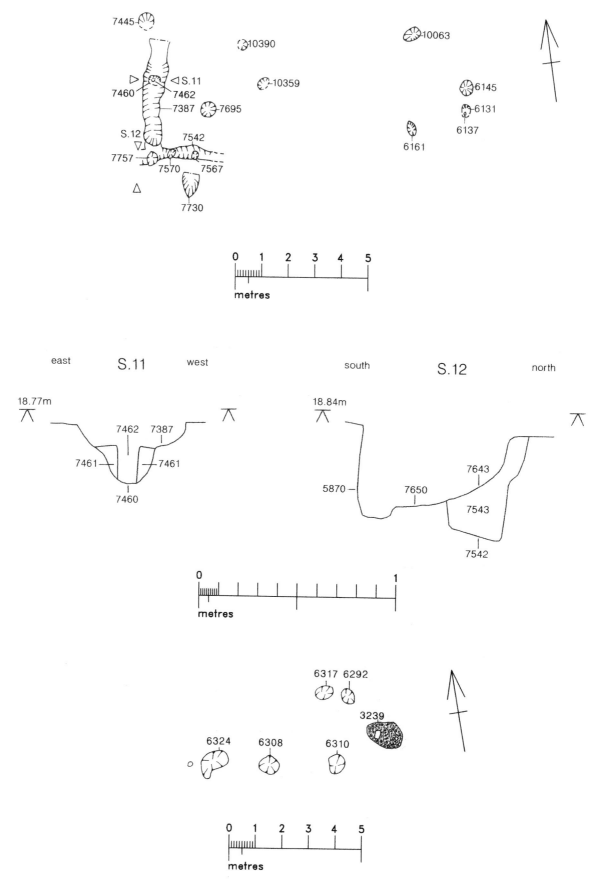

FIG. 5.6. Plans and selected sections of buildings 24 and 39. The upper plan and sections refer to building 24, the lower plan to building 39 (R. Smith).

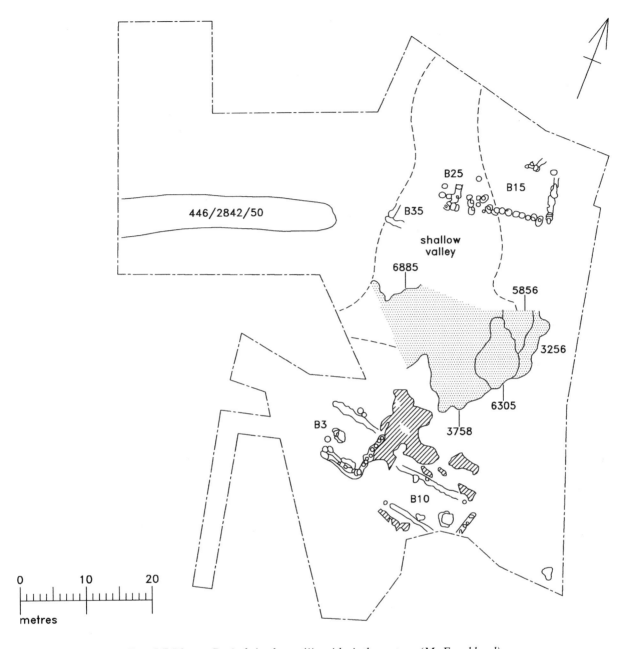

FIG. 5.7.Plan – Period 4, phase 4ii, mid ninth century (M. Frankland).

residual nature of elements of the pottery assemblage in the central dumps. This can also be said for a further sherd of the Iron Age pot, vessel 20, from deposit 5503. A piece of this vessel first appeared in phase 3bv deposits, in the area of building 8, possibly indicating its transport into the site during the early ninth century. However, further movement of new material into the excavated area during Period 4 is also demonstrated by the disposal of the sherds from the whiteware vessel DR351. Several other representatives from multi-context vessels also occurred, and these are presented together with those discussed above in FIG. 5.8. Six of the ten vessels listed in this table had joins with sherds from earlier phases.

The other components of the artefact assemblage from the large central refuse dumps are far greater in number

Vessel	Ware type	Contexts
22	Ipswich	3758
27	Maxey Fabric E	3758
29	Maxey Fabric E	3758 5503
28	Maxey Fabric U	3758 5503
21	Greensand-tempered	3758 5503 6885
13	Walberb	3758
68	Maxey	5503
30	Maxey Fabric E	5503
15	Sandstone-tempered	5503
20	Iron-Age	5503

FIG. 5.8. Table showing multi-context pottery vessels found in Period 4 dumps (Jane Young).

than the pottery finds. Furthermore, whilst there were similarities in the character of the pottery assemblage within the dumps – particularly between 3758, 6885 and 5503 – there were some distinct differences in the character of other artefacts, within these deposits. These differences were particularly apparent between deposits 3758 and 6885 on the one hand, and 5503 on the other. The vast majority of the finds from the two former deposits relate to weaving. Together, the two deposits yielded the vast majority of the 244 individually recorded loom weight fragments from Period 4 (an assemblage weighing 13,929g out of a total 15,794g from the period as a whole, with 223 of the 244 recorded finds), with a large number of near-complete loom weight fragments and even some whole weights (Walton Rogers, Volume 2, Chapter 9; Walton Rogers, Volume 4, Chapter 6; see ADS archive for distribution plots).

Significantly, the vast majority of the loom weights were also of a new lighter type than those of earlier periods on the site, probably reflecting the production of a specialist cloth (Walton Rogers, Volume 2, Chapter 9 and Volume 4, Chapter 6). Other weaving- and cloth finishing-related finds from 3758 and 6885 included two pin-beaters (RFs 11504, and 5357); three pairs of small iron shears (RFs 5482, 5660 and 9952); and copper-alloy, bone and iron needles (RFs 5615, 5687 *et al.*). A much smaller quantity of material relating to processing textile fibres and spinning was also recovered, comprising one spike from a wool comb and six spindle whorls (Walton Rogers, Volume 2, Chapter 9; Volume 4, FIG. 6.8). Other key craft-working tools from these deposits include a pair of iron pincers or a 'locking tongs' (RF 12169), probably used to hold partly formed artefacts during iron- or non-ferrous metalworking (Ottaway, Volume 2, Chapter 11; Coatsworth and Pinder 2002, 52– 53; FIG. 5.9*). In contrast to dumps 3758 and 6885, only several loom weight fragments were found in deposit 5503, although a very similar number of spindle whorls were recovered. Other differences include the absence of coinage from 3758 and 6885, whereas three primary and secondary series *sceattas* were recovered from 5503, two of which had been imported from the Rhine mouths area of Frisia. These coins were also residual from the early to mid eighth century, having an estimated collective minting range between AD 700 and 740 (Archibald, Volume 2, Chapter 13).

Significant similarities, however, do exist between some of the artefact characteristics of dumps 3758 and 5503, in addition to those seen in the pottery assemblage and evidence for spinning. For example, a range of dress accessories was recovered from both deposits, although in different proportions. Thirty pins and an exceptional gilt silver-alloy disc brooch (RF 5467; FIG. 5.10*), dating from the end of the eighth or early ninth century, were found in 3758; whilst a copper-alloy buckle (RF 6099), a triangular copper-alloy hooked tag (RF 13256), and five pins were recovered from 5503. Vessel glass fragments

were also found in both 3758 and 5503; and a stylus and window glass fragments were recovered from both deposits. The stylus from 3758 (RF 7518) was made from copper-alloy, including a gilt-foil eraser mount, with interlace decoration; and the stylus from 5503 (RF 6143) was made in silver (Pestell, Volume 2, Chapter 3; FIG. 5.11*). There was also a similar number of bone and antler comb fragments in the two deposits; although significantly, the fragments from 3758 are much smaller and more abraded than those from 5503. Indeed, the latter deposit contained a whole winged comb – RF 6139 (Foreman, Volume 2, Chapter 1: FIG. 5.12*). Taken as a whole, apart from the three coins and the fragments of pottery from previously deposited and re-worked vessels, the majority of the artefacts in the dumps could have been manufactured at any time between the end of the eighth and mid ninth centuries.

Whereas the pottery from deposits 5503, 3758 and the other dumps suggests some similarity in the character of the deposits, with regard to a re-worked residual component, there are also other indications that provide hints of the relative extent of deposit disturbance and re-deposition. For example, there is an evident contrast in the fragmentation pattern between comb fragments from 3758 and 5503, with much smaller fragments coming from the former deposit, and a whole comb and larger fragments coming from the latter (Foreman, Volume 2, Chapter 1). The fragility of these artefacts, and their likelihood of fracture within refuse, might suggest that 3758 contained material that had been more extensively re-worked. A direct contradiction to this hypothesis, however, is provided by the largest artefact component in 3758, namely the loom weights. Petrological analysis of the loom weights suggests that they were made from local clay and were un-fired, and hence prone to extensive fragmentation on disturbance in refuse (Vince, Volume 2, Chapter 9). The large quantity of near-complete, and even whole, clay loom weights from 3758 suggests a more complicated scenario for deposit formation, with a far larger primary or little-disturbed refuse component in comparison to residual elements.

A proportion of the pottery, many of the bone combs, some of the dress jewellery, and the coins were almost certainly re-worked and re-deposited from earlier contexts. Nevertheless, the combs in 5503 and the well-preserved state of the loom weights in 3758 (and 6885) also suggest the presence of material that can be regarded as recently deposited, in contemporary use during the middle decades of the ninth century. The new lighter loom weights that first appeared in this phase also support the idea of the majority of the material in the dumps having a contemporary derivation. This would also accord with the presence of significant quantities of Early Lincolnshire Fine-shelled pottery, the production of which seems to have begun in the early decades of the ninth century.

In summary, the central refuse deposits from phase

4ii, particularly those from dumps 3758 and 5503, did possess significant quantities of residual finds. With the exception of the combs, these residual artefacts were highly susceptible to survival during deposit disturbance, e.g., the pottery sherds and the coins. More importantly, however, 3758 and 6885 especially, contained a much larger proportion of finds that are likely to have been contemporary with the period of deposit formation. The textile-manufacturing remains, in particular, seem to have been contemporary features of Period 4, with the new loom weight type providing a strong indication of contemporary use. It is noteworthy too that a concentration of other craft-working tools, like the pincers (locking tongs), also came from deposits of this phase. Other craft-working debris, in addition to the tools and loom weights, included significant quantities of iron-working slag and relatively large fragments of hearth bottoms from smithing (Starley, Volume 2, Chapter 10). These were recovered from deposits 3758, 5503 and 6885.

By the end of phase 4ii, the ditch (446/50) in the north-western sector of the site had also been completely filled (FIG. 5.1). It is extremely difficult to date the stages in the digging and re-cutting of this large feature, due to its excavation by a combination of machine and hand techniques (see FIG. 2.2, this volume). Fortunately, however, it is possible to provide a firmer assessment of when it had disappeared as a feature, due to the presence of both specifically and broadly datable artefacts, within its lower and uppermost fills. The uppermost fills of the ditches, deposits 51 and its machined equivalent 3107 (FIGS 5.13 and 5.14), contained two silver pennies (RFs 4164 and 406) of Æthelberht, King of Wessex, minted between AD 858 and 865 (Archibald, Volume 2, Chapter 13). These same uppermost fills also contained Early Lincolnshire Fine-shelled ware pottery sherds in small numbers. Together with strap-ends, decorated in Trewhiddle style zoomorphic decoration (RFs 10785 and 10905), from an amalgamation of the machine-excavated, lower ditch fills – designated 10772 (Thomas, Volume 2, Chapter 1), the latest datable indicators suggest a date in the mid ninth century for the completed filling in of the ditch. Single sherds of medieval pottery were also found in each of the uppermost deposits, 3107 and 51. This probably reflects the use of the levelled site as an activity area associated with a large oven in Period 7, followed by subsidence into the large, earlier cut feature of the Anglo-Saxon ditch.

Like the refuse dumps in the centre of the shallow valley, the refuse tipped into ditch 446/50 also yielded an exceptional range, quality and quantity of artefacts, as well as a considerable number of animal bones (Barrett, Dobney, Jaques and Johnstone, Volume 3). Some of these bones can be seen in the photograph of the ditch section, shown in FIG. 5.15*). The date range and character of certain artefacts have some similarities with the central dumps, in terms of an element of residual objects dating from the early eighth century onwards. There are,

however, more stark differences between the compositions of the ditch deposits and the central refuse dumps than there are similarities.

For purposes of analysis, and due to the presence of early to mid ninth-century material in both upper and lower fills of the ditch, the material from the ditch fills will be considered together. Overall, they have a very similar artefact composition. A total of 181 sherds of pottery were recovered from the machine-cut ditch sections, reflecting fragments of 165 vessels. Eight of the vessels had cross-joins with fragments from other deposits, and crucially all the other cross-joining fragments of these vessels were recovered from later contexts, most of which were in the vicinity of the former ditch. In each case the fragments from the ditch fills represent the earliest occurrence of these vessels. The vessels from the ditch also included a far greater proportion of Ipswich ware vessels when compared with the central dumps (fragments of 11 vessels from the ditch, compared to two from the dumps); as well as an additional four imported Continental pots, including the grey-burnished vessels 56 and 58 (Vince, Volume 2, Chapter 12). The vast majority of the pottery vessels were in Maxey-type fabrics (128 vessels in 28 forms). The ditch fills also contained both leached and unleached sherds, suggesting that leaching probably took place before deposition in the ditch, thus reflecting a mixed origin for the material. Overall, the indications of the re-working of the pottery before tipping it into the ditch, the different proportion of certain pottery types, the first appearance of certain vessels, and the absence of any cross-joins with earlier pots all suggest that the material originated from outside the excavated area. In addition, the recovery of Ipswich ware in the lower ditch fills, the presence of sherds from three Early Lincolnshire Fine-shelled ware vessels, and the Trewhiddle-decorated strap-ends all suggest a filling of the ditch over a relatively short period, between the early and mid ninth century.

The other artefact components of the ditch fills also suggest a different origin for the material in the ditch, compared with that from the central dumps, as well as a possible zoning of certain activities in the immediate vicinity of the feature. The points of similarity between the artefact profiles are limited. They occur primarily in relation to the recovery of *sceattas* of the primary and secondary series (RFs 4165 and 254; Archibald, Volume 2, Chapter 13) and window glass (e.g. RFs 5545 and 5774) from the ditch fills and central dumps (Cramp, Volume 2, Chapter 4; FIG. 5.16*, this volume). Here too, however, there are slight differences in the sense that the ditch also yielded mid ninth-century coins, in addition to lead window cames from fill 3107. A further area of similarity is reflected in the presence of a new artefact type found for the first time in phase 4ii, in both the central dumps and ditch; namely, lead net weights. These are as likely to have related to the netting of wildfowl as fishing, during this phase (Wastling, Volume 2, Chapter 6).

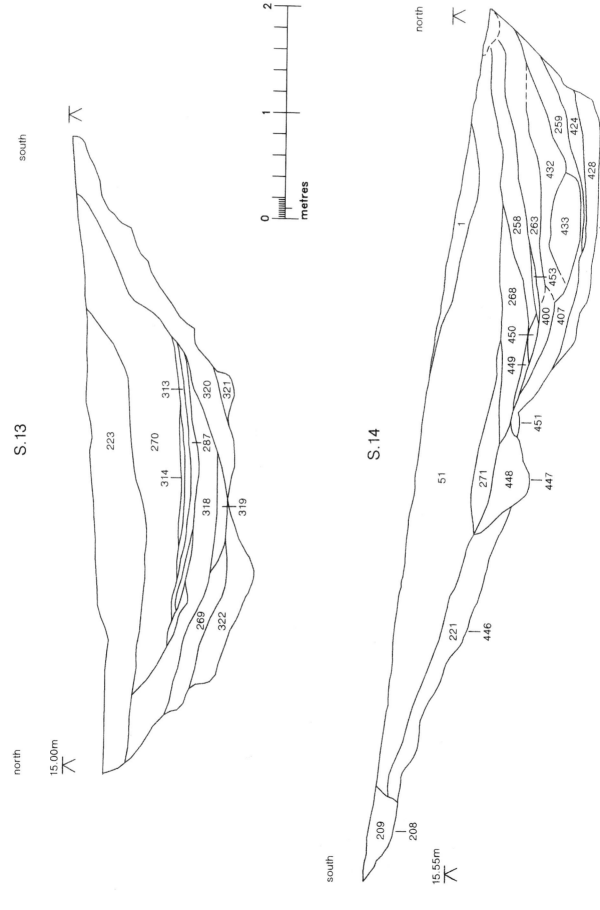

Fig. 5.13. Sections of Ditch 446/50/2842 (M. Frankland).

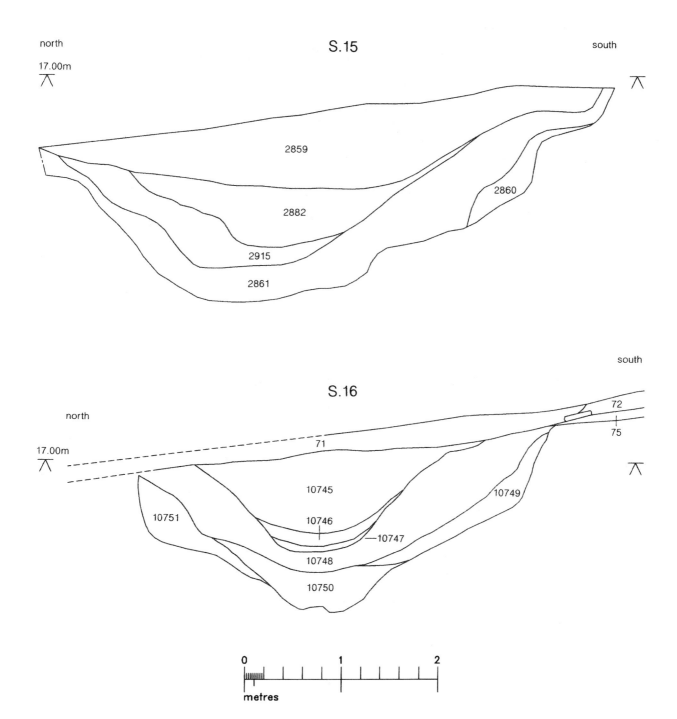

FIG. 5.14. Sections of Ditch 446/50/2842 (M. Frankland).

The major differences between the ditch deposits and the central dumps are stark. Weaving-related artefacts are almost completely absent from the ditch. Instead, heckle teeth are much more numerous, reflecting either an origin for some of the ditch deposits in an area associated with fibre processing, or possibly, fibre processing in the area of the ditch whilst the area was being used as a refuse zone (Walton Rogers, Volume 2,

Chapter 9; see ADS archive for distribution plot). At the same time, imported Eifel quern fragments were absent from the central dumps but were abundant in the ditch fills (Parkhouse, Volume 2, Chapter 6; ADS archive distribution plot). A similar contrast can also be seen in the distribution of other artefacts. Only one comb fragment came from the ditch, in contrast to fragments of at least 13 combs from the dumps; and one fragment of vessel glass was recovered from the ditch, whereas 15 fragments came from the dumps. A particular contrast is also evident amongst the dress accessories. Overall, they were much more abundant in the ditch fills, with a number of differences also exhibited in accessory type. For example, five hooked tags and three strap-ends came from the ditch, in comparison with one hooked tag and the disc brooch (RF 5467) from the dumps. Eleven iron and copper-alloy buckles also came from the ditch fills, whilst only one came from the dumps, from 5503. Greater similarity, however, was seen in the number of pins, with 52 coming from the ditch, and 35 from the dumps.

There are also differences in the character of the craft-working debris found within the two refuse zones, in addition to the stark contrast in textile-manufacturing activities. The central dumps yielded a relatively small collection of artefacts and debris not related to weaving and spinning – comprising the pincers/hand vice and limited iron-smithing debris. In contrast, the ditch fills proved to be the focus of deposition for most of the iron-working debris from this period. These remains comprised abundant smithing detritus, in the form of slag and fragments of hearths. Furthermore, for the first time in the occupation sequence, several fragments of furnace bottoms, furnace slag, tap slag, and roasted ore, from iron smelting were recovered (Starley, Volume 2, Chapter 10). Hammerscale from smithing was also recovered from both the ditch fills and central dumps, in small quantities. Alongside this iron-working evidence, indications of non-ferrous metalworking were also retrieved, in the form of a mould fragment (RF 14355) and two pieces of a crucible (RF 14354). Both of the latter were found in the uppermost fill of the ditch (fill 51). This evidence for high-temperature craft activities was also supplemented by an indication of woodworking, in the form of a single-sided adze (RF 11793) from fill 10772 (Volume 4, Fig. 6.3).

Overall, therefore, there is a clear contrast in the artefact composition of the ditch deposits and the central refuse dumps, although they would appear to have a very similar date of accumulation, with *termini post quos* suggesting their formation between the early and middle decades of the ninth century. Their very different artefact profiles suggest different respective origins for the material found within them. The central dumps contained vast quantities of probably contemporary weaving waste, with smaller amounts of both re-worked and newly deposited material, suggesting a largely local derivation. In contrast, the ditch deposits did not contain any demonstrably re-worked material from the excavated area; and their very different artefact composition suggests that they represent a composite product of refuse material transported from other parts of the settlement. The totality of the evidence provides one of the most comprehensive pictures of the range of specialist craft-working activities undertaken on the settlement at any time in its occupational history. Similarly, the refuse deposits also provide an extensive sample of the imported

commodities reaching the settlement from other parts of England, such as East Anglia and possibly York, as well as from continental Europe, between the eighth and mid ninth centuries.

As stated earlier, it is unclear whether the buildings to the north and south of the shallow valley were still standing whilst the two foci for refuse dumping were utilized. However, the indications from the fills of the foundation trenches, and the demolition cuts of these features, indicate that the buildings were probably levelled as part of the site clearance, seemingly reflected by phase 4ii as a whole.

The filled-in foundation trenches of building 3, and the fill of a 'robber' cut which seems to have been excavated to demolish the earth-fast structure, contained 38 sherds (268g) of pottery, representing fragments of a maximum of 30 vessels. Most of these sherds came from Maxey-type wares, which were probably residual by this period. A sherd from an Ipswich ware vessel was also recovered, and five fragments from a single Early Lincolnshire Fine-shelled ware vessel were found in the fill of the demolition trench 4134. This indicates that on the demolition of building 3, Early Lincolnshire Fine-shelled ware was in regular use on the site – a fact that is also indicated by its presence in significant quantities, in both the ditch and central dump deposits. A copper-alloy 'safety-pin-type' brooch (RF 3181) was also found in the fill of 4134 (Rogers, Volume 2, Chapter 1). This brooch was only the second of its type recovered from Flixborough – the earliest came from deposit 10962, dating from between the mid eighth and early ninth centuries (phases 3biii to 3bv).

Following the demolition of building 10, a group of 42 sherds of pottery (weighing 442g) was incorporated into the fills of its former foundation trenches. Fragments of six Romano-British vessels were also present, including one piece of the late fourth-century jar, vessel 2, fragments of which had been disturbed and re-worked on the plots occupied by buildings 3 and 10 since the seventh century. Fragments of two Ipswich ware vessels were also recovered from deposits 4815 and 2469, reflecting the fact that Period 4, between the early and mid ninth century, was the *floruit* for the receipt of Ipswich ware, within the occupational history of the settlement. The remainder of the pottery consisted mainly of Maxey-type wares, including sherds from some demonstrably residual forms, such as the medium-sized, type Vii bowl – vessel 3a. The absence of pottery in quartz-tempered fabrics and certain Maxey-type vessels (type IV) in fabric E, also serves to highlight the different composition of the pottery from features associated with the demolished building 10, in contrast to the dumps of the preceding phase (3b). Also found in the foundation trenches of the former building were fragments of Eifel lava quern and a spiral-headed, copper-alloy pin (RF 4729). In addition to the gravel paths leading to the doors of this building, in the middle of its long walls (Fig. 5.3), the presence of two clench bolts (RFs 3373 and 3466) within the foundation trench 3319 and post-hole 3463 provides further evidence of the location of these entrances, since they may have held together elements of a door.

To the north of the central refuse zone, the artefact remains from the foundations of buildings 15 and 25 were more limited, and no finds were recovered from the partial gravel sill base of building 35. The post-holes of building 15 yielded only pottery fragments, 54 sherds (weighing 1406g) from 33 vessels. The vast majority of the sherds were of Maxey-types, with single examples of Romano-British, sandstone- and local shell-tempered sherds. Likewise, only Maxey-type pottery sherds were found in association with building 25, seven sherds (weighing 124g).

6   Period 5: Mid to Late Ninth to Early Tenth Century

Christopher Loveluck and David Atkinson

with contributions by Jane Young and Peter Didsbury

6.1 Introduction

The demolition and site clearance, represented by the activities of phase 4ii, reflected the onset of major changes in the character of the structural remains and the use of space within the excavated area, between the mid to late ninth and early tenth centuries AD (defined as Period 5 of the occupation sequence). The long-lived, east to west building plots to the north and south of the shallow valley were abandoned, with one exception. In their place smaller buildings were constructed, predominantly with post-hole foundations, mainly in the southern half of the excavated area. The vast majority of the buildings were less than 10m in length and less than 6m in width; and they were constructed on a variety of alignments, ranging from north-south to east-west. To accompany the foundation of new building plots in the south of the site, there were also significant changes in the use of the former northern building plots, during this period. The site of former building 15 was occupied by a series of fired-clay and stone ovens, before becoming a northern refuse dumping zone. Following the filling in of ditch 446/50, several post-hole structures were also constructed, cutting the line of the former ditch. On the basis of parallels from other Mid to Late Saxon phases of settlements, such as Wicken Bonhunt and West Heslerton, it is possible that the latter structures represent granaries or haylofts (Wade 1980, 97–98; Powlesland pers. comm.).

The area of the shallow valley saw some continuity in use, in the sense that it was still used for refuse dumping, in the earlier part of Period 5 (phase 5a). Unlike the dumps from earlier phases, however, the construction of gravel paths across the dumps suggests that the area was a focus for discard over an extended period. This contrasts with the dumping episodes of shorter duration, probably reflected in the phase 3biv–v and phase 4ii refuse deposits. In the later part of the period (phase 5b), the central part of the site was again used for buildings, and new areas of refuse accumulation formed on parts of the former northern and southern building plots. The structural alterations and changes in the use of space between the mid to late ninth and early tenth centuries are presented within two structural phases, 5a and 5b below. Identification of these two phases of activity was based on a combination of two distinct changes in the use of space in certain parts of the site, together with two phases of construction and replacement on others. Certain structures, however, including the probable granaries and buildings 27 and 28, could have remained standing for one or both of phases 5a and 5b. As with the discussion of settlement morphology and deposit formation for earlier periods, the two structural phases which involved changes in settlement layout, in addition to deposit accumulation, have been designated using alphabet labels.

6.2 Phase 5a – mid to late ninth century

The filling of the ditch, the large-scale refuse dumping in the central shallow valley, and the comprehensive levelling of all the buildings during phase 4ii, precipitated a series of discontinuities within the excavated area. With the exception of the central southern building plot, previously occupied by building 10, all the locations for the construction of replacement structures were newly defined (FIG. 6.1). The organisation of the site in phase 5a can be defined within three zones. These consisted of a southern zone of buildings, probably having residential, storage, and possibly craft-working functions; secondly, a central refuse zone, defined to a certain extent by gravel paths; and thirdly, an area of fired-clay and stone ovens, in the northern extremity of the site.

In the southern zone of structures, only building 29 succeeded an earlier building on the same broad plot and

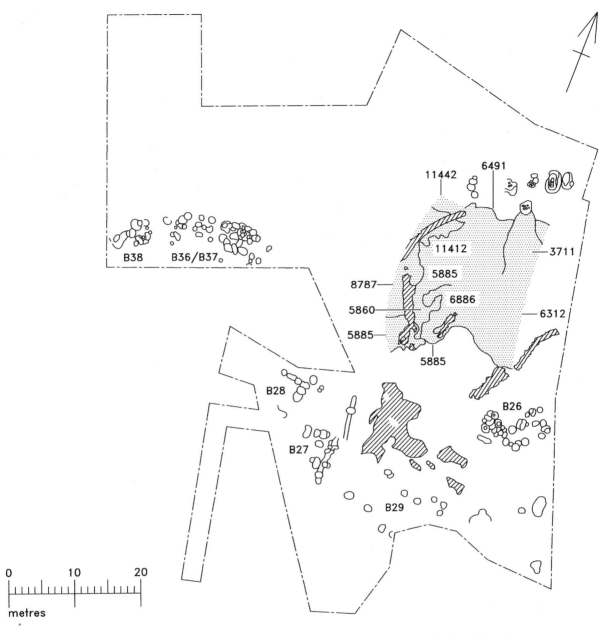

FIG. 6.1. Plan – Period 5, phase 5a, mid to late ninth century (M. Frankland).

alignment, although the building footprint shifted approximately 3m to the south (FIG. 6.1). This building is represented by a series of large, broadly opposing post-holes in its long walls (FIG. 6.2). It was at least 9m in length, and between 6 and 6.5m in width. To the west of building 29, two structures were constructed, within combinations of post-hole and trench foundations (FIG. 6.2). Building 27 was built on part of the plot previously occupied by building 3, but unlike the latter structure it seems to have been constructed on an approximate north to south alignment. Even though the foundation plan is partial, due to erosion of the slope of the spur, it is possible to infer that this building was a small structure, 5m wide and at least 7m long. Slightly to the north-east, the partial foundations of another small building were also un-

covered, on a site not previously used for a structure, namely building 28. It is not possible to estimate the length of this building, but it was 6m in width.

To the east of building 29, the possible building reflected by hearth 668 from Period 4 was not replaced; and instead the area was used for digging several pits (FIG. 6.1). Immediately to the north of this zone of pits a new building was erected in a location not previously used for buildings, in the shallow valley. This new structure, building 26, was again a small building and was constructed on a north-northeast to south-southwest alignment, within post-hole foundations (FIG. 6.1). It also possessed a fired-clay hearth base (1671) in the centre of the building, and a concentration of inter-cutting post-holes beyond its southern end, which have defied

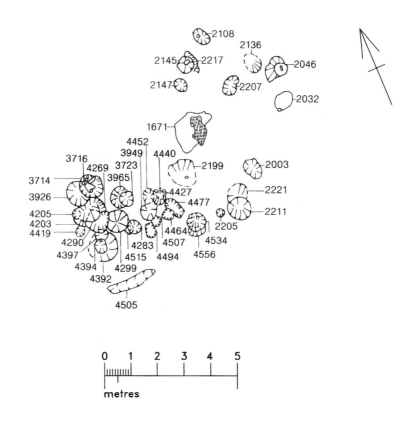

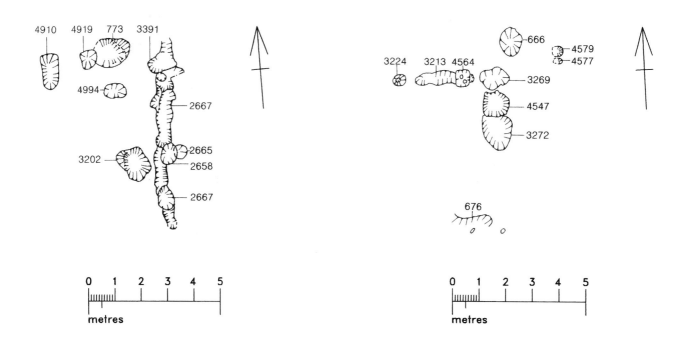

F*ɪɢ. 6.2. Plans of buildings 26, 27, and 28. The top plan shows building 26; bottom left shows building 27; bottom right shows building 28 (R. Smith).*

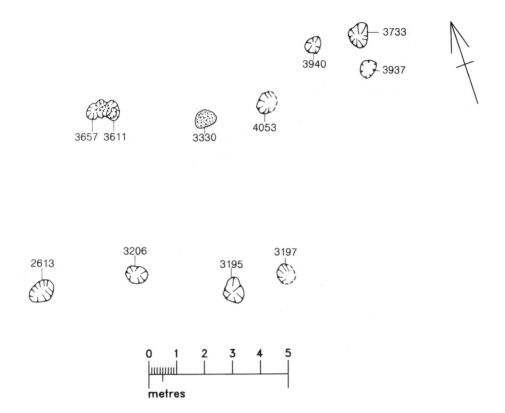

Fig. 6.3. Plan of building 29 (R. Smith).

interpretation (FIG. 6.2). Like the other buildings from phase 5a building 26 was also small, approximately 8m by 5m in size. Indeed, the buildings from Period 5 are the smallest within the Anglo-Saxon settlement sequence. The sections of the foundation features for all the above buildings from phase 5a can be found in the ADS archive.

In the north-western extremity of the excavated area, a series of structures were built set within post-hole foundations – some of which overlay the filled-in ditch in this area. Unlike the evidence from other structures identified on the site, buildings 36, 37 and 38 reflect clusters of post-holes concentrated in broadly square or sub-rectangular concentrations (FIG. 6.1). These structures share their closest similarities with above-ground granaries identified on several other Mid to Late Anglo-Saxon sites and on Continental settlements from the 'Migration' to the Carolingian periods (see Loveluck, Volume 4, Chapter 3). In size, the series of sub-rectangular post-hole concentrations range from between 3m by 3m for building 38, to 3.5 by 4m for building 36. As FIG. 6.4 shows, however, the concentration of post-holes reflected by the designation building 36 may reflect two building phases, with a possible corner of a small building cutting the earlier post-hole concentration. The possible line of the building is indicated on the plan, reflecting a building approximately 5m in width and of indeterminate length.

In the area of the former northern building plots, a

series of bases and partial walls of domed and sub-rectangular, fired-clay and stone ovens were uncovered, constituting a zone of ovens during phase 5a (FIG. 6.1). Replacement of the ovens is evident on two occasions, thereby reflecting the presence of at least three ovens in this area at any time during the mid to late ninth century. The position of the oven foundations is shown in FIG. 6.5, indicating their location within the northernmost part of the site, labelled as Area D during excavation (see Chapter 2, this volume, FIG. 2.3). Ovens 8635, 8686, 6488, 7288 and 7364 represent a composite picture of most of the ovens from the two phases in the construction of these features. A possible screen for the ovens is also suggested by a small line of post-holes to the west of the ovens, shielding them from the prevailing wind (10839, 10336, 10797 and 10869).

Ovens 8635 and 8686, and either 7288 or 7364, were the earlier of the ovens. Plans and sections of these ovens, showing aspects of their construction and their place within the stratigraphic sequence in the northern part of the site are presented in FIGS 6.6–6.8. The successive plans of oven 7288 are particularly instructive as an illustration of the method of construction of these ovens. The north-south section of 8686 also demonstrates very clearly the cutting of the foundations of building 12 from Period 6 (feature 6960) through the earlier ovens. During the second phase of oven construction, 8686 was totally replaced by oven 6486 (FIG. 6.6). In contrast, it is less

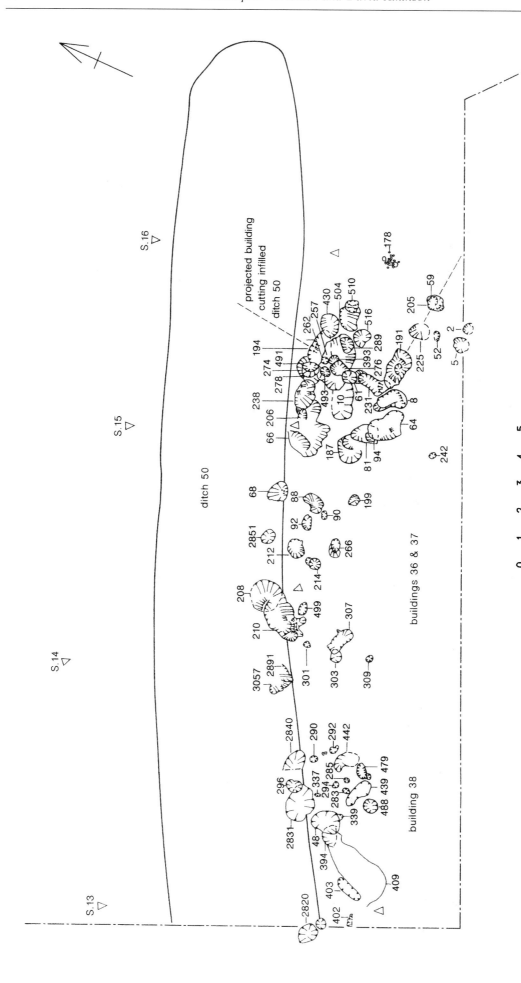

Fig. 6.4. *Plans of buildings 36, 37 and 38 in area G of the site (R. Smith).*

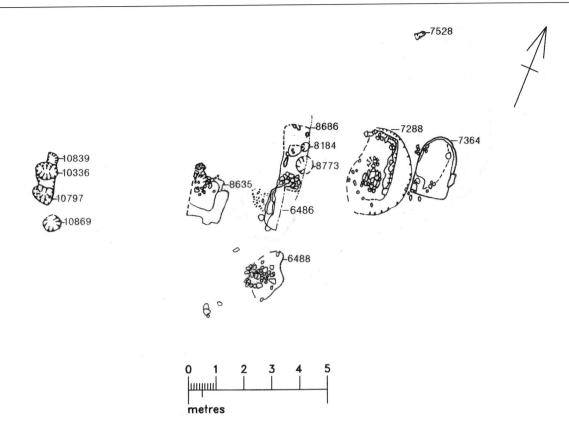

Fig. 6.5. Plan of the zone of ovens from phase 5a in area D of the site (R. Smith).

clear to which phase in oven construction 6488 belongs. Its location as the southernmost oven, however, and the fact that deposit 3711 seems to represent a discrete trail of ash sweepings from this oven, suggest that it belonged to the second phase of construction (Fig. 6.1).

In the intervening area between the zones of ovens and buildings a large refuse area formed, probably for a combination of communal dumping and the tipping of ash from the ovens (Fig. 6.1). This area of dumps was crossed and partly defined by two gravel paths (given the context/stratigraphic unit numbers 4040, 5245, 3237, 6393, 11008 and 12242), linking the buildings with the ovens (Fig. 6.9*). The eastern of the two paths, in front of building 26, seems to have formed the eastern boundary of the refuse dumping area; whereas refuse was tipped either side of the western path leading to the ovens. The fact that the gravel paths were built also indicates that this refuse zone was open and utilised for a considerable period, unlike some of the earlier refuse dumps, most of which reflected re-organisation of the site associated with demolition and clearance.

Unlike the refuse dumps formed during phases 3biv to v and phase 4ii, which tended to consist of large distinct deposits, the dumps associated with phase 5a were formed from a larger number of smaller refuse contexts/stratigraphic units. Fig. 6.1 shows the location of most of the larger deposits from the phase. Due to their small and composite nature, the artefact profiles from these refuse contexts are considered together below.

A total of 236 sherds of pottery was recovered from the dumps from phase 5a. The assemblage consisted almost entirely of Maxey-type pottery, mainly abraded body sherds; and a small number of fragments from other vessels in a range of wares were also recovered. These included sherds of Ipswich ware, Early Lincolnshire Fine-shelled ware and pieces of handmade vessels, in a number of fabrics. Significantly, sherds of five vessels, including the greensand vessel 21 (broken and deposited by the mid to late eighth century) were also found in these refuse deposits, reflecting the continued re-working and disturbance of elements of earlier refuse material from within the excavated area. Other types of artefact also suggest the re-working of residual finds from earlier phases, but, importantly, they also indicate the probable transport of deposits into the site from unexcavated parts of the settlement as well.

Overall, the majority of the non-pottery finds from the phase 5a dumps relate to textile manufacture, like their phase 4ii forbears. Unlike the deposits from the latter period, however, there was no apparent zoning in the disposal of refuse relating to particular stages in textile production. Small numbers of loom weight fragments were found in most of the dumps, giving a total of 72 fragments, weighing approximately 2,400g – a much

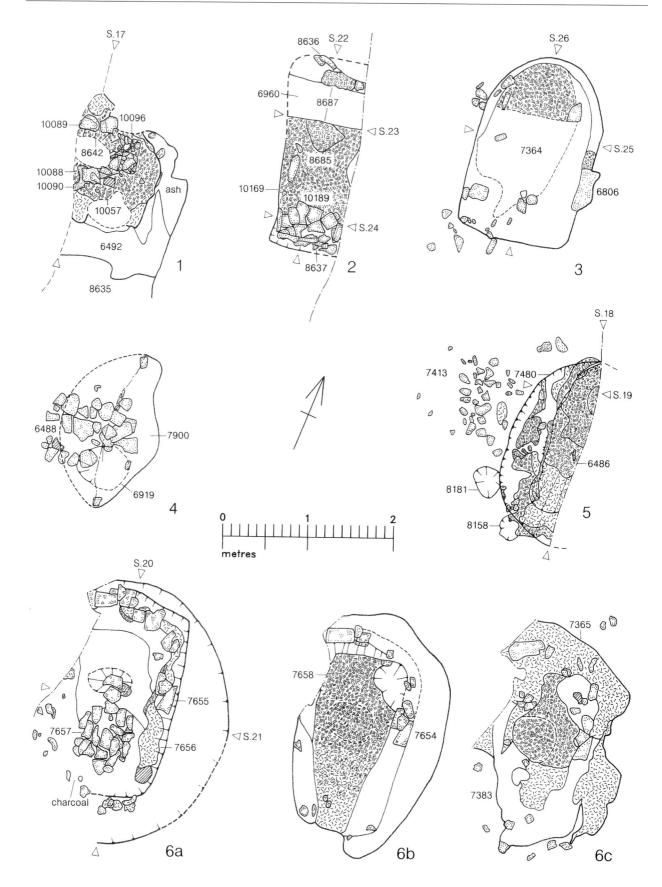

FIG. 6.6. Plans of stone and fired-clay ovens from phase 5a.
1. Oven 8635; 2. Oven 8686; 3. Oven 7364; 4. Oven 5114; 5. Oven 6486; 6a–6c. Successive construction phases of oven 7288 (M. Frankland).

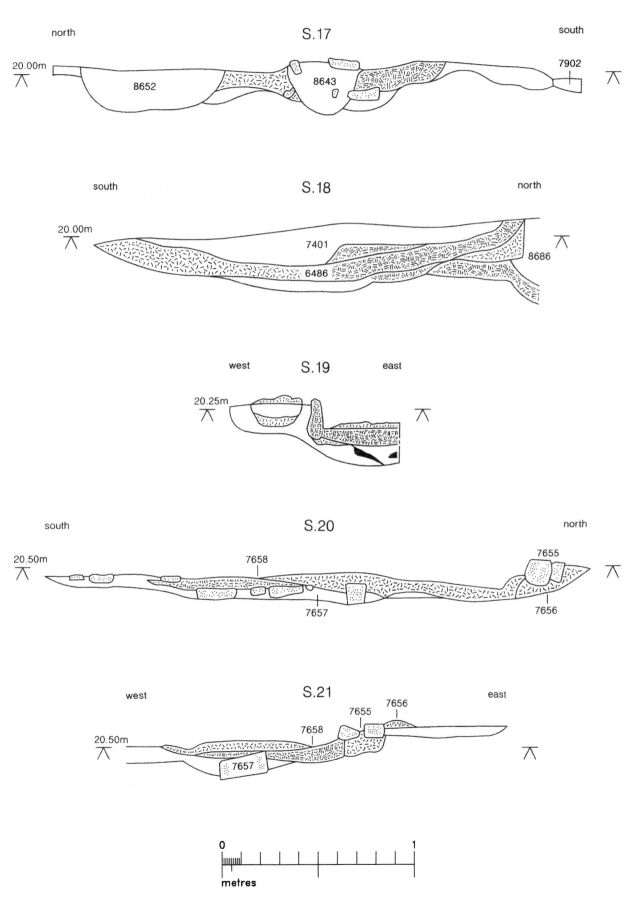

FIG. 6.7. Sections of stone and fired clay ovens from phase 5a (M. Frankland).

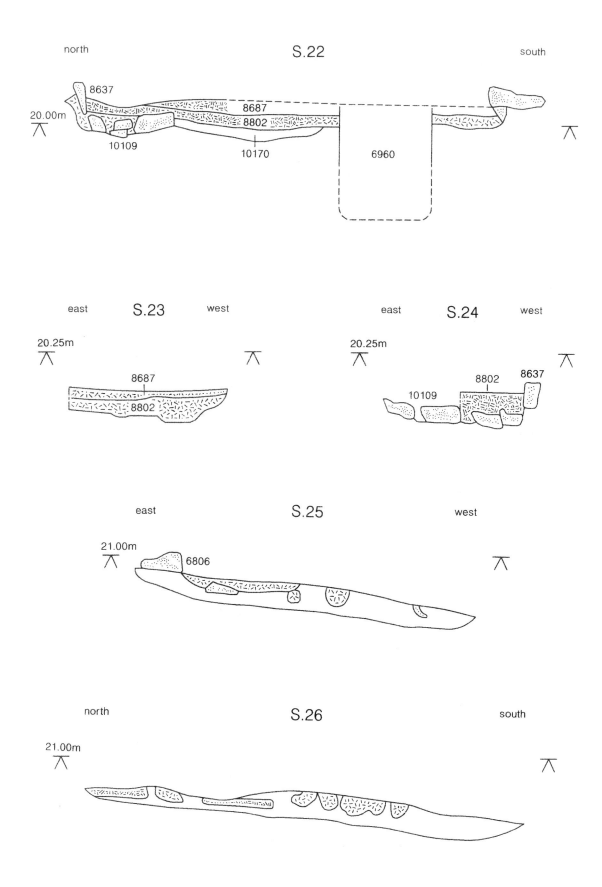

Fig. 6.8. Sections of stone and fired clay ovens from phase 5a (M. Frankland).

smaller number and overall weight than from phase 4ii, which yielded approximately 16,100g (Walton Rogers, Volume 2, Chapter 9; Walton Rogers, Volume 4, Chapter 6). Nevertheless, the individual loom weights themselves were of the smaller and lighter type, first seen in phase 4ii. At the same time, heckle and wool comb teeth, and spindle whorls (RFs 5830, 6601, 4980, 10076 and 11051) were found in the same dumps as weaving and cloth-finishing evidence, represented by small pairs of shears (RFs 5707 and 6004) and needles (such as RF 8497). Fragments of predominantly double-sided bone and antler combs were also regular occurrences (Foreman, Volume 2, Chapter 1), as were small quantities of Eifel lava quern fragments. Similarly small numbers of imports from continental Europe were also found in certain dumps: namely two silver coins – Series E 'porcupine' *sceattas* (RFs 12072 and 12987) from the Rhine mouths area; and a small number of fragments from glass vessels (RFs 5799 and 6020). The coins were minted between AD 700 and 730, and are demonstrably residual (Archibald, Volume 2, Chapter 13); and the glass vessels fragments are equally likely to have been re-worked from earlier deposits.

Overall, during the mid to late ninth century, no demonstrably new imports from the Continent arrived or were deposited in the excavated area. This is not to say, however, that no artefacts were transported into the site. The occurrence of two fired-clay sling-shots (RFs 4605 and 8198), thought to be of Iron Age date, were deposited in the dumps, probably having originated in a part of the Anglo-Saxon settlement which disturbed Iron Age or early Roman remains (Wastling, Volume 2, Chapter 14). Nevertheless, despite the presence of residual material, there is no reason to doubt the contemporary nature of at least some of the textile-manufacturing evidence. Indications from the debris of other craft-working activities, however, in the form of very small and abraded mould fragments and a limited range of iron-working debris, do suggest that a significant component of the material was re-worked from phase 4ii deposits, and that the scale and diversity of craft-working declined overall.

A similar picture is presented by the finds recovered from structures which were demolished sometime between phases 5a and 5b, comprising buildings 26, 29, and the ovens and oven 'screen'. The post-hole fills of building 26 yielded only 12 sherds of pottery from 11 vessels. This reflects the new nature of this building plot, which did not disturb earlier deposits to a great extent. The vast majority, if not all the pottery was residual, consisting of Maxey-type wares, and single fragments from Romano-British and Early Anglo-Saxon 'Charnwood'-type vessels. The only other find from the building was part of a copper-alloy needle (RF 1771), incorporated into hearth 1671. Similarly, the pottery from the post-holes of building 29 was also limited, comprising two sherds of Maxey-type ware, although a greater range of finds came from deposits 2610 and 2611 outside the

western end of the building. These included two fragments of vessel glass and further textile manufacturing evidence, in the form of heckle or wool-comb teeth, and a pair of shears (RF 3432). Four sherds of pottery were recovered from the fill of post-hole 10336, which composed part of the oven 'wind-screen'. These comprised a piece of Ipswich ware and Maxey-type ware, and further pieces of the Walberberg vessel 13 and the greensand vessel 21. Hence, an extensive re-worked component is evident amongst the pottery assemblage on this southern building plot in phase 5a. Pieces of vessel 13, in particular, had been broken and deposited by the early to mid eighth century, and dispersed from the northern to the southern building plots through the eighth and ninth centuries.

6.3 Phase 5b – late ninth to early tenth century

Following the wholesale re-planning of settlement layout during phase 5a, further changes in the organisation of space occurred between the late ninth and early tenth centuries. The second phase of ovens was eventually demolished and overlain by the large refuse deposits 6472 and 6803, and the dumps and gravel paths were cut through and overlain by new structures, buildings 30/31 and 14 (FIG. 6.10). The area formerly occupied by building 29 was also used as a southern refuse area, after its demolition. A series of pits was also dug on the site of building 26, before the construction of building 4 on the same plot. A large fired-clay and stone hearth (850) might also suggest a building to the south-east of building 4, but only sporadic limestone post-pads provide very ephemeral evidence for a structure, in addition to the hearth. It is not possible to say whether buildings 27 and 28 still existed or not, during phase 5b, and the same is true for the probable granaries. Although, the later structure identified within 'building 36' may relate specifically to phase 5b (FIG. 6.4). The use of much of the north-east and south-east corners of the site for refuse dumping also marks a further break with the past in the excavated area, akin to the discontinuity evident in the abandonment of the long-lived building plots during the preceding phase.

The character of the foundations of the new and replacement buildings from phase 5b reflects continuity with the buildings from phase 5a, as well as the re-appearance of continuous trench foundations. The plan of building 4, which replaced building 26, represents approximately half of the structure – the remaining part lying beyond the eastern edge of the excavation (FIG. 6.11). Building 4 is almost a direct rebuild of the earlier building, with the same foundation style and a similar internal fired-clay hearth base (1512), despite the digging of the pits in between the demolition of one structure and the construction of the other. Even though it is not possible to be certain of its length, the building was 6m wide and had an excavated length of 7m. If the hearth

FIG. 6.10. Plan – Period 5, phase 5b, late ninth to early tenth centuries (M. Frankland).

was located centrally, as in building 26, this could suggest a building of approximately 12m in length. Consequently, the late ninth-century building could have been significantly larger than its immediate predecessor, although if the hearth was constructed in the eastern end of the building, as in building 31 and others from the occupation sequence, it could have had a length of only between 8 and 9 metres.

In the central area of the site, buildings 30/31 and 14 were built on the now raised surface of the shallow valley. Building 30/31 also shows hints of having two phases of construction, like buildings 26 and 4. The earlier phase of the structure (building 30) seems to have had post-

hole foundations and the subsequent replacement, building 31, had continuous trench foundations on at least two sides (FIG. 6.12). It also possessed a circular, fired-clay and stone hearth base (4194) in the centre of the eastern half of the building. In terms of dimensions, building 31 was approximately 8.5m by 5m. In contrast, only one phase of construction seems to be reflected in the continuous foundation trenches of building 14, immediately to the east of building 30/31. Where it is possible to tell, this building was constructed by setting wall sections into narrow slots within the wider trenches, based on stone post-pads (FIG. 6.12). The building was 12m long and 7m wide.

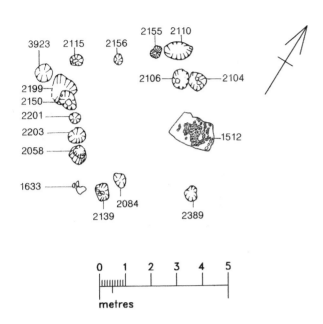

FIG. 6.11. Plan of building 4 (R. Smith).

Amongst these buildings, which like those from phase 5a were predominantly smaller than their eighth- and earlier ninth-century forbears, the new areas of refuse accumulation were created to the north and south of buildings 14 and 4 (FIG. 6.10). The shallow deposit 3597 may reflect an accumulation created when moving deposits and walking to the new southern refuse zone, covering and extending outwards from the former location of building 29. In phase 5b, this former building plot comprised a series of distinct deposits, the largest of which are labelled on FIG. 6.10; namely, dumps 1727, 1728, 2518, 2776 and 3081. To the north of building 14, many of the demolished ovens were covered by much larger spreads of refuse, which extended down the eastern margin of the excavated area, notably deposits 6472 and 6803 (FIG. 6.10).

The finds from the refuse deposits and features associated with the buildings from this phase reflect two categories of material: re-worked refuse from earlier periods, and newly deposited contemporary material. Treating the artefact profile from the refuse dumps as a whole, a large quantity of pottery was recovered (393 sherds); yet, the main wares present were residual Maxey-types. Approximately 50 percent of the Maxey-type sherds were also too badly abraded or leached to be attributed to a fabric type, indicative both of deposit re-working and exposure to chemical weathering on the surface of middens. The dumps also contained residual Romano-British pottery in small quantities, including a further sherd of the fourth-century jar, vessel 1, from 2776; and two sherds of early Roman Samian ware from 1728 (Didsbury, Volume 2, Chapter 14). One of the Samian

sherds (RF 2592) certainly dated from the Hadrianic or early Antonine periods (early to mid second century AD). This contrasting Romano-British assemblage is likely to reflect both the continued re-working of the late Roman pottery of local derivation and the continued importation of early Roman pottery into the excavated area, within Anglo-Saxon refuse from unexcavated parts of the settlement. The latter probability is also suggested by the presence of another Iron Age or early Roman, fired-clay sling-shot (RF 3131), from deposit 3081 (Wastling, Volume 2, Chapter 14).

In addition to the residual pottery and the indications of deposit movement, the refuse deposits from phase 5b also contained small quantities of Late Saxon pottery types, including sherds of Early Lincolnshire Fine-shelled ware, 'Lincoln Kiln-type' ware, 'Torksey-type' ware and one sherd of a locally made Late Saxon vessel (Young, Volume 2, Chapter 12; Vince and Young, Volume 2, Chapter 12). None of the Late Saxon sherds exhibited any diagnostic features allowing any refinement of dating within a range extending from the late ninth to the late tenth centuries. Nevertheless, their presence in small numbers reflects the importation of pottery at a period broadly contemporary with the structures of phase 5b, such as Lincoln Kiln-type ware and Torksey-type ware, via regional exchange networks from further down the Trent valley and the nascent urban centre of Lincoln.

Other artefact remains from the dumps also reflect the residual component seen in the pottery assemblage. Deposit 1728, overlying building 29 from phase 5a, yielded a small, inscribed lead plaque (RF 1781), with the names of seven individuals (both male and female) carved into it. On the basis of the palaeographic style of the letters, the plaque is thought to date from between the late eighth and early ninth centuries AD (Brown and Okasha, Volume 2, Chapter 3; FIG. 6.13*). The closest parallels for the style of script come from charters of Offa of Mercia, and certain inscribed monuments from North Yorkshire and County Durham (Brown and Okasha, Volume 2, Chapter 3). A small number of copper-alloy pins were found in the same dump, together with a gilt silver pin which had openwork zoomorphic decoration (RF 1887; FIG. 6.14*). One of several copper-alloy 'saftety-pin-type' brooches (RF 1968) recovered from deposits of this phase was also found in deposit 1728 (Rogers, Volume 2, Chapter 1).

Overall, however, the number of artefacts found within the dumps, other than pottery, was relatively small compared with other phases of the Flixborough occupation sequence. The same can be said of the quantities of animal bones recovered, much smaller than from phases 3b, 4ii or 5a. Nevertheless, both the northern and southern dump deposits consistently contained small quantities of glass vessel fragments, together with pieces of Eifel lava querns, although all of these finds could have been residual. The majority of the diagnostically datable metal items encountered were also residual. These included a

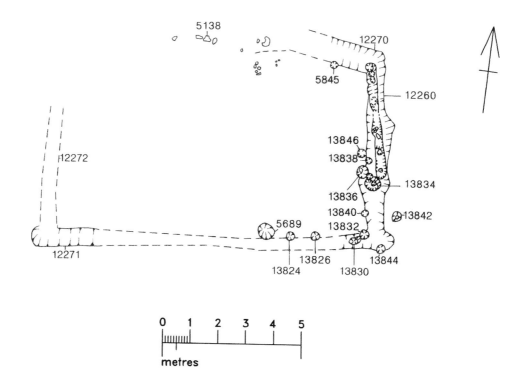

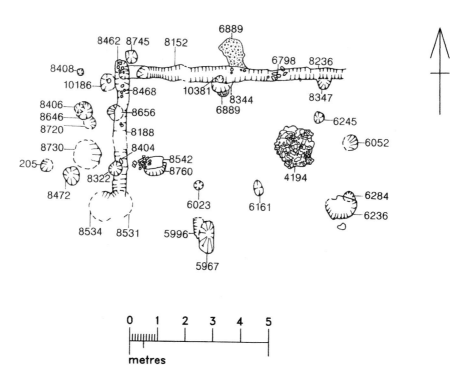

Fig. 6.12. Plans of buildings 14 and 30/31. The upper plan shows building 14, the lower building 30/31 (R. Smith).

seventh-century hanging bowl escutcheon (RF 5717) from dump 5553 (Youngs, Volume 2, Chapter 2); a set of chain-linked pins (RF 3454) from 3417 (Rogers, Volume 2, Chapter 1); and a styca (RF 10988) of Aethelred II of Northumbria, AD 840-844, (Pirie, Volume 2, Chapter 13).

Textile-manufacturing debris was also far less abundant than in the refuse deposits from phases 4ii and 5a. A small number of loom weight fragments, a spindle whorl (RF 5419), a pin-beater (RF 7203), and several heckle teeth comprised the entire assemblage from the dumps of phase 5b, although building 30/31 was associated with a significant concentration of textile-manufacturing finds. This decline in the quantity of debris, however, does not reflect a residual nature for all of the evidence for textile manufacture. The late ninth or early tenth century saw another change in the type of loom weight used in making textiles, in this case a reversion to the use of a larger, heavier weight, for producing coarser cloth (Walton Rogers, Volume 2, Chapter 9; Walton Rogers, Volume 4, Chapter 6). Large fragments of these weights were found in relatively small numbers in phase 5b and Period 6, reflecting smaller-scale textile production, probably for domestic needs (Walton Rogers, Volume 4, Chapter 6). They are unlikely to be residual from phases earlier than 4ii, due to the large size of the un-fired fragments and their propensity to break up when disturbed. Consequently, fragments of the new type of loom weight in conjunction with the Late Saxon pottery types form a broadly contemporary artefact component, within the deposits dating from the late ninth to early tenth centuries AD.

The refuse dumps from this phase also yielded all the stratified 'safety-pin-type' brooches from the excavated occupation sequence, with the exception of RF 3181 which had a different form, and was recovered from phase 3biii. The brooches from phase 5b include a silver example (RF 10994) from 6472 (Rogers, Volume 2, Chapter 1). It is possible that the three examples from phase 5b are all residual, although their concentration in late ninth- to early tenth-century deposits and their 150-year absence between the mid eighth and late ninth centuries, may also reflect a trend in their chronological use.

The artefact assemblages incorporated into the fills of the former foundations of buildings demolished within or at the end of phase 5b present a similar picture to that from the refuse dumps. A large number of residual finds were encountered alongside smaller quantities of artefacts dating from the late ninth and tenth centuries. Buildings 27, 28 and structures 36, 37 and 38 could have been demolished at any time within phase 5a or 5b. Buildings 27 and 28 yielded 31 sherds from the deposits filling their foundations, most of which were small, worn pieces of Maxey-type ware. Fragments of two Ipswich ware vessels also came from features associated with building 27, again reflecting the ninth-century *floruit* for the

arrival and use of Ipswich ware at Flixborough. In contrast, buildings 36, 37 and 38 contained a far greater number of pottery sherds within their post-hole fills. The pottery fragments were also larger and less abraded, suggesting a lesser degree of post-depositional damage, and possibly a more contemporary date of use.

The post-holes from buildings 36 and 37 contained fragments from a maximum of 71 vessels. These included sherds of Early Lincolnshire Fine-shelled ware, Ipswich ware, local Mid Saxon wares, and single sherds of an imported Continental grey ware and white ware vessel respectively. Although five sherds of vessels with cross-joins to fragments from other deposits were encountered, none had links with those from underlying deposits in the ditch. The size and freshness of some of the sherds and this lack of re-worked material probably reflect contemporary refuse. A spindle whorl (RF 193), iron heckle tooth and several loom weight fragments were also incorporated into the fills. The post-holes of granary (building) 38 also produced 13 sherds from 10 vessels, including three pieces of Ipswich ware and a fragment of a Late Saxon jar in a grey quartz fabric, again suggesting a late ninth- or early tenth-century date range for some of the material.

The features and structures undoubtedly belonging to phase 5b showed a consistent presence of small quantities of late ninth- to early tenth-century pottery and other finds, alongside a larger number of identifiable residual artefacts. The pits 2001, 2040 and 2089, which separated the demolition of building 26 (phase 5a) from the construction of building 4 (phase 5b), all contained sherds of Late Saxon Torksey-type ware pottery. Although, the fills of post-holes from building 4 themselves did not contain any pottery. Hearth 850, however, possibly representing a building to the south of building 4, did incorporate a sherd of Late Saxon Torksey-type ware into its fired-clay base, alongside residual sherds from Early and Mid Anglo-Saxon vessels.

In the central part of the site within the shallow valley, the features of building 14 yielded few finds. They consisted of three sherds of pottery and an iron stylus (RF 12268), with a silver-foil repoussé mount on its eraser end. This mount was decorated with interlace decoration, suggesting a date of manufacture between the eighth and ninth centuries (Pestell, Volume 2, Chapter 3; FIG. 6.15*). It is not possible to tell whether another iron stylus (RF 12144) from refuse deposit 6490 was in contemporary use before discard.

Deposits associated with buildings 30/31, however, yielded a larger assemblage of artefacts, some of which are possibly indicative of activities undertaken within the building. These included a concentration of finds associated with spinning, weaving and cloth finishing, comprising approximately 35 loom weight fragments (weighing 234g); three spindle whorls (RFs 8450, 10174 and 13724); and two bone needles (RFs 6037 and 6047). All these finds were retrieved from fills of post-holes and foundation trenches, predominantly from the western end of building 31 (in the case of the spindle whorls and loom weights). This assemblage is the largest collection of textile-manufacturing evidence from phase 5b, and it may reflect the use of the building for that purpose.

Other finds from occupation deposits within building 31, or foundation trench fills, included a collection of 38 sherds of pottery from up to 33 vessels; a fragment of a glass vessel; and a residual silver *sceat* (RF 8233; Series G, type BMC3a), attributed to Quentovic – modern Vismarest, near Etaples-sur-Canches, in northern France, and minted between AD 715 and 725 (Archibald, Volume 2, Chapter 13). The pottery consisted of a combination of disturbed residual material from underlying dumps and a smaller number of vessels in contemporary or near-contemporary use. A sherd of the greensand vessel 21 (first encountered within a mid eighth-century deposit) and Maxey-type wares certainly reflect re-worked components; whereas fragments of Early Lincolnshire Fine-shelled ware and Ipswich ware may have come from vessels in contemporary use in the late ninth or early tenth centuries. A further sherd of mid second-century Samian ware, from post-hole 8730, may also indicate the continued importation of non-local, disturbed material into the excavated area, although it could have been disturbed from refuse in immediately preceding phases.

The craft-working evidence from phase 5b is difficult to interpret, with the exception of the small quantities of textile-manufacturing debris from the refuse dumps and the larger concentration from building 31. A 'lunette' knife for leather-working (RF 10841) came from the fill of a foundation slot (10834), which could date from either phase 5a or 5b; whilst the artefact itself could also be residual from an earlier period (FIG. 6.16*; Ottaway, Volume 2, Chapter 8; Loveluck, Volume 4, Chapters 6 and 9). Iron-working evidence was more abundant, although quantities were not great. Debris from smithing was recovered from the refuse dumps and from the fills of the foundations of buildings 36, 37 and 38, in particular. Most of the debris from the refuse dumps related to smithing, in the form of hearth fragments, although furnace fragments, tap slag and roasted ore were also present in very small quantities. In the area of the granaries, however, furnace fragments, tap slag and ore were found in larger quantities, although their number was still very limited in comparison to the much greater quantities that were deposited in Period 6 (Starley, Volume 2, Chapter 10).

Some of the smithing evidence is likely to have been contemporary with phase 5b, but the smelting debris could have been disturbed from phase 4ii deposits, in the vicinity of the ditch. Similarly, several small, fired-clay mould fragments (RFs 14268, 14270 and 14357) from post-holes of buildings 36, 37 and 38 may also reflect disturbance of the deposits filling the earlier ditch, which contained non-ferrous metalworking debris. Nevertheless, other deposits from phase 5b – namely refuse dumps 2562, 5553 and 6490 – also contained mould (RFs 14416 and 14410) and crucible (RF 14415) fragments, so not all the non-ferrous metalworking debris was necessarily residual (Wastling, Volume 2, Chapter 11). Overall, however, it is difficult to be certain whether most of the iron-working and non-ferrous metalworking evidence was residual or contemporary.

7   Periods 6 and 7: Tenth to Fifteenth Century

Christopher Loveluck and David Atkinson

with contributions by Jane Young and Peter Didsbury

7.1 Introduction

At some point between the early and mid tenth century, the relatively small buildings and granaries which had characterised Period 5 were demolished. In their stead, the largest buildings seen in the excavated occupation sequence were constructed, all with continuous trench foundations. As with the re-planning of the site between the mid and late ninth century, the alterations in layout during Period 6 represent a significant discontinuity in the use of space. The southern and western extremities of the excavated area seem to have been abandoned for structural purposes after the demolition of buildings 27, 28, 36, 37 and 38. Instead, the more central building plots used in phase 5b exhibit continued use, and the northern part of the site was also used for buildings again (FIG. 7.1). During the period between the early and middle decades of the tenth century (phases 6i and 6ii), there was also a further re-organisation of the site, with a change in building alignment and an apparent movement of the zone of buildings eastward, towards the now demolished church of All Saints. This is reflected by buildings 32 and 33, the latest in the stratigraphic sequence, and by the use of the former site of building 7 as a refuse area (FIG. 7.2).

Subsequently, between the mid tenth and early eleventh centuries, the whole of the excavated site seems to have become a focus for refuse dumping, derived from a habitation area probably located immediately to the east, on the site that would become the medieval village of North or Little Conesby. The Anglo-Saxon settlement sequence labelled with reference to the modern village of Flixborough, during excavation, was probably the predecessor of the North Conesby settlement, now in Flixborough parish. The analysis of the structural and depositional developments within Period 6 is presented within three sub-phases, defined not by the replacement of buildings, but by the change in the use of areas for refuse dumping. Consequently, as in earlier chapters, the changing episodes or phases of deposit accumulation, within the one main structural period, have been differentiated with the use of Latin numerals.

7.2 Phase 6i – early to mid-tenth century

By the early decades of the tenth century, the small buildings of Period 5 had certainly been demolished. It is possible that they were levelled prior to the end of phase 5b, when part of the former southern building plots became a focus for refuse accumulation (FIG. 6.10). Whatever the exact chronological sequence of their demolition, none of the building plots used in the southern part of the excavated area during phase 5b influenced the location of buildings during the succeeding period. In contrast, the more recently defined plots in the central part of the site (those for buildings 14 and 30/31) were utilised as general foci for succeeding buildings, during the early to mid tenth century. Building 4 was replaced on the same general plot by building 34, and building 7 was constructed in the central building zone, overlying much of building 30/31 (FIG. 7.1). A large external refuse deposit (1680) accumulated to the west of building 34, and this may represent an external midden. It is also possible that the southern refuse zone from phase 5b remained in use, and that 1680 reflects an extension of this refuse area. In the northern part of the site, however, a further discontinuity to add to the changes in the south and west of the site is also apparent. Building 12 was constructed overlying the former ovens, and their succeeding refuse dumps; whilst at some point in this phase the north-south aligned, building 32 was built along the north-eastern extremity of the site, also cutting refuse deposit 6472 from phase 5b (FIG. 7.1). The construction of the latter building also represented a change in alignment of the buildings during phase 6i, from

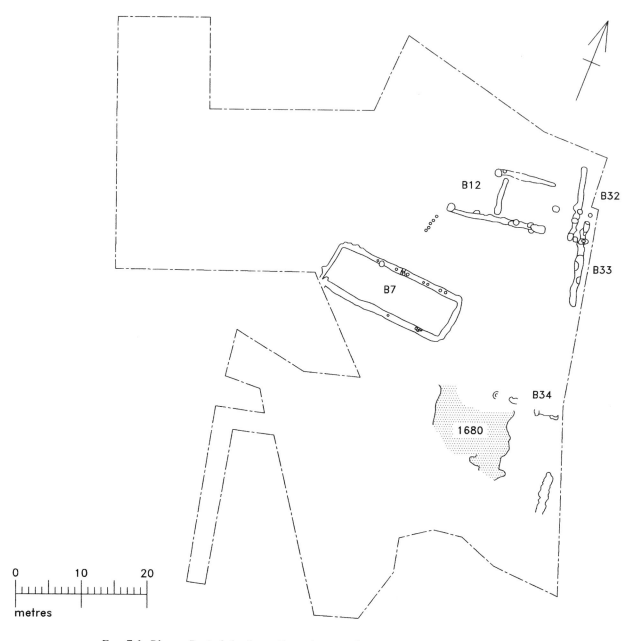

FIG. 7.1. Plan – Period 6, phase 6i, early to mid tenth century (M. Frankland).

structures set on approximate north-east to south-west axes, to a north to south alignment for the latest buildings.

Accompanying this re-planning of settlement layout in Period 6, the size of the buildings underwent a dramatic increase, moving from the period with the smallest buildings in the occupation sequence to the period with the majority of the largest structures. Furthermore, there was also a change to the almost total adoption of continuous foundation trenches for long walls of buildings, although buildings 12, 32, 33 and 34 also possessed combinations of trench and post-hole bases for their short walls. It is possible to give detailed estimates of building size in only two instances, in relation to buildings 7 and 12. The remaining buildings (numbers 32, 33 and 34)

yielded only partial plans, as their 'footprints' extended beyond the eastern edge of the excavated area. This phenomenon of an increased number of buildings constructed on the eastern extremity of the site, together with the alignment change and the abandonment of the former western building plots, seems to reflect the start of a gradual and very limited settlement shift eastwards, through the tenth century.

Building 7 was constructed within a continuous rectangular foundation trench, just over three times as long as it was broad, being 19.7m in length and 6.5m in width (FIG. 7.3). The foundation trenches of the building were approximately 0.5m in depth, and they cut through underlying deposits dating from phases 3b, 4ii and 5a.

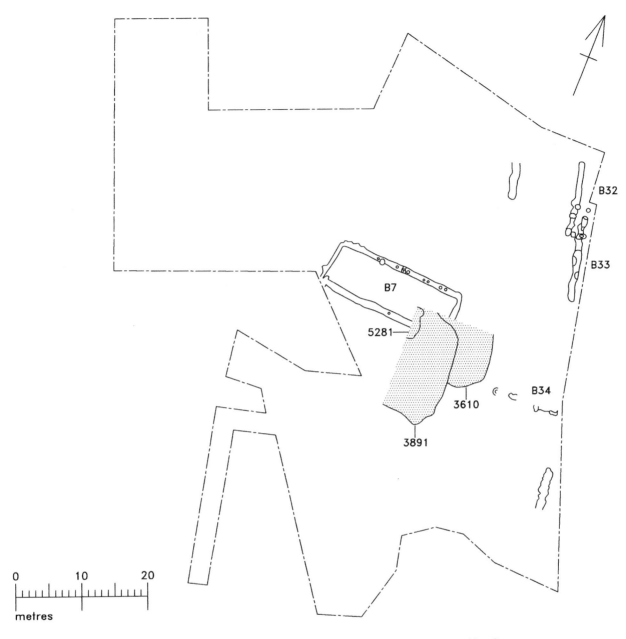

FIG. 7.2. Plan – Period 6, phase 6ii, mid tenth century (M. Frankland).

FIG. 7.4 shows foundation trenches 5870 and 5987 from building 7 cutting through truncated deposits from phases 4ii and 3b, with subsequent deposits from phases 6ii and 6iii overlying the demolished and filled foundations of the building. FIG. 4.19, in chapter 4, also shows foundation trench 5987 cutting the former trench (5977) of building 9, from phases 3biv–v. In other areas the trenches are noted as cutting through the phase 5a dumps and the foundations of building 30/31, from phase 5b. The earth-fast superstructure of the building was based on limestone and ironstone post-pads, and within post-holes, placed along the long walls (FIG. 7.3). FIG. 7.4 shows a selection of sections of these foundation trenches, with their post-pads and post-holes. The sections of

trenches 5870 and 5987 show a range of the post-pads and composite stone post-settings, together with packing stones. They also hint at the possibility of two phases for building 7, since some of the post-settings (e.g. 5926) are placed well above the surface of the foundation trench, within its fill.

Building 12 in the north of the site was constructed within continuous foundation trenches, where it is possible to tell, with an additional, central north-south trench dividing the building into two parts of similar size (FIG. 7.5). The foundations of the building, which were between 0.5 and 0.6m in depth, cut through the ovens from phases 5a and 5b, as well as earlier deposits. FIG. 7.6 shows a number of the sections of the foundation

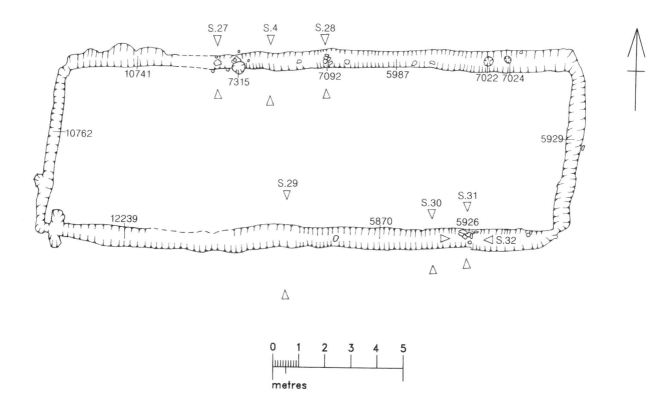

FIG. 7.3. Plan of building 7 (R. Smith).

trenches (6960, 7211 and 9936) either cutting the ovens or deposits from phase 5b and earlier periods (others are presented in the ADS archive). Although the north-western corner of the building was removed by a twelfth-century ditch (85) from Period 7, it is still possible to give an estimate of the size of the building: it was at least 15m in length and 7m in width. The foundation trenches showed signs of having been dug in stages, although as part of one construction event, reflected in the different context numbers attached to the southern long wall (FIG. 7.5). Large post-holes had also been dug into the foundation trenches, some of which had stone post-settings. Indeed, it is possible that the shorter, end-wall parts of the building were based within post-holes, not trenches. As with building 7, there are also hints that building 12 was subject to at least one phase of renovation or rebuilding. The sections of foundation trench 10334 show stone post-pads within the middle of the trench fill, as does the section of post-hole 10315, suggesting the rebuilding of elements of the southern long wall (FIG. 7.6).

A line of stake-holes, heading south from building 12 towards building 7, also indicates some internal division of the excavated area with fences during Period 6 (FIGS 7.1 and 7.7). Beyond the possible fence line, to the west of building 12 there was also a series of refuse pits, 7076 and 7089 amongst others (FIG. 7.1).

Due to the partial nature of the plans of buildings 32, 33 and 34, less can be said about their overall dimensions in comparison with buildings 7 and 12, but a series of traits associated with these buildings can be gleaned from their plans and the profiles of their foundations. Building 32 was constructed on a north to south alignment, unlike the other buildings of phase 6i. It is possible that it could be either contemporary with building 12, to its west, or a later construction of phase 6ii. The north-south long wall, set in a continuous foundation trench was at least 10.5m in length, and the southern end wall was set in post-holes (FIG. 7.8). Unfortunately, it is not possible to estimate the width of the building. Its successor, building 33, represented by a north to south foundation trench and post-holes, constituted the latest structural evidence from the Anglo-Saxon phases of occupation. This was probably contemporary with phase 6ii and reflects a movement of the residential zone of the settlement to the east. It is only possible to conclude that the building had a length of approximately 13 metres. The foundations of building 34 were subject to similar partial recovery. The building was constructed on broadly the same plot as the former building 4, within a combination of continuous trench and post-hole foundations. An unknown portion of the building ran underneath the eastern limit of the excavation. Nevertheless, it is possible to say that it was at least 11m in length and between 7 and 7.5m in width. Like

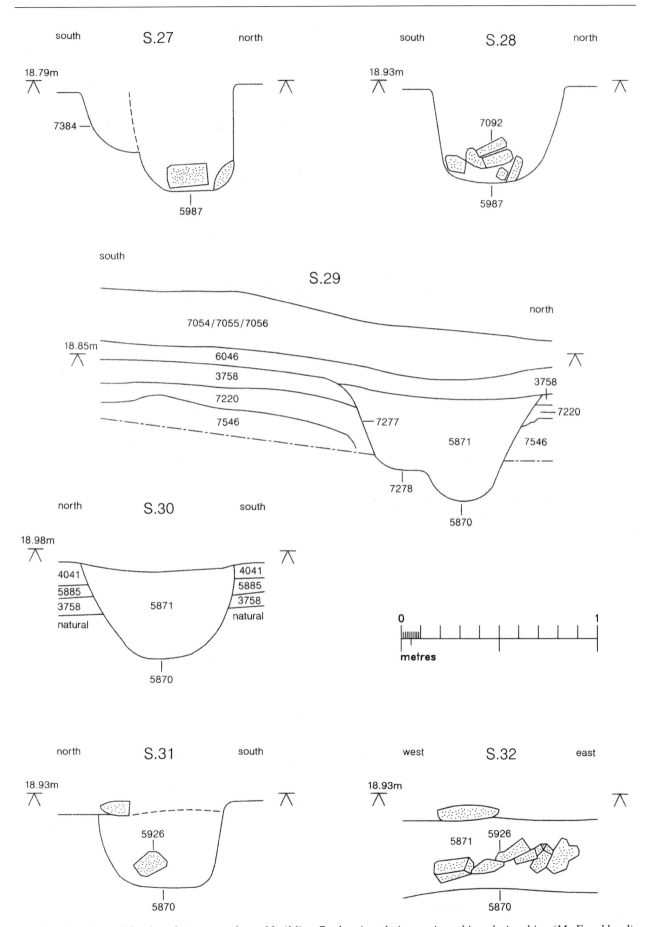

FIG. 7.4. *Sections of the foundation trenches of building 7, showing their stratigraphic relationships (M. Frankland).*

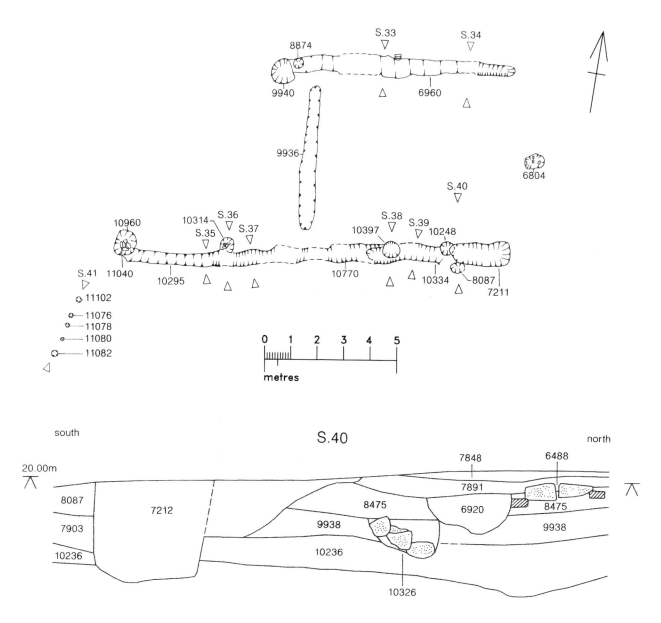

FIG. 7.5. Plan and section of building 12 (R. Smith, M. Frankland).

buildings 7 and 12, none of the buildings from the eastern margin of the site contained internal fired-clay hearths at ground level, marking a distinct difference with buildings from Periods 4 and 5.

The character of occupation during phase 6i can be summarised as one of residential habitation with limited contemporary refuse disposal, apart from the midden area to the west of building 34. As a consequence, the range and quantity of finds, in terms of artefacts, animal bones, and industrial debris were limited. The refuse deposit 1680, and a smaller dump 2488, both yielded several sherds of Torksey and Lincoln Kiln-type pottery wares, which could date from any time between the late ninth and late tenth centuries (Young, Volume 2, Chapter 12).

A small number of Early Lincolnshire Fine-shelled ware and Ipswich ware sherds were also recovered, together with a much larger collection of residual Maxey-type wares. Other finds included three clench bolts from 2488, and fragments of Eifel lava querns and a piece of vessel glass from 1680.

As a prelude to the re-organisation of the site during phase 6ii, buildings 7 and 12 were demolished and large numbers of finds were incorporated into the fills of their foundations. Much of the material, however, was residual, since the deep foundations of these buildings cut through and disturbed earlier artefact-rich deposits. This was especially true of building 7, which cut through deposits from phase 5b to 3b. The pottery from its foundation

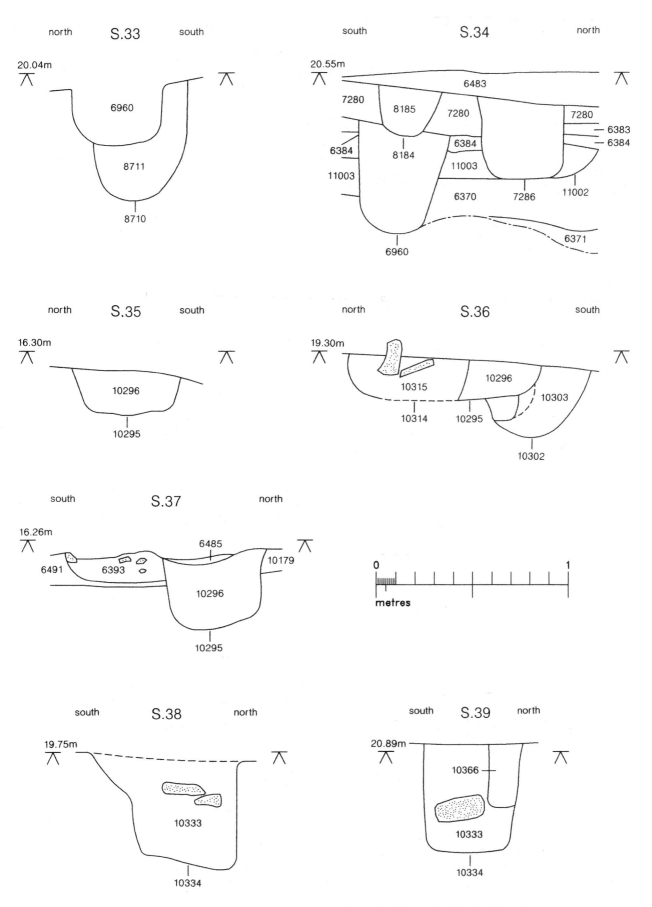

FIG. 7.6. *Sections of the foundation trenches of building 12 (M. Frankland).*

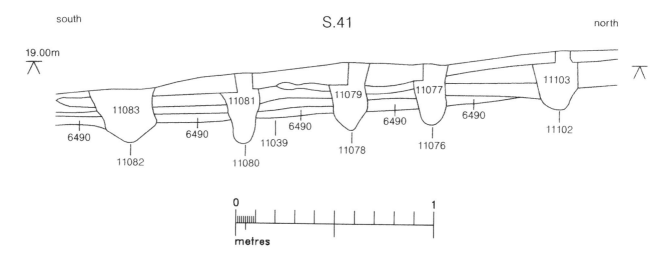

FIG. 7.7. Section of the fence line associated with building 12 (M. Frankland).

trenches comprised a group of 70 sherds, mainly consisting of residual and disturbed Maxey-type wares, although a single, worn sherd of Late Saxon Torksey-type ware was also recovered. Other artefacts from building 7 included two heckle or wool-comb teeth, loom weight fragments weighing 289g, including 18 recorded weights, two small mould fragments (RFs 14391–2), and five fragmentary bone and antler combs, in both single-sided and double-sided forms, one of which was almost complete (RF 5939). Bearing in mind the fact that the foundations of building 7 cut through deposits, such as 6312, 3758 and 5503, which contained large numbers of loom weights and comb fragments, it is highly likely that the bulk of the material from the trenches originated in earlier phases. The same can be demonstrated for the finds recovered from the filled foundations of building 12. A collection of 58 sherds from a maximum of 48 vessels was recovered, most of which were of disturbed and residual Maxey-types, alongside sherds from three Ipswich ware vessels. A single loom weight fragment was the only other find associated with the foundations of this building.

7.3 Phase 6ii – mid tenth century

The two large structures comprising buildings 7 and 12, with their indications of a secondary phase of renovation and rebuilding, could have remained standing for well over three or four decades of the tenth century, even allowing for the chemically hostile nature of the soil environment in which they stood. They had undoubtedly been demolished, however, prior to the first deposition of diagnostic pottery forms dating from the late tenth or early eleventh centuries, found for the first time within the latest Anglo-Saxon deposits of phase 6iii. Consequently, the vertical stratigraphy and the diagnostically datable artefacts dictate that these buildings had been

demolished and sealed by the vast refuse dumps of phase 6ii, before they in turn were covered by the deposits of 6iii. Therefore, it is suggested that buildings 7 and 12 were demolished prior to the creation of the refuse dumps of phase 6ii, sometime in the middle decades of the tenth century (FIG. 7.2).

The decades after the early tenth century, and prior to the 970s, are particularly enigmatic on many sites in eastern England due to the absence of certain datable forms of evidence, particularly coins minted after the end of the ninth or early tenth centuries (Loveluck 2001, 118–119). In many cases, coinage does not re-appear until the 970s, with West Saxon issues of Edgar and Edward the Martyr. In the absence of contemporary coinage and abundant jewellery with diagnostically datable decoration, dating has to rely on the pottery. Dating of the pottery is achieved, in turn, by reference to other datable artefacts, such as coins. Consequently, when artefacts such as coinage disappear at sites like Flixborough, between the end of the ninth century and the 970s, the dating references for the pottery disappear too. Hence there is a tendency to identify late ninth- to early tenth-century pottery forms, i.e. until the coinage disappeared; and pottery forms from the mid to late tenth century onwards, when coinage supply resumed (see Young, Volume 2, Chapter 12; and Vince and Young, Volume 2, Chapter 12). Exceptionally, however, the Flixborough occupation sequence houses phases (6i and 6ii) which were sandwiched in between periods dated by small quantities of pottery, currently attributed to between the late ninth and early tenth century (phase 5b), and the late tenth to early eleventh century (phase 6iii) respectively (Loveluck 2001, 118–119). The structures and deposits of phases 6i and 6ii, therefore, provide a relative sequence of activities between phases 5b and 6iii.

On the basis of this relative chronological sequence

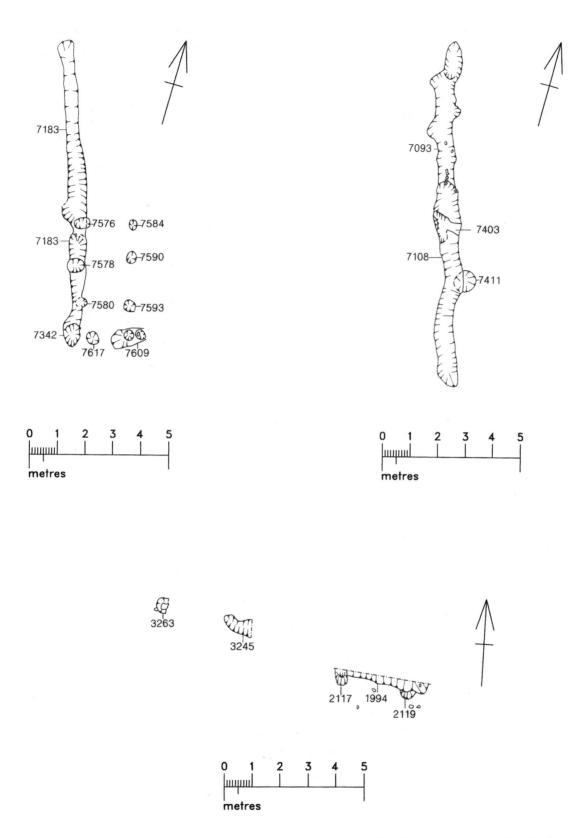

FIG. 7.8. Plans of buildings 32, 33, and 34. The upper left plan shows building 32; upper right building 33; lower plan shows building 34 (R. Smith).

after the early tenth century, buildings 7 and 12 were demolished sometime in the middle decades of the tenth century. The area formerly occupied by building 7 extending westwards from deposit 1680 was then covered by large refuse dumps (3891 and 3610 in particular), containing vast quantities of animal bones, large quantities of both smelting and smithing debris from iron-working, and large numbers of other artefacts (FIG. 7.2). During the same period, several gullies of indeterminate nature were also created, cutting the filled foundation trenches of building 12 (8460), and to the south of building 34 (1758 and 5322). Building 33 may have replaced its predecessor, building 32, at the same time. Overall, the almost total demolition of the previous buildings within the excavated area reflects further movement of the settlement eastwards, perhaps towards a mid tenth-century, stone precursor of All Saints' church, similar to the example excavated by Glynn Coppack at Burnham, in North Lincolnshire (Coppack 1986, 47–50). This also reflects the already mentioned shift towards the site of the medieval settlement of North or Little Conesby. The name 'Conesby' – the Old Danish *Kuningrsby* – meaning 'King's Farm', may have become associated with the settlement at any time between the late ninth and eleventh centuries AD (Cameron 1998, 33; Cameron, Volume 4, Chapter 4).

The main dumps from phase 6ii contained over 600 sherds of pottery, in addition to the thousands of animal bones and iron-working evidence. On the basis of the pottery alone, little might be considered as contemporary material. The assemblage included sherds of the Continental imports vessels 42 and 56 (Vince, Volume 2, Chapter 12), fragments of which had first been deposited in the large ditch during the refuse dumping of phase 4ii. Presence of sherds of these vessels may indicate some re-working of deposits from that area. Significantly, however, a similar set of circumstances to those from the large refuse dumps 3758 and 5503, from phase 4ii, pertained to deposits 3610 and 3891 in regard to the unrepresentative nature of the pottery as an indicator of the extent of residual material present. While there is a residual element of finds within 3610 and 3891, both newly developed artefact types and previously unseen objects were also deposited in these dumps, alongside small quantities of tenth-century pottery, which all suggest a large contemporary component of early to mid tenth-century material.

A significant quantity of fragments of unfired clay loom weights was recovered from these dumps (weighing almost 3 kilos, and including at least 28 recorded finds). Many comprised large fragments or near-complete weights, and some complete examples were also present (Walton Rogers, Volume 2, Chapter 9; Walton Rogers, Volume 4, Chapter 6). The majority of the fragments or complete examples represented the larger, heavier 'bun-shaped' loom weight which had first appeared in phase 5b, although smaller numbers of the much lighter loom

weights from phases 4ii, and perhaps 5a, were also present. The heavier weights from phase 5b and Period 6 weighed 500g on average, whereas the smaller weights from phases 4ii weighed only 200g on average (Walton Rogers, Volume 4, Chapter 6). The much higher proportion of the larger, unfired loom weights and their appearance and rise in number from phase 5b suggest that they were contemporary with phases 6i and 6ii. Furthermore, the presence of the near-complete and whole loom weights also suggests limited post-depositional re-working, since a significant degree of disturbance and deposit movement could be expected to have produced greater fragmentation of these large, unfired clay objects.

New types of artefacts previously unseen at Flixborough were also present in the major refuse dumps from phase 6ii, in the form of lead weights. Some of these weights were probably used in bullion exchange, presumably of silver. These weights included a solid cylindrical weight (RF 3727) from 3610 (FIG. 7.9*), and a perforated conical weight from 3891 (RF 4147). Both of these weights are directly paralleled with others from the tenth and eleventh centuries in north-eastern England, Wales and Ireland (Kruse 1992, 79; Redknap 2000, 61; Wastling, Volume 2, Chapter 13). A larger, bell-shaped weight (RF 3884) with an iron handle was also recovered from dump 3891, and this too may have had a function related to weight-based exchange. Weights such as the above were not encountered in any earlier deposits at Flixborough, and others which were recovered either in deposits from 6iii or as unstratified finds are of a type well-known from the late ninth and tenth centuries AD (Kruse 1992, 79; Redknap 2000, 61).

It can be concluded, therefore, that the lead weights were used between the early and mid tenth century, during the period when contemporary coinage did not reach the site. An unstratified silver 'finger' ingot (RF 12198) is also likely to derive from this period. Again, this ingot has many tenth-century parallels in Scandinavian-influenced parts of northern Britain, Wales and Ireland (Bayley 1992; Graham-Campbell 1992; Sheehan 1998, 151–157). Only two Anglo-Saxon coins were recovered from this phase, from the smaller refuse deposits 3255 and 7280. The coin from 3255 was a West Saxon silver penny (RF 3568) of Alfred the Great (AD 871–899), probably minted between AD 871 and 875 (Archibald, Volume 2, Chapter 13); and the coin from 7280 was a Northumbrian styca (RF 7503) of Eanred, minted between AD 830 and 835 (Pirie, Volume 2, Chapter 13). Although undoubtedly residual, it remains a possibility that such coins, particularly the silver coin, could still have been used in bullion-based exchange.

Alongside the new, heavier loom weights and the lead weights, fragments of nine vessels currently dated to between the late ninth and early eleventh centuries AD were recovered from the dumps, in addition to fragments of 11 Early Lincolnshire Fine-shelled ware vessels which could also have been in contemporary use in this phase.

Only one vessel was typologically distinct, a Lincoln Kiln-type dish, from 3610. At Lincoln, this type of vessel was confined to deposits dating from between the late ninth and early/mid tenth centuries (Young, Volume 2, Chapter 12). The sherd was fresh and unworn, although small. Other smaller dumps and deposits yielded only four sherds that may be of contemporary Late Saxon date.

In summary, therefore, the refuse dumps from phase 6ii contained a large number of demonstrably residual pottery sherds and a much smaller number of contemporary Late Saxon fragments, reflecting different patterns of pottery use and supply in the Mid and Late Saxon periods. Small numbers of other artefacts, probably of a residual nature, were also recovered: for example, glass vessel, lava quern, and bone comb fragments, although not all the combs need have been residual. The decorated, double-sided comb RF 6864 from refuse deposit 6797 could have been manufactured at any time between the mid ninth century and early to mid tenth century (Foreman, Volume 2, Chapter 1). Alongside the small quantity of contemporary pottery, however, the new heavier loom weights far outnumbered the residual, smaller loom weight fragments. Together with the other new types of artefact, such as the lead weights, they suggest a significant quantity of relatively undisturbed contemporary material.

Further evidence of the contemporary nature of the majority of the non-pottery finds from phase 6ii is provided by the iron-working debris. The deposits of this period yielded far greater quantities of iron-working debris than all earlier periods within the occupation sequence. At the same time, significant quantities of iron-smelting evidence were present for the first time. The iron-working debris was also found in large fragments, including large pieces of hearth bottoms (e.g. RF 5330) from iron-smithing and a furnace bottom and large slag blocks (e.g. RF 5329) from iron smelting, particularly from dump 3891 (Starley, Volume 2, Chapter 10). These constitute some of the largest fragments of such features from Flixborough, and they reflect both iron smelting and smithing on the settlement during phases 6i and 6ii. The dramatically increased quantities of iron-working waste, and the very different composition and size of the pieces of debris, suggest that much of this material was contemporary with the tenth-century phases on the settlement.

Non-ferrous metalworking evidence was also recovered, although its quantity was very limited in comparison to the iron-working evidence. It consisted of four fired-clay mould fragments from dumps 3610, 3891, 6499 and 6797 (Wastling, Volume 2, Chapter 11). Bearing in mind the presence of residual imported pottery, possibly re-worked from the ditch fills of phase 4ii and which also contained mould and crucible fragments, it is unclear whether these were residual or contemporary losses. Overall, in comparison with the evidence from artefacts and debris from phases 3b, 4ii and even 5a, the diversity

of contemporary craft-working activities seems to have decreased by Period 6, with small-scale textile manufacture and more significant iron-working being the only craft activities undoubtedly represented. Although, it is also possible that the exceptional collection of woodworking tools, housed within two lead tanks, also dates from the tenth century or later (Cowgill, Volume 2, Chapter 7; Ottaway, Volume 2, Chapter 7; Darrah, Volume 4, Chapter 3; Loveluck, Volume 4, Chapter 6; FIGS 1.11 and 1.12, this volume).

On the demolition of the remaining buildings sometime in phase 6ii, and the filling in of the enigmatic gullies and slots, a further small assemblage of Late Saxon pottery was incorporated into the cut features. Significantly, however, the overall number of finds from all the features associated with buildings 32, 34, and the gullies 8460, 1758 and 5322 was small. As a result, the small amount of contemporary finds makes up a relatively high proportion of the finds. The foundations of building 32 contained only six small and residual Maxey-type sherds; and those of building 34 contained 12 sherds, five of which were of residual Maxey wares alongside a single sherd of Lincoln Kiln-type ware, dated to between the late ninth and late tenth centuries. Gulley 1758 contained a sherd of Torksey-type ware and Early Fine-shelled ware, probably contemporary with phases 6i and 6ii; and 5322 contained a fragment of a Torksey-type ware vessel, dated to between the late ninth and late eleventh centuries, with two residual sherds. Again, a small number of Torksey-type sherds were also recovered from several other cut features, such as pit 77, which also contained the bone of a black rat in one (923) of its fills (see Volume 3, and Dobney, Volume 4, Chapter 7). Very few artefacts, other than sherds of pottery or occasional loom weight fragments, were recovered from the above features.

Overall, the deposits and structures from phase 6ii reflect the increasing use of the excavated area as a refuse zone during the course of the tenth century, with a gradual shift of the habitation area eastwards. The refuse deposits indicate conspicuous consumption of animal resources, seen in the vast quantities of animal bones, together with a small but significant level of exchange within the region of Lincolnshire. This was represented by the presence of Lincoln Kiln-type and Torksey-type pottery in particular, together with lead weights probably used for the weight-based exchange of silver bullion. Demonstrably contemporary imports from the Continent were absent; and at the same time, the craft-working base of the settlement also seems to have decreased overall, with a small level of textile production and more significant iron-working.

7.4 Phase 6iii – mid tenth to early eleventh century

The final actions of the Anglo-Saxon occupation sequence in the excavated area are represented by a phase of refuse dumping across the whole site. When possible, distinct deposits such as refuse dump 6300 were excavated stratigraphically (FIG. 7.10). The latest refuse layers, however, described as 'dark soils' during excavation, appeared to be homogeneous deposits over the whole site; and as a consequence, they were divided into approximate five-metre-square grids, and excavated in two spits. The locations of the recorded north-western and south-eastern 'dark soil' deposits are shown in FIG. 7.10. The upper arbitrary context/stratigraphic unit numbers in each square represent the numbers applied to the upper spits, and the lower numbers to the lower spits. The area enclosed by the dashed line in the north-eastern part of the site represents the zone excavated by machine (see FIG. 2.2, this volume); and the locations of the former Mid Saxon ditch and the later twelfth-century ditch, from Period 7, have been presented as geographical reference features within the excavated area. Not all 'dark soils' are represented on FIG. 7.10, although their locations and place in the stratigraphic matrices can be examined on the ADS archive and the site archive.

These refuse deposits contained large quantities of artefacts and animal bones, although there was significant zoning in the character and date of certain types of artefact from deposits, in different parts of the site. Considering the pottery as a starting point, the deposits from phase 6iii as a whole contained a group of 1148 sherds. Analysis of the distribution of different types of pottery demonstrated several differences in the composition of ceramics within the 'dark soils', between the south-eastern and north-western parts of the site respectively (site excavation areas E and G approximately; FIG. 2.3, this volume). These differences are presented in the form of percentage occurrence of different pottery types within these two broad areas, in FIG. 7.11.

The material from the northern and western zones of the excavated area (site area G in particular) survived in variable condition, with some quite large sherds occurring as well as tiny worn scraps. The fabrics of nine of the Maxey-type sherds were unidentifiable due to leaching, and a further six had partial internal or external leaching, reflecting chemical weathering within or prior to incorporation in these refuse deposits. At least 11 of the Maxey-type vessels were large jars or bowls. Most significantly, sherds of diagnostic Late Saxon wares, such as Torksey-type and Lincoln wares were completely absent, and there was a high proportion of Ipswich ware amongst the assemblage (FIG. 7.11). Ten fragments were recovered from vessels cross-joining to pieces from other deposits; although sherds of only two vessels (42 and 58) joined to material occurring before phase 5b. Consequently, most of this pre-tenth-century assemblage seems to have been transported into the excavated area from other parts of the settlement from the late ninth century onwards.

In the southern and eastern part of the site (area E approximately), a large number of sherds were un-

identifiable due to leaching, again reflecting their chemical weathering probably in surface refuse deposits. The leached material included sherds of Early Lincolnshire Fine-shelled ware, Lincoln Kiln-type and Lincoln Fine-shelled ware. The most notable aspect of the group from this area is the presence of a high proportion of Late Saxon pottery types, approximately 19% of the assemblage. Only five multi-context vessel fragments were recovered, with only two vessels (10 and 40) joining with examples occurring before phase 5a. These differences between the pottery components of the finds in the north-western and south-eastern parts of the site suggest that whilst their accumulation might have been part of the same process of refuse dumping, the origins and dates of the material housed within the deposits were quite different. The latest Anglo-Saxon pottery types occurred in deposits within the southern and eastern margins of the site, again probably reflecting the eastern shift of the settlement through the tenth century. Another feature, however, of the upper spits of the deposits from 6iii was the recovery of small numbers of sherds dating from between the twelfth and fourteenth centuries. These occasional sherds of medieval pottery occurred in both the north-western and south-eastern parts of the site, and their presence in the upper excavation spits probably reflects the use of the 'dark soils' as the activity surfaces associated with the medieval oven and pits of Period 7.

The concentrations of the latest Anglo-Saxon pottery types in deposits located in the southern and eastern margins of the excavated area are also mirrored by the continued occurrence of significant numbers of the heavier, 'bun-shaped' loom weights of Period 6, in the same areas (FIG. 7.10). Deposit 6300, in particular, contained fragments of these loom weights, sited along the eastern margin of the site. The presence of wool-comb teeth and increasingly heavier bone pin-beaters is seen as coinciding with the production of heavier woollen cloth on the site, during the tenth century (Walton Rogers, Volume 2, Chapter 9; Walton Rogers, Volume 4, Chapter 6). This distinct refuse deposit also contained a large number of fragments of hearth bottoms from iron-smithing as well as some smelting waste, like the deposits encountered in phase 6ii. The 'dark soils' also contained iron-working debris in small but consistent quantities. However, in addition to the contemporary Late Saxon pottery, textile-manufacturing remains and iron-working debris, there were also residual finds present in the southern and eastern deposits, as they were in those to the north-west.

Deposit 6300 contained three fragments of a single, imported clear glass bowl, decorated with yellow reticella trails (RFs 5348, 6895 and 7012), which are from the same vessel as a fragment (RF 1991) from a deposit from phase 5b (Evison, Volume 2, Chapter 2; FIG. 7.12*). This reflects the re-working of fragments of an artefact which had already been broken and incorporated into refuse by

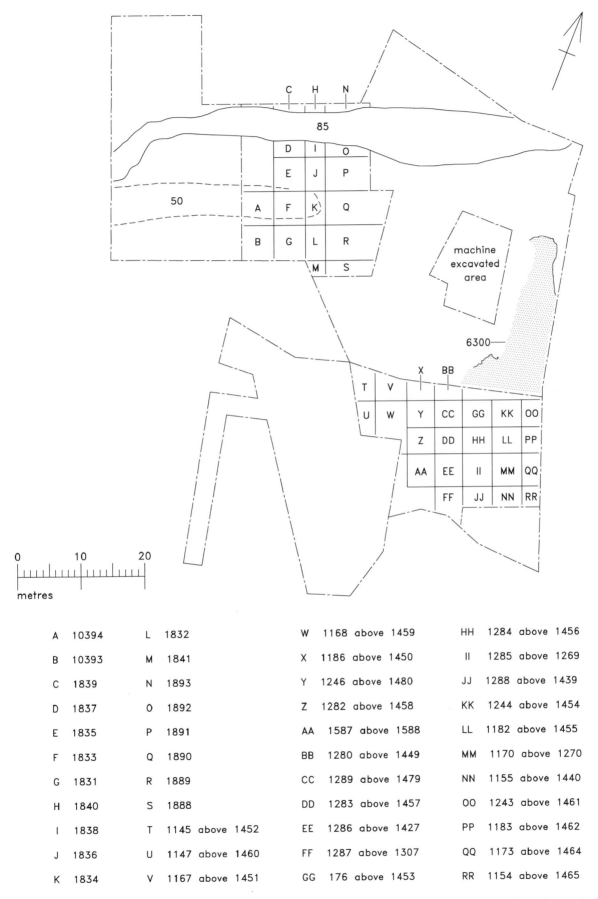

A	10394	L	1832	W	1168 above 1459	HH	1284 above 1456
B	10393	M	1841	X	1186 above 1450	II	1285 above 1269
C	1839	N	1893	Y	1246 above 1480	JJ	1288 above 1439
D	1837	O	1892	Z	1282 above 1458	KK	1244 above 1454
E	1835	P	1891	AA	1587 above 1588	LL	1182 above 1455
F	1833	Q	1890	BB	1280 above 1449	MM	1170 above 1270
G	1831	R	1889	CC	1289 above 1479	NN	1155 above 1440
H	1840	S	1888	DD	1283 above 1457	OO	1243 above 1461
I	1838	T	1145 above 1452	EE	1286 above 1427	PP	1183 above 1462
J	1836	U	1147 above 1460	FF	1287 above 1307	QQ	1173 above 1464
K	1834	V	1167 above 1451	GG	176 above 1453	RR	1154 above 1465

FIG. 7.10. Plan – Period 6, phase 6iii, mid tenth to early eleventh centuries. The gridded squares show the method of excavation of the 'dark soil' deposits for this phase; the key shows relevant context numbers (M. Frankland).

Pottery types	Area E	Area G
Roman	4%	0.5%
Anglo-Saxon Handmade	3%	-
Maxey-type Fabric A	0.5%	3%
Maxey-type Fabric B	18%	51%
Maxey-type Fabric E	3%	10%
Maxey-type Fabric U	2%	7%
Maxey-type no fabric	29%	6%
Imports	-	4%
Ipswich ware	6%	19%
Early Lincolnshire Fine-shelled ware	4%	0.5%
Lincoln Kiln-type	7%	-
Late Saxon Lincoln Sandy	1%	-
Torksey-type	11%	-
Lincoln Fine-shelled ware	0.5%	-
Medieval or later	9%	0.5%
Total sherds	**247**	**151**

FIG. 7.11. Table showing the percentage of pottery types from 'dark soil' deposits in areas E and G of the site (Jane Young).

the late ninth century. Other fragments of glass vessels were recovered from the same deposit (FIG. 7.13*), along with a blue glass tessera (RF 14334), comb fragments, lead weights, an iron strap-end (RF 9768), and two silver pennies. One of these pennies was an issue of Æthelwulf of Wessex, struck between AD 852 and 858; and the other was an intrusive silver penny of King Henry III (AD 1216–1272), incorporated via succeeding churning of the surface during Period 7 (Archibald, Volume 2, Chapter 13). The refuse dump 6300, therefore, exhibits a composite nature of residual finds, contemporary tenth-century material and some intrusive elements.

The other southern and eastern 'dark soils' had artefact profiles which were very similar, with regard to non-pottery finds. Overall, they represent deposits that had been re-worked and had accumulated immediately to the east of the contemporary later tenth-century habitation area of the settlement. Likewise, the deposits located in the north-west of the site also represent accumulations of re-worked refuse, although their greater distance from the settlement zone may account for the absence of contemporary material, as the tenth-century progressed. It is also possible that the north-western 'dark soils' may, to a certain extent, represent refuse deposits from phase 5b to phase 6ii, which appeared as part of a homogeneous mass with later southern and eastern deposits, when first uncovered by machine during excavation.

Nevertheless, a number of contrasts are apparent between the discrete deposits of phases 6i, 6ii, and 6iii (such as 6300), and those defined within the 'dark soils' of phase 6iii. The later refuse deposits yielded far more dress accessories, many of which were probably residual from the eighth- and ninth-century phases. For example, two hooked tags came from deposits of phases 6i and 6ii;

whereas nine came from the 'dark soils' of 6iii, such as the silver-gilt example with animal ornament RF 1816 (FIG. 7.14*, Thomas, Volume 2, Chapter 1). Similarly, strap-ends had been absent since the mid ninth century, until four were deposited in phase 6iii; and 112 pins came from the 'dark soils' (e.g. FIG. 7.15*), whilst approximately 80 came from phases 6i and 6ii (Rogers, Volume 2, Chapter 1).

Further contrasts can also be seen in the occurrence of artefacts such as residual coins and probably residual styli. After phase 5a, contemporary coinage did not reach Flixborough until the 970s, suggested by an unstratified penny (RF 14198) of Edward the Martyr (Archibald, Volume 2, Chapter 13). Indeed, no coinage reached its final deposition context relatively near to its period of minting after phase 4ii. The largest group of stratified but demonstrably residual coins was recovered from the phase 6iii deposits, comprising five in number. A like pattern is also seen in the occurrence of styli. After a concentration in deposits from the early to mid ninth century, only two examples occurred in deposits between phase 4ii and phase 6iii, and one of the latter (RF 12268) was demonstrably residual, with silver interlace ornament (FIG. 6.15; Pestell, Volume 2, Chapter 3). In phase 6iii, however, a further three styli were incorporated into the 'dark soil' refuse deposits. The increased presence of certain types of residual finds in comparison with those from Periods 5 and 6 suggests that a significant proportion of the artefacts reflect the clearance of deposits from unexcavated parts of the settlement, and subsequent transport into the communal refuse zone. Such activities seem to have occurred concurrently with, or slightly before the accumulation of contemporary tenth-century refuse along the eastern and southern margins of the excavated area, probably adjacent to the mid tenth- to eleventh-century habitation area.

7.5 Period 7 – twelfth to fifteenth century

The latest defined period in the occupation sequence can be summarised briefly as peripheral settlement activity, between the twelfth and fourteenth centuries AD. The features within the excavated area took the form of a large ditch (85/6362), dug on a broadly north-east to south-west alignment, in the northernmost extremity of the site (FIG. 7.16). This feature cut through the 'dark soils' of phase 6iii, and truncated or destroyed the northern sides of several of the buildings on the northern building plots, last occupied by building 12, in Period 6. It contained a range of residual finds, as well as thirteenth- to early fourteenth-century glazed, Orangeware pottery fragments (Didsbury, Volume 2, Chapter 14).

In the southern half of the site, the base of a stone and fired-clay oven (1342 *et al.*) was uncovered, with a range of associated features (FIG. 7.17). These took the form of a large clay-lined pit (1699) and a slot (1710), possibly reflecting some sort of oven screen (FIG. 7.17). A possible

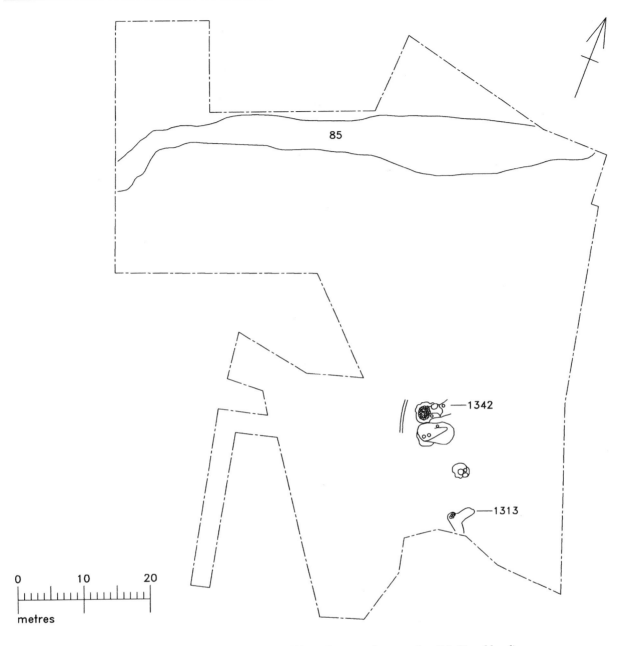

FIG. 7.16. Plan – Period 7, twelfth to fourteenth centuries (M. Frankland).

corner foundation for some sort of building was also located on the southern edge of the excavated area (1313). The fills of the large clay-lined pit yielded two pottery sherds, one dating from the late twelfth century, and the other dating from either the thirteenth or fourteenth centuries AD (Didsbury, Volume 2, Chapter 14).

Overall, the range of medieval pottery sherds in features constructed or dug in Period 7, and incorporated into the surfaces of the 'dark soils' from phase 6iii, provides an assemblage dating from the twelfth to the fourteenth centuries (and possibly into the early fifteenth century). This might suggest a break in the use of the excavated area following the eastward migration of the eleventh-century Anglo-Saxon focus, towards the site of

All Saints' church and the settlement of Conesby. Subsequently, the re-appearance of activity on the site during the twelfth century could have coincided with a re-planning of the settlement in the Anglo-Norman period, with the construction of a moated manor house at the eastern end of the settlement, seemingly during the thirteenth century (Bradley 2005), leaving All Saints' church as the western pole of the settlement. A settlement continuum throughout the medieval period is certainly confirmed by its inclusion in the Domesday survey (Longley and Foster 1924, 149; Roffe, Volume 4, Chapter 8); and by further documentary evidence, dating from between the twelfth and fifteenth centuries (Loveluck and Cameron, Volume 4, Chapter 4).

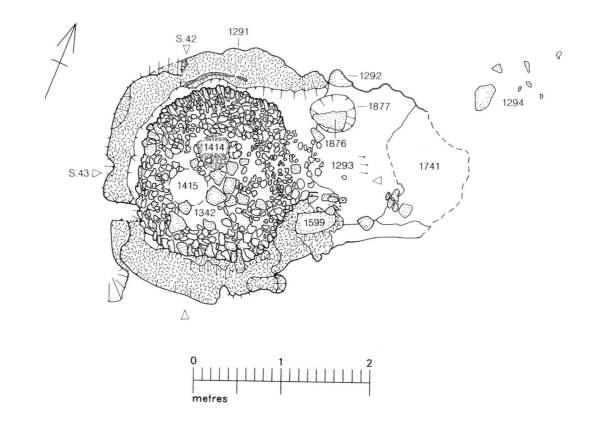

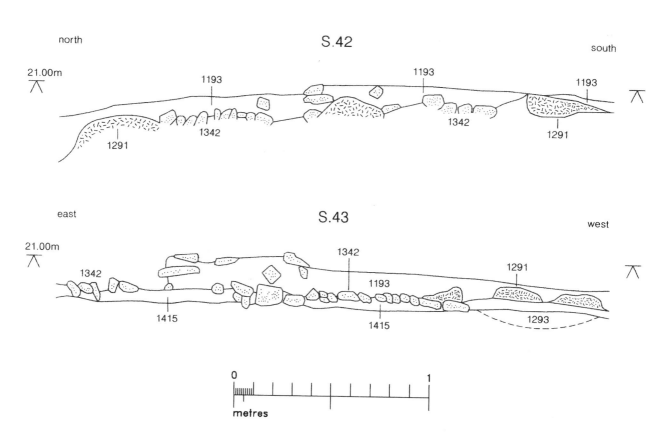

FIG. 7.17. Plan of the medieval oven and associated features (R. Smith, M. Frankland).

8   The Inhabitants

Helen Geake, Simon Mays and Patrick Ottaway

8.1 The human burials

by Helen Geake

The human burials found at Flixborough fall into two groups. Eleven burials were found in 1988 about 60m to the south of the main excavation area (the 'southern' group), and six burials were found in 1988–91 around the building plots in the south-eastern corner of the main excavation area (the 'northern' group). Further burials may lie outside both of the excavated areas. Burials of the date-range spanned by the Flixborough settlement are rare compared to the numbers known from the earlier or later Anglo-Saxon period, and so the evidence is worth discussing in detail.

The southern group

The southern group were in a hostile soil environment, subject to acid leaching, and were therefore poorly preserved (Canti, Chapter 2 this volume). No grave cuts were visible, so no stratigraphic relationships could be observed, but the burials are fairly well spread out and may all have respected each other. Graves 1 and 9 are particularly close and could possibly have formed a double grave. Some of the burials are very close to the edges of the excavation, so there is no reason why the cemetery should not continue beyond the excavated area. In addition, spaces between the burials may have contained further bodies (particularly those of children) which have not survived the soil conditions.

All of the identified graves were aligned similarly, with the heads roughly to the west; there was some variation in orientation from slightly north to slightly south of west. All of the burials were supine and extended, but the poor preservation means that it is impossible to discern many aspects of the treatment of the body from the layout, such as tight wrapping from a winding sheet (where the bones are tightly squeezed together), or decay within a void, created perhaps by a coffin (where the

bones have rolled apart as the body decayed), or the burial of two or more bodies in the same grave cut.

The osteological data on the burials from the southern group are limited by the poor bone preservation. All that can really be said is that all were adults, that they certainly included both men and women, and that one skeleton had osteoarthritis (see section 8.2, below). These characteristics are commonly found within earlier Anglo-Saxon cemeteries; infants and children are usually under-represented. Suggestions to explain away the under-representation of children have ranged from the greater susceptibility of younger bones to poor preservation conditions or of shallower graves to agricultural damage, to the possibility that the bodies of children were buried elsewhere or otherwise disposed of. The hostile soil conditions in the southern area at Flixborough, combined with the truncation due to cultivation and the small excavation area, mean that we cannot safely draw any conclusions about the range of inhabitants at Flixborough, or the age-related zoning of burial, from this group.

Apart from the coffin fittings, there is no independent dating evidence from the southern group of burials.

Coffins

One of the few aspects of the southern group of burials that it is possible to discuss in detail is the presence of iron coffin fittings. Iron coffin fittings were found associated with one burial, Grave 1, and further un-stratified coffin fittings were recovered from the topsoil. The nature of these fittings is discussed in section 8.3 (below), and they are well-known from eighth–tenth century-contexts.

Coffins and other containers or structures within the grave are known from furnished Anglo-Saxon graves, particularly rich ones such as Taplow and Sutton Hoo mound 17, but they appear to become more common as grave-goods decline. In the absence of an interrogatable database for all Anglo-Saxon burials, a statement such as this must always be tentative, but one example comes from Apple Down in West Sussex, where the large late fifth- to seventh-century Cemetery 1 had no coffins, but the 11 poorly furnished, seventh-century or later, graves in Cemetery 2 contained up to nine coffins (Down and Welch 1990). Iron coffin fittings are also known from earlier furnished graves (Evison 1987, 99–100), but again appear to become more common later (Ottaway 1996, 99–113). Ottaway suggests that coffins (or other containers such as re-used chests) with iron fittings may be indicators of high social status (see p.122 below; Ottaway 1996, 113).

The increase in the use of coffins, and other containers or covers for the body, may be linked to changes in funerary ritual and display. It seems likely that an early Anglo-Saxon funeral involving grave-goods would have centred around the viewing of the *tableau* of the body laid out in the grave with the grave-goods neatly displayed around it. This would provide a setting within which the consistent placing and ordering of the costume and additional grave-goods could be viewed and appreciated by the community, helping to reinforce their symbolic content. Those earlier furnished graves which do have coffins often have large and complex grave *tableau* in which the coffin is just one element; it does not serve to hide the other grave-goods.

As grave-goods declined, the viewing of the *tableau* within the grave may have become less important; there would have been less for the mourners to see. A modern funeral, by contrast, centres around the lowering of the body into the grave; this kind of activity is made more decorous by the use of a container or wrapping which hides the body itself.

The northern group

The northern group of burials came from the area of buildings 1 and 2 (Loveluck and Atkinson, Chapter 4, this volume). In contrast to the southern group, the six northern burials enjoyed a much more favourable soil environment and generally survived in better condition. They included an adult woman in her twenties, a peri-natal infant, a three- to four-year-old, a nine-year-old and two eleven- to twelve-year-olds (see section 8.2, below). All of the children could have been under twelve, the probable age at which Anglo-Saxon children may have achieved adult status (Crawford 1991). Although the northern burial area was close to the edges of the excavation and may well have continued further to the south and east, it can be stated with confidence that the excavated group had a high proportion of children.

Grave-cuts were easily observable for the northern group, and four graves could be seen to be associated with building 1, a building of unusual and perhaps high-status construction which was demolished and rebuilt on the same site. The earlier phase of this structure is known as building 1a, and the later as building 1b. These four graves (1960, 3580, 4010 and 3706) were all dug through the demolition deposits of the Period 2 (late seventh to

early eighth century) building 20, which pre-dated the period 3 (early eighth to early ninth century) building 1a. Grave 1960 (an eleven- to twelve-year-old child) had the clearest stratigraphy; it cut the gravel foundation of building 1a, but was sealed by a padstone belonging to the footings of building 1b. Grave 3580 (the adult woman; FIG. 8.1*) was dug through the occupation layer belonging to the floor of building 1a. Grave 4010 (the nine-year-old; FIG. 8.2*) either cut or abutted the line of the internal wall that divided building 1a into an eastern and a western room; this grave could have been contemporary either with building 1a or 1b, but the balance of probabilities is thought to rest with 1a. The construction of building 1b does not appear to have been influenced by any knowledge of the location of the graves (Loveluck and Atkinson, Chapter 4, this volume). There is not enough stratigraphic data for Grave 3706 (the peri-natal infant) to be certain of its relationships. One further grave, 3878 (an eleven-year-old; FIG. 8.3*), was found outside the south-western corner of building 1a. It has been tentatively linked to that building.

The final burial, 2231/2 (the three- to four-year-old), was found disturbed in the upper fills of post-hole 2230. This post-hole belonged to building 19, a phase 1b (mid to late seventh century) building which was later replaced by building 2. Building 2 stood to the east of, and on the same axis as, building 1, and was contemporary with building 1b. Grave 2231/2 was internal to building 2, and about 13m from the eastern wall of building 1b. The grave is thought most likely to have been contemporary with building 1a, but to have settled or sunk downwards into the soft filling of the earlier post-hole.

All of the undisturbed graves, apart from Grave 3706 (the peri-natal infant), were aligned with building 1 and so were nearly west-east. Grave 3706 lay south-west to north-east. Three of the graves had enough bone surviving to show details of layout, and all were supine with the head to the west. Grave 3878, the eleven-year-old buried outside building 1, had bent legs and also perhaps bent arms. The best-preserved graves, 3580 and 4010, had conventional layouts, with no good evidence either for wrapping or coffins.

Three of the children (1960, 2231/2 and 4010) had osteological evidence of *cribra orbitalia*, probably associated with gut infections or a heavy intestinal parasite load. There is osteological evidence that the adult woman buried in Grave 3580 had suffered from an episode of disease or poor nutrition at two to three years old (dental enamel hypoplasia), had carried out strenuous physical activity, probably heavy lifting (Schmorl's nodes), and had perhaps suffered from tuberculosis (possible calcified lymph node). There is no osteological evidence for the cause of her death, as advanced tuber-culosis would have caused further bony changes. The nearness of her grave to Grave 3706, the peri-natal infant, may suggest that the two are related and that both the deaths occurred during the infant's birth. This is possible, but can remain no more than conjecture which may be weakened by the different alignment of the infant's grave; it may simply be that the woman died at the same time as one or more of the children, or was considered to be in some way child-like or similarly marginal to adult society.

Special burial areas for children

There are some parallels to the special treatment of children at Flixborough. The best known is Whithorn, where the remains of 56 children were excavated from an area immediately to the east of a building interpreted as a burial chapel (Hill 1997, 162–72). Bone preservation was not particularly good, but the determinable ages of the Whithorn children, like those at Flixborough, ranged from peri-natal to 9–12 years old. There was also a high incidence of *cribra orbitalia* among the Whithorn children, which contrasted with children from the later medieval cemetery nearby. It was suggested by Cardy that among the reasons for this might be a poorer diet, greater numbers of intestinal parasites, different disease patterns, or even Whithorn's early fame as a healing centre (Cardy in Hill 1997, 557–9). As at Flixborough, the Whithorn child burials were associated with a building, but they were outside rather than within it (Hill 1997, 170–2).

The cemetery at Church Walk, Hartlepool, also had an area apparently reserved for children, with a group of 31 children including 19 infants under two years old (Daniels 1992; R. Daniels pers. comm.). Another children's cemetery was found in Pontefract (Geake 1997, 191). Twenty infants were buried close to the western end of a probable church; from a combination of radiocarbon-dating and stratigraphical relationships they are considered to date from the ninth or tenth century. They represented a phase of burial within a cemetery that appears to have begun (from a radiocarbon date derived from a burial in a re-used chest) in the late seventh century, stratigraphically pre-dating the church; the infant burials date from a reorganisation of the cemetery when the church was built. The partially excavated Cemetery 2 at Brandon (not known to have been associated with a church, but focused around a building which may have been a mortuary chapel) also contained a high proportion of infants or juveniles (Carr *et al.* 1988).

Judging by the fairly consistent under-representation of young children in early Anglo-Saxon cemeteries (Crawford 1991), there seems to have been a difference in the treatment of their bodies compared to the bodies of adults. It is possible that this difference continued into the eighth and ninth centuries, albeit in another guise. Although children were still specially treated at this later date, they were no longer invisible, and are identifiable in the archaeological record. John Blair has drawn attention to a possible historical echo of this practice in Bede's *Historia Ecclesiastica*, where infant children of the royal house of Northumbria in the early seventh century are, unusually, recorded as being buried in churches (*HE* II, 14; Blair 2005, 62, note 204).

The status of Building 1

Building 1a measured about 14m by 6m, and had the unusual construction technique of a gravel footing on which a sill-beam was placed. Its subsequent rebuilding appears to have replaced the sill-beam with an interrupted sill-beam placed on intermittent padstones. These construction techniques were probably adopted in an attempt to prolong the life of the sill-beam. Experiments carried out by Stanley West at West Stow in Suffolk, on a similar sandy soil, have shown that the effective life-span of building timbers depends on how dry they can be kept (West 2001). The use of this unusual technique for Building 1 can therefore perhaps be attributed to a desire to prolong its life.

Building 1a had an internal division formed of earth-fast post-holes, dividing it into an eastern room and a western room of approximately equal size. Both building 1a and building 1b had a hearth; in building 1a the hearth was central to the eastern room, but in building 1b the hearth was just to the east of, and lying partly over, the line of the former internal wall.

Building 1, in both its manifestations, therefore looks like an ordinary, if carefully built, domestic building. Could it have been a church? And, if not, why should it have received a small number of human burials around it?

There are few parallels in England to which we can turn for help in interpreting building 1. Timber buildings that are interpreted as early local churches, but which do not have later stone phases, are rare; they tend to be identified by a bicameral plan, with two rooms of unequal sizes, as well as by the presence of graves around them – e.g. at Cowage Farm near Malmesbury (Hinchliffe 1986), or Brandon (Carr *et al.* 1988). Building 1 does not look anything like these. Even if it were to be suggested that the division of the space into two has similarities with these possible bicameral churches, the hearth in the eastern half still has to be explained away.

The structures with which building 1 has the most obvious affinities are Buildings D2 and B5 at Yeavering in Northumberland. Both are of similar size to building 1, are single-celled (although Building B5 later had a western annexe added), and are interpreted as a pagan temple and a Christian church respectively. Both buildings, however, are notable for their lack of domestic occupation debris and hearths (Hope-Taylor 1977, 98 and 168).

Even if building 1 could be a church, the lack of radiocarbon-dating for the southern group of burials at Flixborough hampers our discussion of the status of building 1. If they are contemporary with the northern group, we could ask why (if building 1 was a church) it did not attract the majority of the burials of the Flixborough community. If they are earlier, we might be seeing the establishment of a short-lived church then attracting burials, although why it appears preferentially to attract children is an unanswered question. If the southern group is later, why was building 1 abandoned as a burial focus?

Could the Flixborough building alternatively have been built for more specialist use as a burial chapel? There is a record of a mortuary church being built by Archbishop Cuthbert at Canterbury (Morris 1989, 88), and there is both documentary record and excavated evidence for the eighth-century 'mausoleum' at Repton (Biddle 1986, 16). The building at Whithorn that is interpreted as a burial chapel, which like building 1 was also of unusual construction, was half the size of building 1, with internal measurements of 5m by 4m (Hill 1997, 164–5). It had no hearth. At Wells, the suggested mortuary chapel had internal measurements of no more than 3m by 4m (Blair 1996, 7) and, again, no hearth. All these excavated burial chapels were built of stone, but there is another possible example at Thwing (Manby 1987) which measures only 3.5m by 2m.

Religious buildings of the eighth and ninth centuries, however, should perhaps not be expected to look much like each other. John Blair has drawn our attention to the ephemeral, 'vernacular' nature of early local churches, although evidence for these is rarely earlier than the tenth century (Blair 1996, 12–13). As vernacular buildings they may draw on a much wider range of building traditions than those of episcopal centres or royal monasteries.

Alternatively, building 1 could have had more than one use during its life. None of the burials associated with building 1 has to post-date its rebuilding. It seems possible that the building could have been carefully built and intentionally designed as some kind of focus for burial, and then later converted into a domestic building with the addition of an internal partition and a hearth. The subsequent careful rebuilding and conversion into a single large room would therefore belong to its later domestic use. Another possibility, although one without obvious English parallel, is that for some reason a domestic building attracted human burials.

To sum up, then, the possibilities for building 1 are various; an odd form of church, or an odd form of burial chapel, or a church quickly converted to domestic use, or a domestic building which attracted burials. None of these options is entirely satisfactory on their own, but when they are compared with other evidence for eighth- and ninth-century burial, some patterns may be discerned.

The burials considered together

The relationship between the two groups of burials
Why did some of the people living in the Flixborough area bury their dead around building 1, and others in the southern cemetery? This question is difficult to answer satisfactorily. The study of burial in the seventh to ninth centuries began comparatively recently, and is still at an early and unformed stage. In contrast, the study of early Anglo-Saxon burial began in the late eighteenth century; but, despite its current level of sophistication, there is

still little that can be said about links between particular cemeteries and settlements, or particular groups of people and their burial practices. In many cases it is simply assumed that a discrete settlement would have used a single discrete cemetery, despite the fact that large-scale excavations have shown that the notion of simple nucleated cemeteries or settlements may be the exception rather than the rule – e.g. Mucking (Hamerow 1993; Hirst and Clark forthcoming) and Eriswell/Lakenheath (Martin *et al.* 1998, 229–31; 2000, 520–1; 2002, 219–21).

It may be expected, then, that few suggestions can be made about the relationship between the two areas of burial at Flixborough. There appears to have been little difference in status between the two areas, but, as social status does not appear to have been expressed through the Flixborough graves, this is unsurprising. A suggestion could be made from the osteological evidence that the burials around building 1 were of lower status than those in the southern group; children and a woman who appeared to have had a stressful or physically arduous life could be interpreted as socially marginal. But without comparable osteological evidence from the southern group, this suggestion is essentially unsupportable. It is possible that children (particularly the newly baptised) could be seen, instead, as more innocent or more holy than society in general.

The most obvious explanation is that the two areas are simply the result of the excavation strategy; two areas were examined within one cemetery. There is no reason not to favour this suggestion; there is no evidence for a gap in the distribution of the graves, and the nature of the burials (apart from the ages of the people buried) is very similar. There is of course no particular reason in favour of this argument, either, given that unfurnished west-east supine burials are all bound to look rather similar. Furthermore, no additional graves were disturbed during construction of earth-fast buildings, or the cutting of pits and other features in the southern zone of the site, during the ninth century. Some of these features cut the area to the south of building 1; for example, building 10a, and no graves or human skeletal remains were disturbed (Loveluck and Atkinson, Chapters 4, 5 and 6, this volume; Loveluck, Volume 4, Chapter 3). Whether or not the burials all belong to one large cemetery, however, we still have a detectable degree of zoning within it, as the northern group contains a very low proportion of adults.

The relationship between the excavated burials and earlier or later burials at Flixborough
The presence of residual sixth-century metalwork in later phases at Flixborough hints at the possibility of an earlier settlement or cemetery nearby. There was a brief flurry of interest in the reasons behind the establishment and abandonment of migration-period cemeteries in the 1970s and 1980s (Faull 1976; Morris 1983, 52–4), but little work on this subject has appeared recently; there seems

to be a consensus that the reasons were complex, and therefore not amenable to generalisation. One generalisation can, however, be made. By about AD 720 it seems that all cemeteries with origins in the sixth century had been abandoned. No burial site which can be demonstrated to have been in use in or after the mid eighth century had pre-seventh-century origins, and very few were founded before the middle of the seventh century (Geake 1997, 18).

There are, however, cemeteries founded in the seventh century which are still in use today. It is a moot point whether these grew up around churches founded in the seventh century (as at Waltham Abbey), or whether later foundations were added to a pre-existing cemetery (as appears to have been the case at Pontefract). In either case, it is the presence of the church which has guaranteed the survival of the cemetery. At Flixborough the presence of All Saints would have been an attractive focus for burial, and it must be considered likely that the apparent cessation of burial in the excavated area was connected in some way with a precursor to the later medieval church up on the ridge.

The interpretation of settlement character and status from the burials

There has been much speculation about the 'character' of occupation at Flixborough – monastery, aristocratic estate centre, trading centre, village? Although it has now been shown that Flixborough had a complicated and shifting set of characters (Loveluck 2001, and Loveluck 2003, 17–19; Loveluck, Volume 4, Chapter 9), one of the more popular interpretations in the past has been that of an undocumented monastery (Whitwell 1991, 247; Yorke 1993, 146; Blair 1996, 9). As one of the functions of monasteries or minsters was to provide burial *ad sanctos*, the burial evidence is important in a discussion of the settlement's character and status.

A reasonably large number of cemeteries from documented monastic centres have now been excavated (see list below). Few, however, have reached final publication, and it is often difficult to disentangle later from earlier burials in cemeteries which can be very long-lived. In addition, excavation areas tend not to include the whole of a cemetery; a sea of endless inter-cutting graves is expensive and often not considered particularly rewarding to excavate (Morris 1983, 50–1; O'Brien 1996, 161–2).

Despite this, it seems possible that two characteristics of the cemeteries known from documented seventh- to ninth-century monasteries are their comparatively large size and their rigorous organisation. These features are visible at Monkwearmouth, Jarrow, Winchester Old Minster, Repton, Brixworth and Hartlepool; there are hints of similar size and organisation at Whitby (Stopford 2000, 104) and Ripon (Hall and Whyman 1996). The excavated areas at Flixborough do not share these characteristics.

Another possible characteristic of a monastic cemetery

is an age, sex and pathology range which differs from a normal mixed community. Although the sample at Flixborough is very small, it contains both sexes, and all ages, and does not have any unusual disabling pathologies. From this small sample of excavated burials, then, Flixborough has little claim to be an undocumented monastery of the type with which we are familiar.

The wider picture

The human burials from Flixborough, although small in number, can therefore shed light on questions of the settlement's character and zoning. They can also help to answer questions about the feelings of the living population towards their dead. When looked at in the context of comparable sites across the Anglo-Saxon culture-province and beyond, they can help in the study of wider questions; about changing attitudes to the burial of the dead, the development of churchyard burial, and the rise of Christianity as the driving force behind political and personal life in early medieval England and Europe.

There are a number of potential sites with evidence for human burial similar to that at Flixborough. A rough count reveals at least 70 sites across England and southern Scotland with comparable groups of unfurnished burials dating from the seventh to early ninth century (bibliographies for most sites in Geake 1997; page references are to this, except where stated otherwise).

The list includes large cemeteries from sites of recorded monasteries, such as the famous sites of Monkwearmouth (184–5), Jarrow (185), Whitby (190–1; Stopford 2000), Hartlepool (148), Whithorn (151; Hill 1997), Repton (149) and Winchester Old Minster (156); and also the less well-known sites of Dacre (148), Carlisle (148), Rochester (165), Cirencester (153), Lichfield (Nenk *et al.* 1995, 241), Wells (177), St Mary Major in Exeter (150), St Augustine's Abbey in Canterbury (162), and perhaps Brixworth (171) and Breedon-on-the-Hill (167).

Other large groups of burials, particularly those close to buildings which can be interpreted as churches, are also thought of as early churchyards. Examples include Waltham Abbey (previously thought to have been founded as a monastery by Harold II) and Nazeingbury (interpreted as an unrecorded nunnery and hospital), both in Essex (152 and 151); various cemeteries in the *Hamwic* area of Southampton (155–6); Castle Green, Hereford (157); St Pancras, Canterbury (162); Red Castle, Thetford (171); Yeavering (172–3); Christ Church, Oxford (174); Beckery, Somerset (176); Brandon, Suffolk (177–8); and The Booths in Pontefract (191).

No church has yet been suggested for some similar large cemeteries. Examples without churches include Sedgeford (Faulkner 1997; Cox *et al.* 1998; Biddulph 1999), Burgh Castle (178) and Caister-on-Sea (169–70), all in Norfolk; Beacon Hill, Lewknor, Oxfordshire (Blair 1994, 70–3); Burrow Hill, Butley, Suffolk (178); and Newcastle Castle (185). Saffron Walden (152), a cemetery of at least 200 burials with hardly any grave-goods, which may have been used at any time from the Roman period to the tenth century, may also belong to this group.

There are also groups of burials which appear to pre-date much later churches (e.g. Wicken Bonhunt (153), Elstow Abbey (144), and St Bride's Church in London (169)), as well as burials which are in the vicinity of an existing or historically known church and are often presumed to have been related to it – e.g. Addingham (191; Adams 1996), Ailcy Hill and perhaps the Ladykirk, both in Ripon (Hall and Whyman 1996), Aylesbury (145; Allen and Dalwood 1983), Northampton (Williams *et al.* 1985) and Rivenhall (152).

Smaller groups of burials are found in and around prehistoric earthworks (most famously in East Yorkshire – Thwing, Kemp Howe, Garton-on-the-Wolds and also possibly Fimber (all 158-9) – but also at Bevis's Grave long barrow at Bedhampton in Hampshire (154), and at the Milfield South henge in Northumberland (172)). Cuddesdon in Oxfordshire may also fall into this group; although it was spectacularly badly recorded when it was first encountered in 1847, Dickinson has since recon-structed it as a number of unfurnished and undated burials focused on a rich or 'princely' barrow-burial of the early seventh century (174; Dickinson 1974).

There are also small enigmatic groups of burials which cannot be related to any known activity and are of uncertain (but presumed Anglo-Saxon) date. Examples include Avon Farm, Saltford (144); Calver Low, Derby-shire (148); Bourton-on-the-Water, Gloucestershire (153); Littleton, Hampshire (154); Garton II (Green Lane Crossing), East Yorkshire (158); Framlingham, Suffolk (178); Alfriston I, Sussex (183); Monkton Deverill (186) and Roche Court Down III (187), both in Wiltshire; and Lamel Hill on the outskirts of York (190). These sites have often been dated by means of a single grave-good, usually a knife or buckle. Similar, but completely unfurnished, graves have occasionally been radiocarbon-dated to the seventh to early ninth centuries, such as the four burials from Saltergate, Lincoln (168), and two from South Gate, Winchester (156).

These small groups of graves, perhaps with a few grave-goods, are hard to distinguish from less sparsely furnished cemeteries such as Portsdown I, Hampshire (154); Dorchester IV (174) and Yelford (176), both in Oxfordshire; Blackhorse Road, Letchworth (157); Bromfield, Shropshire (176); Bury St Edmunds I (178); Glynde (183) and Ocklynge Hill (183–4), both in Sussex; and Winkelbury in Wiltshire (188). The continuum may run right up to famous cemeteries with many well-furnished graves, such as Buckland, Dover (Evison 1987) or Harford Farm (Penn 2000). It is difficult, however, to draw conclusions when excavation areas are small, and we do not know if we are dealing with a small part of a larger cemetery which may have had many well-furnished graves in another area, or a cemetery which never consisted of more than a few poorly furnished graves. We

can, for instance, say that furnished graves datable to later than about AD 720 are not found, but that does not mean that sparsely furnished (and hence difficult to date) graves could not continue to have been used later than this.

There are of course many other completely unfurnished burials, or groups of burials, which have never been dated satisfactorily, due to the difficulty of obtaining strati-graphic dates on plough-damaged sites, the expense of radiocarbon-dating, and the lack of research interest in single burials or small groups (although this may now be changing; see Blair 2005, 243–4). Because of the doubts about their date, they cannot feature in this discussion. Examples are by their nature hard to collect, but include, for example, Ormesby in Norfolk (Nenk *et al.* 1997, 279; for other examples, see Blair 2005, 244, note 274, and 465, note 175). Without radiocarbon-dating, these burials seem doomed to earthly limbo.

When this corpus of sites with few or no grave-goods is compared to the numbers of Anglo-Saxon burial sites as a whole, it is evident that we are extrapolating from a rather small sample. There are now over 350 known burial sites of seventh- to early ninth-century date (Geake 1997), but most have been identified through their grave-goods and are therefore the fairly well-furnished sites of the seventh and early eighth centuries. The comparative rarity of burials securely dated to the eighth and ninth centuries, before the widespread establishment of churches in the tenth century, has long been noted (Morris 1983, 49–62; Geake 2002; Blair 2005, 228). It seems possible that small groups of poorly furnished or unfurnished burials may have been the norm at this date in both England and on the Continent, and that the small numbers of known sites are due to the comparative difficulty of recognising them.

Theories based on this small group will inevitably be tentative, but there are some hypotheses that can be suggested. It seems that settlements and burial places became much more closely integrated, which may reflect a differing attitude of the living towards the dead (Morris 1983, 53). This is very different from the general pattern during the fifth and sixth centuries, where the impression in some places is, of the reservation of large blocks of landscape solely for the dead. There are, of course, always exceptions – there are a very few earlier Anglo-Saxon settlements, such as Carlton Colville in Suffolk (Mortimer and Tipper in Martin *et al.* 1999, 368–9), where a group of graves has been found surrounded by living space – but the situation at Flixborough, with graves scattered around what appear to have been domestic buildings, is a new development. It seems possible that this integration of the dead and the living in one area may have developed into the later medieval pattern of a church and graveyard within a settlement.

The observed pattern of integration of the dead and the living, however, may not have been particularly intentional. The hypothesis which best fits the evidence at present is one of relatively varied burial location. There seems to have been a rigorous control of the siting and arrangement of Anglo-Saxon graves throughout the Migration Period (Geake 2003). In the following centuries, it has often been noted that the Church took very little interest in regulating burial (Bullough 1983, 186–7; Morris 1983, 50). By the tenth or eleventh century, however, effective control appears to have been regained, with highly organised burial in churchyards. What happened in between?

On present evidence there appears to have been some variety or, perhaps, confusion. After the closure of cemeteries with furnished graves around AD 720, a variety of strategies were adopted. Burial *ad antecessores*, rather than *ad sanctos*, seems to have been used by a few, particularly perhaps in East Yorkshire; burial around churches by others. Blair sees a slow increase in the numbers of lay burials in church-related cemeteries, joining the burials of clerics there (Blair 2005, 58–65 and 228–45), but the difficulty of distinguishing lay and clerical burial hampers our interpretation here. Many of the dead of the eighth and ninth centuries may be going unrecognised, having been casually disposed of (as at South Gate, Winchester; Geake 1997, 156) or buried in small, perhaps family plots. The major monasteries, with their large and well-organised cemeteries, may have provided some measure of security for those allowed to bury their dead within, but the overall picture until the mass building of local churches is one of uncertainty, or perhaps choice, over where burial should take place.

The significance of the few known eighth- and ninth-century burial sites is enormous. Due to the importance of the afterlife in Christian culture, the developing attitudes of the living to the dead should reflect the growing status of Christianity in both personal and political life. Other apparent continuities, such as the differential treatment of children, should alert us to the possible continuing influence of earlier burial practices. Flixborough itself, at present, appears to be unique in England in its focus of burial around an apparently domestic building, or one that quickly became domestic, but it is comparable to other sites of this date in its unexpected and various burial choices. Flixborough undoubtedly has the potential to contribute much more to our study of Mid Anglo-Saxon burial practices, and it is to be hoped that further excavation may one day take place there.

8.2 The osteology of the human burials
by Simon Mays

Introduction

In 1988, 10 inhumation burials were recovered from an evaluation trench, excavated in advance of sand-quarrying. [An additional grave was excavated and recorded in 1988, but no bone survives from this, to be included in this study.] These inhumations appear to represent part of a cemetery of unknown size. Between 1989 and 1991, further excavations at the site revealed substantial remains of part of a high-status Anglo-Saxon settlement. Four inhumations were located within one of the buildings (designated 'building 1'), with a further burial just outside it. There was also a burial in the vicinity of another building ('building 19'). The most intensive phases of occupation within the excavated area date from between the seventh and the early eleventh centuries AD. The burials associated with the settlement date from the period between the early-mid eighth century, and the cemetery burials are also thought to be Mid Saxon.

Methods

Amongst the adults, sex was determined using the morphology of the pelvic bones and skull (Brothwell 1981). It is not feasible to sex immature remains reliably using skeletal morphology. For the adults, stature was estimated from long-bone lengths using the regression equations of Trotter and Gleser (reproduced in Brothwell 1981, 101). Age was determined for the infant burial from long-bone lengths, using the linear regression equations of Scheuer *et al.* (1980), and for the juveniles by using dental development (Gustafson and Koch 1974). In adults, age was estimated from dental wear (Brothwell 1981, fig. 3.9). The more important pathological changes observed are noted in the main body of the report; the more minor ones are listed in archive, held at the English Heritage Centre for Archaeology. Cranial and post-cranial measurements were taken according to Brothwell (1981), and non-metric variants were recorded according to the definitions of Berry and Berry (1967) and Finnegan (1978). These results are held in archive (English Heritage, Centre for Archaeology, Fort Cumberland, Portsmouth).

Results

a) The burials from the cemetery:

FIG. 8.4. *Skeletal survival, demography and dental pathology data for the cemetery burials (Simon Mays).*

Burial	Pres	Compl.	Age	Sex	Stat.	Caries	Tloss
Grave 1	P	<10%	30–40	M?	-	0/4	1/8
Grave 2	P	<10%	25–35	-	-	0/2	-
Grave 3	P	<10%	ADULT	-	-	-	-
Grave 4	P	<10%	25–35	F	-	3/14	0/6
Grave 5	P	<10%	17–25	-	-	0/6	-
Grave 6	P	<10%	-	-	-	-	-
Grave 7	P	<10%	50–60	M	-	1/3	4/13
Grave 8	P	<10%	20–30	-	-	0/2	-
Grave 9	P	<10%	ADULT	-	-	1/1	1/3
Grave 10	P	<10%	ADULT	M	-	0/2	1/6

KEY: Pres = bone preservation, assessed from gross examination of the skeleton on a subjective scale according to the degree of surface erosion on the bones: G = good, M = moderate, P = Poor; Compl. = Approximate skeletal completeness; Age = approximate age at death, in years unless stated; Sex: M = males, F = female, - = unsexed; Stat. = approximate stature in cm; Caries: presented as number of carious teeth over number of teeth present; Tloss = *ante-mortem* tooth loss: presented as number of teeth lost *ante mortem* over number of tooth positions observable.

NOTES: Grave 7: Both hip joints show severe osteoarthritis, with eburnation, pitting and osteophyte formation.

b) The burials from the settlement:

FIG. 8.5. *Skeletal survival, demography and dental pathology for the settlement burials (Simon Mays).*

Burial	Loc.	Pres.	Comp.	Age	Sex	Stat.	Caries	Tloss
1960	Int	P	<20%	11–12	-	-	0/18	0/8
2231/2	Ext	G	<20%	3–4	-	-	0/4	0/10
3580	Int	G	80%+	20–30	F	167	2/31	0/31
3706	Int	G	80%+	38–39wiu	-	-	-	-
3878	Ext	P	20–40%	c11	-	-	3/19	0/20
4010	Int	G	80%+	c9	-	-	0/24	0/24

KEY: as for FIG. 8.4 except: Loc = location: Int = within building, Ext = outside building; Age: for perinatal infant burial 3706: wiu = weeks *in utero*.

NOTES:

1960: There is cribra orbitalia of the porotic type (Brothwell 1981, fig. 6.17). This is likely to be associated with iron deficiency anaemia (Stuart-Macadam 1989), the most common cause of which is not lack of dietary iron, but gut infections or heavy parasite infestation which prevent adequate uptake of iron from food (Stuart-Macadam 1992).

2231/2: There is a small deposit of woven bone on the internal surface of the right parietal, in the sagittal sulcus in the region of the lambda. This is indicative of an intra-cranial infection which was active at time of death. There is also cribra orbitalia (see entry for burial 1960) of Brothwell's (1981, fig. 6.17) cribriotic type.

3580: There is slight new bone deposition in the left maxillary sinus – sinusitis. A flattened ovoid bony fragment, approximately 18 × 10 × 14mm was recovered with the bones from the upper right side of the body of this individual. The outer surface of the fragment is somewhat pitted and irregular. It has a small hollow cavity at its centre. The identity of this calcified mass is unclear. It does not have the smooth outer surface which is seen on calcified hydatid cysts. One possibility is that it represents a calcified lymph node, as may occur, for example, in tuberculosis.

There is a shallow depression on the inferior surface of the body of the second lumbar vertebra, at its anterior margin. The bone in this area is pitted and sclerotic, probably an avulsion injury of the vertebral end-plate (Maat and Mastwijk 2000). This individual also shows Schmorl's nodes on six of the thoracic and three of the lumbar vertebrae. These too are likely to be a result of injury to the back.

There is a small, raised nodule on the medial surface of the right tibia near the junction of its middle and proximal thirds. The bone here is striated and pitted. This represents well-remodelled periostitis, probably secondary to local injury and infection.

There is a depressed band of dental enamel, located between 4.5 and 5.0mm from the cemento-enamel junction on the maxillary first incisor. This represents dental enamel hypoplasia, a disturbance in the formation of the enamel tooth crown. The location of the defect suggests that it occurred when this individual was about 2–3 years old (Skinner and Goodman 1992, fig. 6). Dental enamel hypoplasias form in response to episodes of disease or poor nutrition, so burial 3580 seems to have suffered some such trauma during this period of her childhood.

4010: There is cribra orbitalia (see notes for burial 1960, above), of the trabecular type (Brothwell 1981, fig. 6.17). Hyperplasia of the cancellous bone in the orbits is clearly visible at post-depositional breaks.

Discussion

The bones from context 2231/2, the deposit which had slumped into the fill of a former post-hole of building 19, consist of fragments making up most of a cranium (i.e. the skull without the mandible), plus the first two cervical vertebrae. The cervical vertebrae and the cranium clearly come from the same individual. This deposit may comprise:

a. All that remains *in situ* of an inhumation burial, the lower parts of which have been truncated by later feature(s).

b. Re-deposited material from an inadvertently disturbed inhumation burial.

c. The deliberate deposit of a severed head.

Scenario (c) can be excluded. If the deposit was of a fleshed or partially fleshed head, then one would expect the mandible to be present, particularly as the top two vertebrae were recovered, or else there to be signs of its forcible removal. There were no such cut-marks, nor were there any other signs of anthropogenic interference with the skull. If the interment comprised a severed head, one would also expect to find signs of cut-marks on the vertebrae where the head was severed, but none was found, despite the fact that the excellent preservation of these parts means that had even quite subtle marks been present, they would have been apparent.

Deliberate deposition of the skull in a dry state once the flesh had decayed (as has been found on a Romano-British site: Mays and Steele 1996) is not likely. Under such circumstances, the top two vertebrae would not be expected to travel with it.

Option (b) is unlikely, but not impossible. Although, with re-deposition of bones from an old inhumation, we would not normally expect to find the top two vertebrae still associated with the skull.

Option (a) is the most likely explanation for this deposit – i.e. that the mandible and all parts distal to the second cervical vertebrae were truncated by later activity, leaving only the cranium and atlas and axis vertebrae *in situ*. In a supine burial, the mandible lies somewhat distal to the uppermost cervical vertebra, especially if, as so often happens, the lower jaw falls open during decomposition of the body. It is easy to imagine how the cutting of a later feature might remove the mandible and all parts distal to the top two vertebrae. Deposit 2231/2 therefore probably represents a truncated child burial.

It is notable that in general, bone survival in the cemetery burials is much less good than in most of those from the settlement. In all 10 cemetery burials, only bone fragments, mainly of skull and long-bones, survived. Bone survival was in general much better for the settlement inhumations, with many showing negligible erosion of bone surfaces. Buried bone is sensitive to soil pH: acid soils being hostile to bone, whereas bone survival is often good under alkaline conditions (Mays 1998, 17–18). Soil samples from the cemetery itself are, un-

fortunately, unavailable, so pH values here cannot be directly determined, but analyses of natural soils from the settlement showed that they may be somewhat acidic near the surface where they are subject to leaching (Canti 1992; Canti, Chapter 2, this volume). In the area of the settlement, pH was found to be higher (i.e. it was more alkaline), apparently due to anthropogenic deposits of ash and other material (Canti 1992: Canti, Chapter 2, this volume). It is thus likely that differences in pH of the burial matrix made some contribution to the difference in bone survival between cemetery and settlement burials, although other as yet unidentified factors may also have been involved.

Of the 10 skeletons recovered from the cemetery, age could be estimated to some degree in nine of them. All these were adult. (For the present purposes the dividing line between juvenile and adult ages is placed at about 18 years, with any individual aged under 18 being classified as a juvenile.) All but one of the settlement interments were juveniles (FIG. 8.6).

	Cemetery	Settlement
Juvenile	0	5
Adult	9	1

FIG. 8.6. *Age composition of inhumations in the cemetery and settlement groups (Simon Mays).*

Fisher's exact test indicates that the difference in age composition between cemetery and settlement groups is statistically significant ($p=0.002$). When soil conditions are aggressive, there may be preferential destruction of the bones of immature individuals (Gordon and Buikstra 1981). In the cemetery, the burial environment was clearly more hostile to bone survival than it was in the settlement. It would seem then that the difference in preservation conditions may have been a factor in the difference observed in the demographic composition of the two samples. Another may have been differential recovery. Given the circumstances of excavation, it is quite possible that burials of infants and young children may have been overlooked during the 1988 excavations on the cemetery, and it is also worth noting that this area of the site had suffered from significant soil erosion, which may have acted selectively to remove the often shallower graves of young individuals. Therefore, the demographic difference between the cemetery and settlement burials may simply reflect post-depositional and recovery factors; it cannot be used to argue for differential burial practices in antiquity.

A hypothesis suggested by the principal author was that burial within building 1 might have been the prerogative of one particular lineage (Loveluck, Volume 4, Chapters 3 and 9). Burial together of closely related individuals is detectable from skeletal morphology in small collections of burials only if they come from a family who happen to show some rare skeletal variant. None of the burials from building 1 shows such a variant, so the question of the degree to which they are genetically related must be left open.

8.3 The coffin fittings

by Patrick Ottaway

with contributions by Jacqui Watson

The evaluation excavation in 1988 produced eleven inhumation burials, in one of which (Grave 1) the body was buried in a chest with iron fittings. They included two sets of hinges (Fɪɢ. 8.7, cat. no. 6 and nos 7–8: R12–14), a lock bolt (no. 12: R15) and a stapled hasp (no. 11: R16). The hinge straps are of the usual Anglo-Saxon type. The straps on the chest lid (nos 6 and 8: R12 and 14) had a link at the head which engaged with an eye at the head of the straps on the back of the chest (nos 6 and 7: R12–13), the eyes being formed, as is usual, by drawing out the head of the strap, folding it back over, and welding it to the side. All four straps have the commonest form known in the period, in that they narrow to rounded and pierced terminals at the base. Another strap of this form comes from the 1989–91 excavations (no. 10: RF 10847), and was found by metal-detecting quarry spoil – apparently associated with human bone. What is less common is the absence of a nail-hole near the head of the two straps numbered 6 and 7 (R12–13). This probably means they were held in place by staples, as in the case of hinge straps on a chest from an early Viking Age burial at Forlev, Denmark (Brøndsted 1936, fig. 103). No. 8 (R14) is pierced twice, as is usual, and one of the nails is bent in such a way as to suggest that the thickness of wood of the chest lid was 14mm.

The hinges seem to belong to two large chests or boxes, one being identified as made of oak (nos 6 and 7: R12–13). There was another smaller hinge (no. 8: R14) which possibly represents the back of another box. The wood grain was closely examined for carpentry evidence, but none was found other than that some of the structure may have been made from radial split timber as the main surface preserved is a radial section.

The hasp is L-shaped, the upper arm having been stapled to the lid of the chest, and a U-shaped staple survives *in situ*. The staple fitted to the lower arm would have engaged with the lock bolt (no. 12: R15) to keep the lid locked shut. The lock was of a form in which a sliding bolt was held in place by springs when locked (see Ottaway, Volume 2, Chapter 5). No other ironwork was found associated with the grave, apart from a small collar (no. 4: R18), and the chest timbers were probably jointed or dowelled, rather than nailed together.

Two other pairs of hinge straps (nos 5 and 9: R11 and 22) were found in the cemetery, not associated with any particular grave at the time of excavation, although they probably came from another chest re-used as a coffin. The strap from the back of the chest in no. 5 (R11) was unusual, in having the eye at the head made by punching, rather than as described above; it narrows slightly to a rounded base. The two straps making up no. 9 (R22) both narrow to a rounded, pierced terminal.

Although they are not numerous compared to other types of burial, inhumations employing a chest re-used as a coffin are well known in eighth- to tenth-century contexts (Ottaway 1996, 112–13). Sites where they have been recorded include Thwing, East Yorkshire, which produced 26 examples (Ottaway unpublished a), Carlisle Cathedral (Ottaway unpublished b), Dacre Priory, Cumbria (Ottaway, unpublished c), Monkwearmouth (Cramp 1969), Pontefract (Wilmott, in prep.), Repton, Derbyshire (unpublished, excavated by M. Biddle and B. Kjølbye-Biddle), Ailcy Hill, Ripon (Ottaway 1996), Winchester Cathedral Green (Kjølbye-Biddle pers. comm.), and York Minster (Kjølbye-Biddle 1995).

Chest burials often appear to be concentrated in certain locations in cemeteries (e.g. Dacre and Winchester), whilst in other cases (e.g. Repton, and Ripon) they have been found in a distinct cemetery within a sacred site containing other cemeteries. These factors, taken together with the status of many of the cemeteries themselves as belonging to monastic institutions (Dacre, Monkwearmouth, Repton and Ripon) or cathedrals (Carlisle, Winchester and York Minster), suggest that chest burials were usually reserved for people of distinct status, although how this was defined is unclear.

Catalogue (Fɪɢ. 8.7)

Clench bolt

1. Diamond-shaped rove and shank of rounded cross-section. L.61mm
    FX 88, R28, Context F4.

Staples

2. Rectangular. Arm tips in-turned. L.29, W.54mm
    FX 88, R20, U/S.
3. Incomplete. L.11, W.42mm
    FX 88, R58, U/S.

Collar

4. Sub-rectangular. L.50mm. Wood, grain running along arms and across middle. Possibly the staple was lying on a piece of wood, rather than joining two pieces of wood, end grain to end grain.
    FX 88, R18, Grave 1.

Hinge straps (Fɪɢ. 8.7)

Each pair of hinge straps includes one which was fitted to the chest lid and had a link at the head. This was set in the eye at the head of the strap attached to the chest back. The eye was usually formed by drawing out the head of the strap, looping it round, and welding it back on to the side of the strap, rather than by piercing the head of the strap. Both straps were pierced twice unless

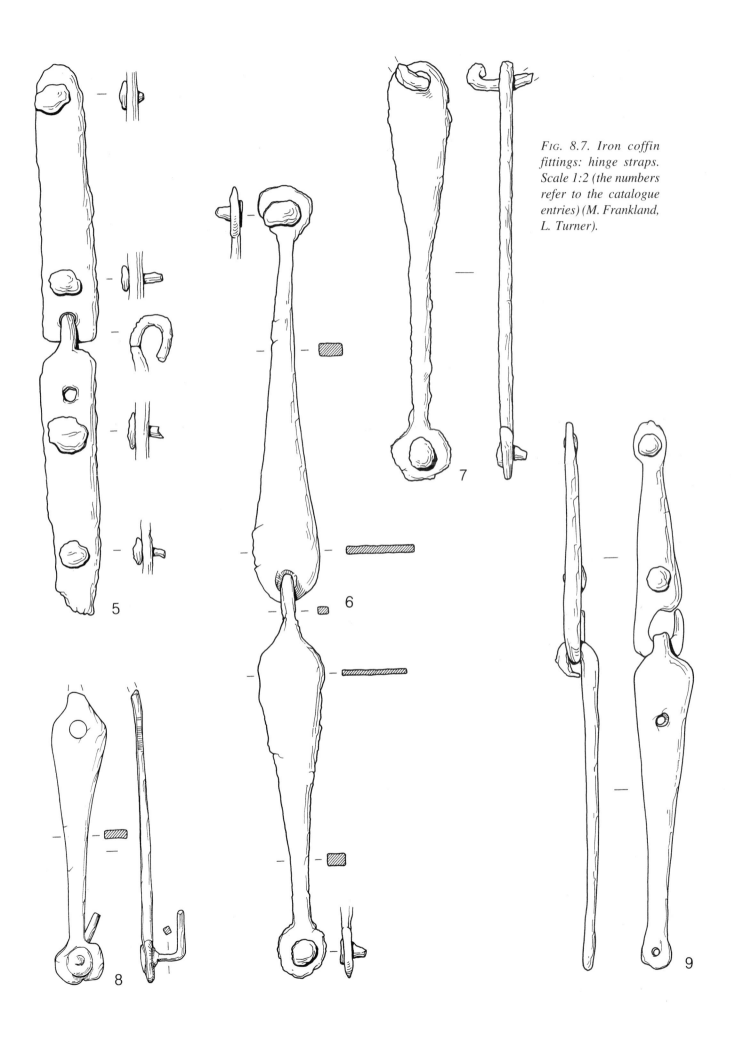

FIG. 8.7. Iron coffin fittings: hinge straps. Scale 1:2 (the numbers refer to the catalogue entries) (M. Frankland, L. Turner).

5

6

7

8

9

otherwise stated – once near the head, and once near the base, or in a terminal at the base.

5. Lid strap. Narrows towards the base which is missing; pierced three times. L.152, W.32mm. Back strap. Flat top, eye probably made by punching. Narrows slightly to a rounded base. L.180, W.34mm Wood remains preserved on one arm, grain running across the short side; RLS of a ring-porous wood. FX 88, R11, U/S.

6. Lid strap. narrows to a rounded, pierced terminal. Not pierced at the head. L.215, W.34mm Linked to back strap which narrows to a neat, rounded and pierced terminal and is not pierced at head. L.200, W.37mm. Wood remains survive on both straps. Wood running across and also around rivet shank. Radial section of *Quercus* sp. (oak). This probably belongs to the same box as no. 7. FX 88, R12, Grave 1.

7. Back strap. Narrows to a neat, rounded and pierced terminal and is not pierced at the head. Fragment of lid strap survives. L.219, W.34mm. Wood running across and also around rivet shank; Radial section of a ring-porous wood. FX 88, R13, Grave 1

8. Lid strap. Link missing, narrows to untidy rounded terminal with nail *in situ*. L.154, W.30mm. Wood running across and also around rivet shank; the wood is not identifiable, but the hinge has been mounted on a board *c.* 14mm thick. This hinge is smaller than nos 6–7, and probably represents the back of another box. FX 88, R14, Grave 1.

9. Lid strap. Narrows to a rounded, pierced terminal. L.180, W.34mm. Back strap. Narrows to a rounded, pierced terminal. Wood preserved on one arm, grain running across the short side; RLS of a ring-porous wood on the long arm, which is probably the back strap. L.131, W.33mm FX 88, R22, U/S.

10. Back strap. Narrows to a rounded, pierced terminal. Area on one side resembles tooled leather. Wood remains, RLS *Quercus* sp. (oak), grain across short width, either on top of leather or wood, with the grain running the other way. L.123, W.25mm RF 10847, Context U/S.

Stapled hasp
11. L-shaped. Head of upper arm has punched eye, U-shaped staple *in situ*. Lower arm widens and is incomplete. Arms: L.53 and 63, W.26mm. Traces of wood running across – just random slivers. FX 88, R16, Grave 1.

Lock bolt
See sliding bolts discussed in Volume 2, chapter 5.

12. Most of the central plate survives along with one arm which has a rolled tip. L.66, W.39mm. FX 88, R15, Grave 1.

Bibliography

Adams, M., 1996. 'Excavation of a pre-Conquest cemetery at Addingham, West Yorkshire', *Medieval Archaeology* 40, 151–91.

Adams Gilmour, L., 1988. *Early Medieval Pottery from Flaxengate, Lincoln,* The Archaeolgy of Lincoln 17/2, Trust for Lincolnshire Archaeology/CBA (London).

Addyman, P., with Fennel, K. R. and Biek, L., 1964. 'A Dark–Age settlement at Maxey, Northants, *Medieval Archaeology* 8 (for 1964), 20–73.

Aitken, M. J., 1974. *Physics and Archaeology* (2nd edition), Oxford: Clarendon Press.

Allen, D. and Dalwood, C. H., 1983. 'Iron Age occupation, a middle Saxon cemetery, and twelfth to nineteenth century urban occupation: excavations in George Street, Aylesbury, 1981', *Records of Buckinghamshire* 25, 1–60.

Bateman, M. D., 1998. 'The origin and age of coversand in North Lincolnshire, U.K.', *Permafrost and Periglacial Processes* 9, 313–325.

Bayley, J., 1992. *Non-ferrous Metalworking from Coppergate,* The Archaeology of York, Vol. 17: The Small Finds, Fasc. 7, York: York Archaeological Trust/ Council for British Archaeology.

Berry, A. C. and Berry, R. J., 1967. 'Epigenetic Variation in the Human Cranium', *Journal of Anatomy* 101, 361–79.

Biddle, M., 1986. 'Archaeology, architecture and the cult of saints in Anglo-Saxon England', in L. A. S. Butler and R. K. Morris (eds.), *The Anglo-Saxon Church,* 1–31, CBA Research Report 60, London: Council for British Archaeology.

Biddulph, E., 1999. 'Sedgeford Historical and Archaeological Research Project, third interim report (1998)', *Norfolk Archaeology* 43, 351–2.

Blair, J. 1994. *Anglo-Saxon Oxfordshire,* Stroud: Alan Sutton.

Blair, J., 1996. 'Churches in the early English landscape: social and cultural contexts', in J. Blair, and C. Pyrah, eds., *Church Archaeology – research directions for the future,* 6–18, CBA Research Report No. 104, York: Council for British Archaeology.

Blair, J., 2005, *The Church in Anglo-Saxon Society,* Oxford: Oxford University Press.

Böhner, K., 1955. 'Frühmittelalterliche Töpferen in Walberberg und Pingsdorf, *Bonner Jahrbücher* 155, 372–387.

Bourdieu, P., 1994. *Raisons Pratiques. Sur la théorie de l'action,* Paris: Seuil.

Bradley, J., 2005. *Archaeological Excavations at Little Conesby Moated Site, Normanby Enterprise Park, Scunthorpe, North Lincolnshire,* Humber Archaeology Report No. 163, Hull: Hull City Council.

Brochier, J. E., 1983. 'Bergeries et feux néolithiques dans le Midi de la France, caractérisation et incidence sur le raisonnment sédimentologique', *Quatar,* Band 33/34, 181–193.

Brøndsted, J., 1936. 'Danish inhumation graves of the Viking Age', *Acta Archaeologica* 7, 81–228.

Brothwell, D. R., 1981. *Digging Up Bones* (3rd edition), Oxford: Oxford University Press and British Museum.

Brown, D. H., 1994. 'Contexts, Their Contents and Residuality', *Interpreting Stratigraphy* 5, 1–8.

Buckland, P. C., 1982. 'The cover sands of north Lincolnshire and the Vale of York', in B. H. Adam, C. R. Fenn & L. Morris, eds., *Papers in Earth Sciences, Lovatt Lectures,* 143–78, Norwich: Geobooks.

Bullough, D., 1983. 'Burial, community and belief in the early medieval West', in P. Wormald, D. Bullough, and R. Collins, eds., *Ideal and Reality in Frankish and Anglo-Saxon Society* 177–201, Oxford: Oxford University Press.

Callmer, J., 1977. *Trade beads and bead trade in Scandinavia, ca. 800–1000 AD,* Acta Archaeologica Lundensia, Series 4, No. 11, Bonn, Lund.

Cameron, K. 1998. *A Dictionary of Lincolnshire Place-names,* Nottingham: English Place-name Society.

Canti, M. G., 1991. *Particle size analysis – a revised interpretative guide for excavators.* Ancient Monuments Lab. Rep. 1/91, London: English Heritage.

Canti, M. G., 1992. *Research into natural and anthropogenic deposits from excavations at Flixborough, Humberside,* Ancient Monuments Lab. Rep. 53/92, London: English Heritage.

Canti, M. G., 2003. 'Aspects of the chemical and microscopic characteristics of plant ashes found in archaeological soils', *Catena* 54, 339–361.

Cardy, A., 1997. 'The Human Bones', in D. Hill, *Whithorn & St Ninian – the excavation of a monastic town 1984–91,* 519–562, Stroud: The Whithorn Trust/Sutton.

Carr, R. D., Tester, A. and Murphy, P., 1988. 'The Middle Saxon settlement at Staunch Meadow, Brandon', *Antiquity* 62, No. 235, 371–377.

Catt, J. A., 1988. *Quaternary geology for scientists and engineers*, New York: John Wiley and Sons.

Chandler, J., 1993. *John Leland's Itinerary – Travels in Tudor England*, Stroud: Sutton.

Clark, A. J., 1992. 'Archaeogeophysical prospecting on alluvium', in S. Needham and M. G. Macklin, eds., *Alluvial Archaeology in Britain*, Oxbow Monograph 27, 43–49, Oxford: Oxbow Books.

Clark, A. J., 1996. *Seeing Beneath the Soil, Prospecting Methods in Archaeology* (revised edition), London: Batsford.

Coatsworth, E. and Pinder, M., 2002. *The Art of the Anglo-Saxon Goldsmith – Fine Metalwork in Anglo-Saxon England: its Practice and Practitioners*, Anglo-Saxon Studies 2, Woodbridge: The Boydell Press.

Coppack, G., 1986. 'St. Lawrence Church, Burnham, South Humberside – The excavation of a parochial chapel', *Lincolnshire History and Archaeology* 21, 39–60.

Coppack, G., 1987. 'Saxon and early medieval pottery', in G. Beresford, *Goltho – The development of an early medieval manor, c. 850–1150*, 134–169, English Heritage Archaeological Reports No. 4, London: Historic Buildings and Monuments Commission for England.

Cox, A., Fox, J., and Thomas, G., 1998. 'Sedgeford Historical and Archaeological Research Project, 1997 interim report', *Norfolk Archaeology* 43, 172–7.

Cramp, R. J., 1969. 'Excavations at the Saxon and monastic sites of Wearmouth and Jarrow, Co. Durham: an interim report', *Medieval Archaeology* 13, 21–66.

Crawford, S., 1991. 'When do Anglo-Saxon children count?', *Journal of Theoretical Archaeology* 2, 17–24.

Daniels, R. 1992. 'The Anglo-Saxon monastery at Hartlepool, England', in *Medieval Europe 1992, Pre-Printed Papers 6: Religion and Belief*, 171–6, York: University of York.

Darby, H. C., 1987. 'Domesday Book and the Geographer', in J. C. Holt, ed., *Domesday Studies*, 101–119, Woodbridge: The Boydell Press.

David, A., 1994. 'The role of geophysical survey in Early Medieval Archaeology', *Anglo-Saxon Studies in Archaeology and History* 7, 1–26.

Dickinson, T. M. 1974. *Cuddesdon and Dorchester-on-Thames, Oxfordshire: two early Saxon "princely" sites in Wessex*, British Archaeological Reports (British Series) 1, Oxford: British Archaeological Reports.

Down, A. and Welch, M. G., 1990. *Chichester Excavations VII: Apple Down and the Mardens*, Chichester: Sussex Archaeological Society.

Dudley, H. E., 1931. *The History & Antiquities of the Scunthorpe & Frodingham District* (1975 edition), Scunthorpe: Scunthorpe Borough Council.

Duggan, N., Fraser, J. and Steedman, K., 2001. *Archaeological Evaluation at the former Normanby Park Steelworks (phase II reclamation area) and the former railway sidings, Conesby Quarry, near Scunthorpe, North Lincolnshire*, Humber Archaeology Report No. 77, Hull: Hull City Council.

Ervynck, A., 1999. 'Possibilities and limitations of the use of archaeozoological data in biogeographical analysis: a review with examples from the Benelux region', *Belgian Journal of Zoology* 129, Issue 1, 125–138.

Evison, V., 1987. *Dover: The Buckland Anglo-Saxon Cemetery*, English Heritage Archaeological Report 3, London: English Heritage.

Faulkner, N., 1997. 'Sedgeford Historical and Archaeological Research Project, 1996: first interim report', *Norfolk Archaeology* 42, 532–5.

Faull, M., 1976. 'The location and relationship of the Sancton Anglo-Saxon cemeteries', *Antiquaries' Journal* 56, 227–33.

Finnegan, M., 1978. 'Non-metric Variation of the Infracranial Skeleton', *Journal of Anatomy* 125, 23–37.

Folk, R. L. and Hoops, G. K., 1982. 'An early Iron-Age layer of glass made from plants at Tel Yin'am, Israel', *Journal of Field Archaeology* 9, 455–456.

Foster, C. W. and Longley, T., 1924. *The Lincolnshire Domesday and the Lindsey Survey*, Lincoln Record Society, Volume 19, Gainsborough: Belton

Frandsen, L. B., 1999. 'Nydro – gamle bro – et vejanlæg fra tidlig vikingetid', in *Mark og Montre*, Årbog for Ribe Amts museer 1999, 39–50.

Gaunt, G. D., 1975. 'The artificial nature of the River Don north of Thorne, Yorkshire', *Yorkshire Archaeological Journal* 47, 15–21.

Gaunt, G. D., 1994. 'Geology of the country around Goole, Doncaster and the Isle of Axholme', *Memoirs of the British Geological Survey*, sheets 79 and 88 (England and Wales), London: HMSO.

Gaunt, G. D., Fletcher, T. P. and Wood, C. J., 1992. 'Geology of the country around Kingston-upon-Hull and Brigg', *Memoirs of the British Geological Survey*, sheets 80 and 89 (England and Wales), London: HMSO.

Geake, H., 1997. *The Use of Grave-Goods in Conversion-Period England, c. 600–c. 850*, British Archaeological Reports (British Series) 261, Oxford: Tempus Reparatum.

Geake, H., 2002. 'Persistent problems in the study of conversion-period burials in England', in S. Lucy and A. Reynolds, eds., *Burial in Early Medieval England and Wales*, 144–155, London: Society for Medieval Archaeology Monograph 17.

Geake, H., 2003. 'The control of burial practice in Anglo-Saxon England', in M. O. H. Carver, ed., *The Cross Goes North*, 259–269, Woodbridge: York Medieval Press/Boydell and Brewer.

Gordon, C. G. and Buikstra, J. E., 1981. 'Soil pH, Bone Preservation and Sampling Bias at Mortuary Sites', *American Antiquity* 46, 566–571.

Graham-Campbell, J. A., 1992. 'The Cuerdale hoard: comparisons and context', in J. A. Graham-Campbell, ed., *Viking Treasure from the North-West: The Cuerdale Hoard in its Context*, 107–115, National Museums and Galleries on Merseyside, Occasional Paper No. 5, Liverpool: National Musuems and Galleries on Merseyside.

Gustafson, G. and Koch, G., 1974. 'Age Estimation up to 16 Years of Age Based on Dental Development', *Odontologisk Revy* 25, 297–306.

Hall, A. R., 1995. *Environmental archaeology and archaeological evaluations*, Working Papers of the Association for Environmental Archaeology, No. 2, York: Association for Environmental Archaeology.

Hall, R. and Whyman, M., 1996. 'Settlement and monasticism at Ripon, North Yorkshire, from the 7th to the 11th centuries AD', *Medieval Archaeology*, 40, 62–150.

Hamerow, H., 1993. *Excavations at Mucking, 2: The Anglo-Saxon Settlement*, English Heritage Archaeological Report No. 21, London: English Heritage.

Hill, J. D., 1995. *Ritual and Rubbish in the Iron Age of Wessex: a study on the formation of a specific archaeological record*, British Archaeological Reports (British series) 242, Oxford: Tempus Reparatum.

Hill, P., 1997. *Whithorn and St Ninian: the excavation of a monastic town, 1984–91*, Stroud: The Whithorn Trust/ Sutton.

Hinchliffe, J., 1986. 'An early Medieval settlement at Cowage Farm, Foxley, near Malmesbury', *Archaeological Journal* 143, 240–259.

Hirst, S. and Clark, D., forthcoming. *The Anglo-Saxon Cemeteries 1 and 2 at Mucking*, London: English Heritage.

Hodges, R., 1981. *The Hamwih pottery: the local and imported wares from 30 years' excavations at Middle Saxon Southampton and their European context*, CBA Research Report No. 37, London: Council for British Archaeology.

Holland, S., 1975. 'Pollen analytical investigations at Crosby Warren, Lincolnshire, in the vicinity of the Iron Age and Romano-British settlement of Dragonby', *Journal of Archaeological Science* 2, 353–363.

Hope-Taylor, B., 1977. *Yeavering: an Anglo-British Centre of Early Northumbria*, Department of the Environment Archaeological Report 7, London: HMSO.

Jones, A., 2002. *Archaeological Theory and Scientific Practice*, Cambridge: Cambridge University Press.

Jones, M. J. and Steane, K. (eds., forthcoming) *The Archaeology of the Lower City and Adjacent Suburbs*, Lincoln Archaeological Studies 4. Oxbow Books, Oxford.

Keeley, H. C. M., Hudson, G. E. and Evans J., 1977. 'Trace element contents of human bones in various states of preservation. 1. The soil silhouette', *Journal of Archaeological Science* 4, 19–24.

Kent, P. E., 1980. *Eastern England from the Tees to The Wash*, British Regional Geology series (2nd edition), London: HMSO.

Kjølbye-Biddle, B., 1995. 'Iron bound coffins and coffin fittings from the pre-Norman cemetery', in D. Phillips and B. Heywood, *Excavations at York Minster 1: from Roman Fortress to Norman Cathedral*, 489–520, London: HMSO.

Kruse, S. E., 1992. 'Late Saxon Balances and Weights from England', *Medieval Archaeology* 36, 67–95.

Le Borgne, E, 1960. 'Influence du feu sur les propriétés magnétiques du sol et du granite, *Annales de Géophysique* 16, 159–195.

Lillie, M. and Parkes, A., 1998. 'The palaeo-environmental survey of the lower Trent valley and Winterton Beck', in R. Van de Noort and S. Ellis, eds., *Wetland Heritage of the Ancholme and Lower Trent Valleys – An Archaeological Survey*, 33–72, Humber Wetlands Project (English Heritage), Hull: University of Hull.

Linford, P. and Lindford, N. 1991. *Archaeomagnetic dating: Flixborough, Humberside, 1991*, Ancient Monuments Lab. Rep. 62/91, London.

Limbrey S., 1975. *Soil Science and Archaeology*, London: Academic Press.

Loveluck, C. P., 1996. *The Anglo-Saxon Settlement and Cemetery remains from Flixborough – revised and summarised assessment and updated project design*, Hull: Humber Archaeology/English Heritage.

Loveluck, C. P., 2001. 'Wealth, Waste and Conspicuous Consumption: Flixborough and its importance for Middle and Late Saxon rural settlement studies' in H. Hamerow and A. MacGregor, eds., *Image and Power in the Archaeology of Early Medieval Britain – Essays in honour of Rosemary Cramp*, 78–130, Oxford: Oxbow Books.

Loveluck, C. P., 2003. 'L'habitat anglo-saxon de Flixborough: dynamiques sociales et styles de vie (VIIe–XIe siècle), *Les Nouvelles de l'Archéologie*, No. 92, 2e trimestre 2003, 16–20, Paris: Maison des sciences de l'homme.

Loveluck, C. P., 2005. '*Terres Noires* and early medieval rural settlement sequences: conceptual problems, descriptive limitations and deposit diversity', in L. Verslype and R. Brulet, eds., *Terres Noires du haut Moyen Âge, Collection d'Archéologie Joseph Mertens XIV*, 86–96, Lovain-la-Neuve: Centre de Recherches d'Archéologie Nationale, Université Catholique de Louvain.

Loveluck, C. P. and McKenna, B., 1999. *The Site of Normanby Steelworks – Assessment of Potential of Archaeological Remains*, Humber Archaeology Report No. 45, Hull: Hull City Council.

Lucas, G., 2001. *Critical Approaches to Fieldwork – contemporary and historical archaeological practice*, London and New York: Routledge.

Lyman, R. Lee, 1994. *Vertebrate Taphonomy*, Cambridge: Cambridge University Press.

Maat, G. J. R. and Mastwijk, R. W., 2000. 'Avulsion Injuries of the Vertebral Endplates', *International Journal of Osteoarchaeology* 10, 142–152.

Mainman, A. J., 1993. *Pottery from 46–54 Fishergate*, The Archaeology of York Series, Vol. 16, Fasc. 6, Council for British Archaeology: London.

Manby, T. G., 1987. 'The Thwing project', in *Excavation and Field Archaeology in East Yorkshire 1986*, Leeds: Yorkshire Archaeological Society, Prehistoric Research Section.

Martin, E., Pendleton, C. and Plouviez, J., 1998. 'Archaeology in Suffolk 1997', *Proc. Suffolk Instit. Archaeol. & Hist.* 39 pt. 2, 209–45.

Martin, E., Pendleton, C. and Plouviez, J., 1999. 'Archaeology in Suffolk 1998', *Proc. Suffolk Instit. Archaeol. & Hist.* 39 pt. 3, 353–86.

Martin, E., Pendleton, C., Plouviez, J. and Thomas, G., 2000. 'Archaeology in Suffolk 1999', *Proc. Suffolk Instit. Archaeol. & Hist.* 39 part 4, 495–531.

Martin, E., Pendleton, C., Plouviez, J. and Geake, H., 2002. 'Archaeology in Suffolk 2001', *Proc. Suffolk Instit. Archaeol. & Hist.* 40 pt. 2, 201–33.

Mays, S., 1998. *The Archaeology of Human Bones*, London: Routledge/ English Heritage.

Mays, S. and Steele, J., 1996. 'A Mutilated Human Skull From Roman St Albans, Hertfordshire, England', *Antiquity* 70, 155–61.

Morris, R. K., 1983. *The Church in British Archaeology*, CBA Research Report 47, London: Council for British Archaeology.

Morris, R. K., 1989. *Churches in the Landscape*, London: J. M. Dent.

Mortimer, J. R., 1905. *Forty Years' Researches in British and Saxon Burial Mounds of East Yorkshire*, London: A. Brown and Sons.

Muir, R., 2000. *The New Reading the Landscape – Fieldwork in Landscape History*, Exeter: University of Exeter Press.

Nenk, B., Margeson, S., and Hurley, M., 1995. 'Medieval Britain and Ireland in 1994', *Medieval Archaeology* 39, 180–293.

Nenk, B., Haith, C., and Bradley, J., 1997. 'Medieval Britain and Ireland in 1996', *Medieval Archaeology* 41, 241–328.

O'Brien, E., 1996. 'Past rites, future concerns', in J. Blair and C. Pyrah 1996, eds., *Church Archaeology – research directions for the future*, 160–166, CBA Research Report 104, York: Council for British Archaeology.

Ottaway, P. J., 1996. 'The Ironwork', in R. A. Hall and M. Whyman, 'Settlement and monasticism at Ripon, North Yorkshire, from the seventh to eleventh centuries AD', *Medieval Archaeology* 40, 99–113.

Ottaway, P. J., unpublished a. 'Iron objects', in T. Manby, forthcoming, *Excavations at Thwing, East Yorkshire*.

Ottaway, P. J., unpublished b. 'Iron objects', in report on excavations at Carlisle Cathedral by Carlisle Archaeological Unit.

Ottaway, P. J., unpublished c. 'Iron objects', in report on excavations at Dacre Priory by R. Newman, Lancaster University Archaeological Unit.

Penn, K. 2000. *Norwich Southern Bypass, Part II: Anglo-Saxon Cemetery at Harford Farm, Caistor St Edmund*, East Anglian Archaeology 92, Gressenhall.

Redknap, M., 2000. *The Vikings in Wales – An archaeological quest*, Cardiff: National Museums and Galleries of Wales.

Robinson, M. and Straker, V., 1991. 'Silica skeletons and macroscopic plant remains from ash', in J. Renfrew, ed., *New light on early farming; recent developments in palaeoethnobotany*, 3–13, Edinburgh: Edinburgh University Press.

Scheuer, J. L., Musgrave, J. H. and Evans, S. P., 1980. 'Estimation of Late Foetal and Perinatal Age From Limb Bone Lengths by Linear and Logarithmic Regression', *Annals of Human Biology* 7, 257–65.

Schiffer, M. B., 1987. *Formation Processes of the Archaeological Record*, Albuquerque: University of New Mexico Press.

Sheehan, J., 1998. 'Viking Age hoards from Munster: a regional tradition?', in M. A. Monk and J. Sheehan, eds., *Early Medieval Munster: Archaeology, History and Society*, 147–163, Cork: Cork University Press.

Skinner, M. and Goodman, A. H., 1992. 'Anthropological Uses of Developmental Defects of Enamel', in S.R. Saunders and A. M. Katzenberg, eds., *Skeletal Biology of Past Peoples: Research Methods*, 153–174, Chichester: Wiley-Liss.

Stopford, J., 2000. 'The case for archaeological research at Whitby', in H. Geake and J. Kenny, eds., *Early Deira: Archaeological Studies of the East Riding in the fourth to ninth centuries AD*, 99–107, Oxford: Oxbow Books.

Stuart-Macadam, P., 1989. 'Nutritional deficiency Diseases: A Survey of Scurvy, Rickets and Iron Deficiency Anaemia', in M. Y. Iscan and K. A. R. Kennedy, eds., *Reconstruction of Life From the Skeleton*, 201–222, New York: Alan Liss.

Stuart-Macadam, P., 1992. 'Porotic Hyperostosis: A New Perspective', *American Journal of Physical Anthropology* 87, 39–47.

Tischler, F., 1952. 'Zur Datierung der frühmittelalterliche Tönwaren von Badorf, *Germania* 30, 194–200.

Ussher, W. A. E., 1890. 'The geology of parts of north Lincolnshire and south Yorkshire', *Memoirs of the Geological Survey of Great Britain*, sheet 86 (Old Series), London: HMSO.

Wade, K., 1980. 'A settlement at Bonhunt Farm, Wicken Bonhunt, Essex', in D. G. Buckley, ed., *Archaeology in Essex to AD 1500*, 96–102, CBA Research Report No. 34, London: Council for British Archaeology.

Walton Rogers, P, 2001. 'The re-appearance of an old Roman loom in medieval England', in Walton Rogers, P, Bender Jørgensen, L, and Rast-Eicher, A (eds), *The Roman Textile Industry and its Influence: A Birthday Tribute to John Peter Wild*, 158–171, Oxford: Oxbow Books.

Walton Rogers, P, 2007. *Cloth and Clothing in Early Anglo-Saxon England, AD 450–700*, CBA Research Report 145. York: CBA.

West, S., 2001. *West Stow Revisited: 25 years of reconstruction*, Bury St Edmunds: Suffolk County Council.

Whitwell, J. B., 1991. 'Flixborough', *Current Archaeology* 126, 244–47.

Williams, J. H., Shaw, M. and Denham, V., 1985. *Middle Saxon Palaces at Northampton*, Northampton: Northamptonshire County Council.

Wilmott, T., in prep. 'The Anglo-Saxon church and cemetery on the Booths', in I. Roberts and T. Wilmott (eds), *Pontefract 1: The Growth and Topography of the Medieval Town*, Yorkshire Archaeol. Monogr. (Wakefield).

Yorke, B., 1993. 'Lindsey: the lost kingdom found?', in A. Vince, ed., *Pre-Viking Lindsey*, 141–150, Lincoln Archaeological Studies 1, Lincoln: City of Lincoln Archaeology Unit.

Abbreviations to primary written sources:

HE *Bede's Historia Ecclesiastica*, ed and trans., Colgrave, B. and Mynors, R. A. B., 1969. *Bede's Ecclesiastical History of the English People*, Oxford: Oxford University Press.

Institutional sources:

Geological Survey of Great Britain, Kingston upon Hull (80) 1:50,000 geological sheet (England and Wales), drift edition, 1983.

Index

FIG. 1.2. The Humber estuary and Trent Falls (the delta of the River Trent) from the Lincolnshire Edge at Alkborough, 5km north of Flixborough (C. Loveluck).

FIG. 1.5. Topographic situation of Flixborough and North Conesby today, looking east across the River Trent towards the Lincolnshire Edge escarpment (C. Loveluck).

FIG. 1.6 (above). Aerial photograph showing the sand spurs and shallow valley running into the centre of the excavated area (Humber Field Archaeology).

FIG. 1.11 (left). One of the lead tanks housing the hoard of Mid to Late Anglo-Saxon woodworking tools and other artefacts, recovered as a chance find during quarrying sand, in 1994 (Humber Field Archaeology).

FIG. 1.12 (below). Some of the woodworking tools from the hoard found in the tanks (Bill Marsden).

FIG. 2.4. View of the excavations of 1989–1991, showing the spurs, and buildings and refuse dumps in the central shallow valley (Humber Field Archaeology).

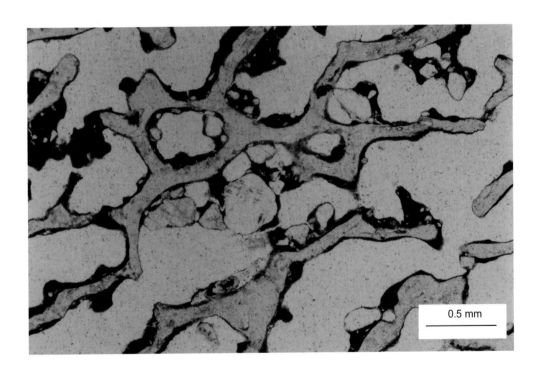

0.5 mm

FIG. 2.10. Highly weathered bone from 2861. Pale network = bone; lighter background = void space; dark adhesions = orange clay (see text). Plane-polarised light (M. Canti).

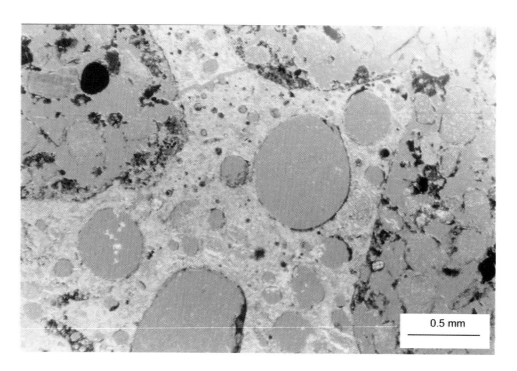

FIG. 2.11. *Fused ash from 6386 showing characteristic vesicular structure. Shaded plane-polarised light (M. Canti).*

FIG. 2.12. *Bone fragment (dark with faint pale streaks) in fine ashy matrix (pink-brown material) of 3711. Compare with the bone fragment in* FIG. *2.10. Crossed-polarised light (M. Canti).*

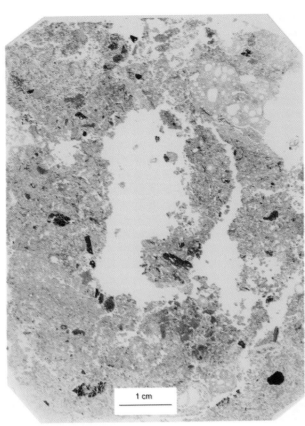

FIG. 2.13. Whole thin-section slide of ash dump 3758 (M. Canti).

FIG. 2.14. Whole thin-section slide of dump 5983 (M. Canti).

FIG. 3.10. Two fragments of an imported glass bowl with yellow marvered trail decoration (RF 5000), recovered in the fill of post-hole 5001, from building 6a (Bill Marsden).

FIG. 3.11. Single-bladed, iron woodworking axe (RF 12107) from occupation deposit 6492 (Bill Marsden).

Fig. 4.3. Buildings 1a and 1b under excavation (Humber Field Archaeology).

Fig. 4.5. Photograph of the grave of an adult female interred within building 1a, with a peri-natal foetus at her feet (Humber Field Archaeology).

FIG. 4.9. Building 1b under excavation (Humber Field Archaeology).

FIG. 4.10. Foundations of buildings 6, 5 and 3, partly superimposed on the same general building plot (Humber Field Archaeology).

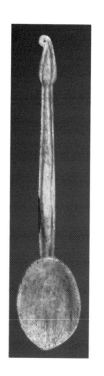

Fɪɢ. 4.22. *Bone spoon with lyre-shaped handle (RF 4135) from refuse deposit 2722, near buildings 1b and 5, phase 3bv (Bill Marsden).*

Fɪɢ. 4.21. *Copper alloy stylus from upper fill 4702 of post-hole from building 1b, following demolition, phase 3bv (Bill Marsden).*

Fɪɢ. 4.23. *Fragments of glass drinking vessel (RFs 8717 and 8723) from filled-in foundations (8708) of demolished building 9, phase 3bv (Bill Marsden).*

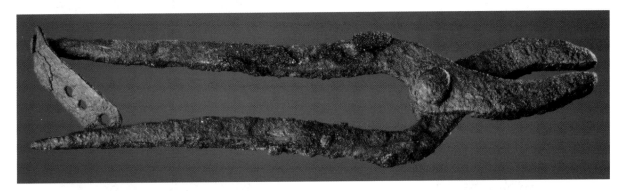

FIG. 5.9 (above). Locking tongs/hand-vice (RF 12169) from refuse dump 3758, phase 4ii (Bill Marsden).
FIG. 5.10 (below). Late eighth- to early ninth-century disc brooch (RF 5467) from refuse dump 3758, phase 4ii (Bill Marsden).

FIG. 5.11 (right). Silver stylus (RF 6143) from refuse dump 5503, phase 4ii (Bill Marsden).
FIG. 5.12 (below). Single-sided 'winged' composite comb (RF 6139) from refuse dump 5503, phase 4ii (Bill Marsden).

Fig. 5.15. Photograph of the section of Ditch 446/50/2842 (courtesy of T. P. O'Connor).

Fig. 5.16. Two clear (very light blue) fragments of window glass from refuse from phase 4ii: RF 5545 (right side of the photograph) was found in dump 5503; RF 5774 was found in ditch fill 3107 (Bill Marsden).

FIG. 6.9. Gravel paths and refuse dumps in the centre of the site, from phase 5a (Humber Field Archaeology).

FIG. 6.13. Radiograph of the inscribed lead plaque (RF 1781), with the names of seven individuals, both male and female, found in refuse dump 1728, from phase 5b (courtesy of the British Museum).

FIG. 6.14. Silver-gilt pin (RF 1887) with openwork zoomorphic terminal, found in refuse dump 1728, from phase 5b (Bill Marsden).

FIG. 6.15. Iron stylus (RF 12268) with decorated silver sheet mount on the eraser, from phase 5b (Bill Marsden).

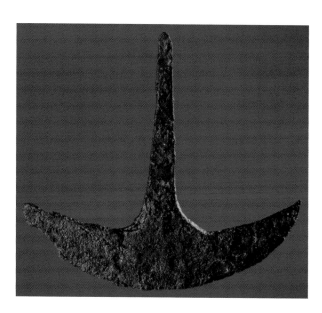

FIG. 6.16. 'Lunette' knife (RF 10841) for leatherworking, from phase 5a–5b (Bill Marsden).

FIG. 7.9. Cylindrical lead weight (right; RF 3727) used in silver bullion exchange from refuse deposit 3610, from phase 6ii; and a silver 'finger' ingot (RF 12198), found as an unstratified find (Bill Marsden).

FIG. 7.12. Three fragments of a clear glass bowl (RFs 5348, 6895, and 7012), decorated with yellow reticella decoration, from refuse deposit 6300, from phase 6iii (Bill Marsden).

FIG. 7.13. Fragment of a glass vessel (RF 6887) with red 'feathered' patterning, and a black and yellow reticella trail; and a blue glass tessera (RF 14334), both from refuse deposit 6300, from phase 6iii (Bill Marsden).

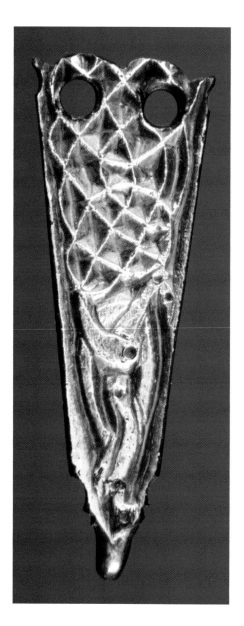

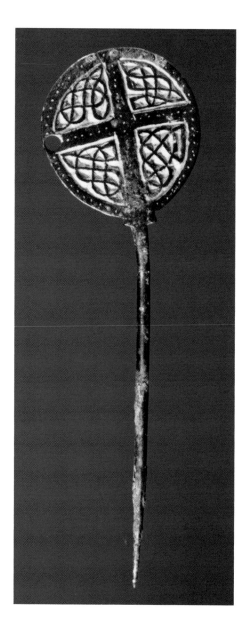

Fᴵɢ. 7.14. Late eighth-century silver-gilt hooked tag (RF 1816) with zoomorphic decoration, from 'dark soil' 1450, from phase 6iii (Bill Marsden).

Fᴵɢ. 7.15. Gilt copper alloy, disc-headed pin (RF 7835), with eighth-ninth-century interlace decoration, from 'dark soil' 7817, from phase 6iii (Bill Marsden).

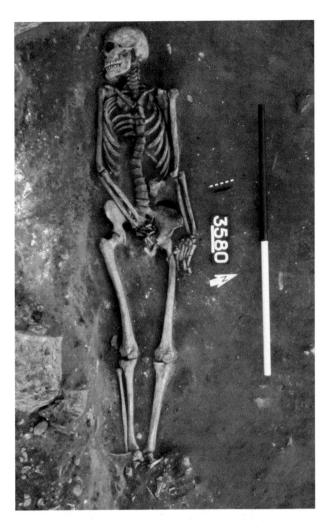 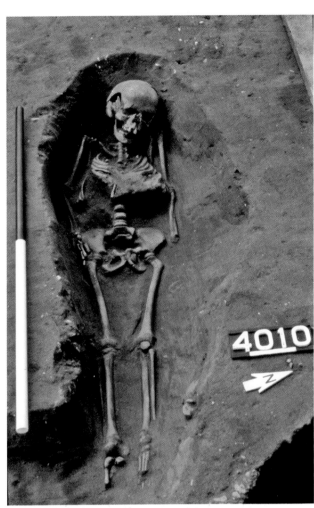

Fig. 8.1. Grave 3580, adult female (25–35 years old) with peri-natal foetus in a separate grave at her feet (Humber Field Archaeology).

Fig. 8.2. Grave 4010, nine-year-old child (Humber Field Archaeology).

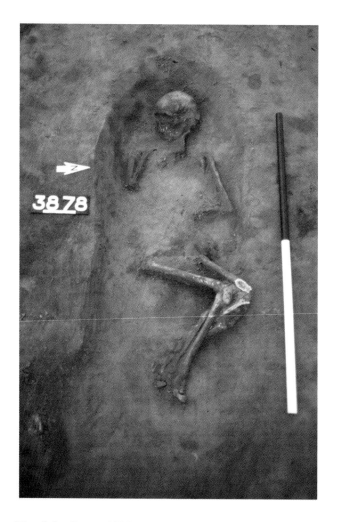

Fig. 8.3. Grave 3878, eleven-year-old child (Humber Field Archaeology).